THE MOUNTAIN BIKER'S GUIDE TO
THE SOUTHEAST

Dennis Coello's America by Mountain Bike Series

THE MOUNTAIN BIKER'S GUIDE TO THE SOUTHEAST

Dennis Coello's America by Mountain Bike Series

Coastal South Carolina
Coastal Georgia
Florida

Lori Finley

Foreword, Introduction, and Afterword
by Dennis Coello, Series Editor

MENASHA
RIDGE
PRESS

FALCON™

Library of Congress Cataloging-in-Publication Data
Finley, Lori, 1958–
    The mountain biker's guide to the Southeast : coastal South
Carolina, coastal Georgia, Florida / Lori Finley ; foreword,
introduction, and afterword by Dennis Coello. — 1st ed.
        p.   cm.
— (Dennis Coello's America by mountain bike series)
    "A Falcon guide"—P. [4] of cover.
    ISBN 1-56044-256-5
    1. Bicycle touring—South Atlantic States—Guidebooks.
2. All terrain cycling—South Atlantic States—Guidebooks.
3. South Atlantic States—Guidebooks.   I. Title.   II. Series:
America by mountain bike series.
GV1045.5.S66F56   1994
796.6'4'0975—dc20   94-15852
                                                         CIP

Photos by author unless otherwise credited
Maps by Tim Krasnansky
Cover photo by Dennis Coello

Menasha Ridge Press
3169 Cahaba Heights Road
Birmingham, Alabama 35243

Falcon Press
P. O. Box 1718
Helena, Montana 59624

 Text pages printed on recycled paper.

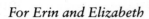

For Erin and Elizabeth

Table of Contents

THE SOUTHEAST *RIDE LOCATIONS*

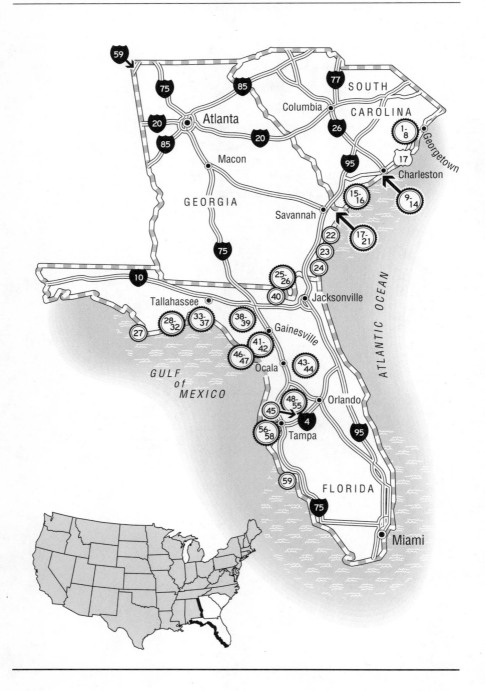

List of Maps

AMERICA BY MOUNTAIN BIKE *MAP LEGEND*

Ride trailhead

Steep grade

Primary bike trail

Direction of travel

(arrows point downhill)

Optional bike trail and trailhead

Other trail

Hiking trail

Interstate highways (with exit no.)

U.S. routes

State routes

Other paved roads

Croom Rital Rd.

Unpaved, gravel or dirt roads (may be 4WD only)

U.S. Forest Service roads

Charleston ◉
Tampa
Cities

Dade City ◉
Trilby
Towns or settlements

Dam
Lake

River, stream or canal

0   1/2   1
MILES

Approximate scale in miles

True North

CHARLES TOWNE LANDING STATE PARK

Parklands

State Border

✈ Airport

▼ Archeological or historical site

Boat ramp

▲ Campground (CG)

≡ Cattle guard

Cemetery or gravesite

♠ Church

Cliff, escarpment or outcropping

Drinking water

Fire tower or lookout

Food

Gate

House or cabin

Lodging

Mountain or butte

Mountain pass

△ Mountain summit
3312 (elevation in feet)

Military test site

✕ Mine or quarry

Museum

Observatory

Park office or ranger station

Picnic area

Power line or pipeline

Restrooms

Stable or horse farm

Swimming Area

Transmission towers

Tunnel or bridge

Acknowledgments

First, I would like to thank all the cyclists who eagerly and willingly provided me with information about trails in their area. Though I never got more than a first name from the majority of them, a few deserve special mention. Ken Foster, owner of Cyclelogical Bike Rentals in Tallahassee, generously shared information about his favorite rides, as well as information about the most popular rides in the panhandle area of Florida. Nestor Gernay at Savannah's Cycle Center gave me the lowdown on most of the rides found in or near his historic city. But doggone him . . . after giving me directions to a trail which involved passing Moon River, I spent the rest of the day humming the old Andy Williams tune. And to think he thought I was too young to be familiar with the song! John "Crawfish" Crawford at the University of Georgia's Marine Extension Service really went the extra mile to help me out. He enthusiastically shared his extensive knowledge of Georgia's coastal areas and trails, and offered me numerous suggestions for mountain bike rides. The folks at Savannah's Wilderness Outfitters kept me in a good supply of quad maps and were also helpful with ride suggestions.

The staff at the Francis Marion, Apalachicola, Ocala, and Osceola National Forests and the rangers at the Withlacoochee State Forest were all friendly and helpful in providing information on mountain biking in their respective forests. Even though a few of the forests do not permit mountain bikes on the single-track trails, the staff was quick to offer alternative rides.

I especially want to offer my heartfelt thanks to Sandra Thomas, Fred Thomas, Herb Clark, Jim Sinclair, Brenda Cox, Owen Riley, and Megan the Wonder Dog. This group of mountain biking buddies has become my family on the trails. They are always willing to travel to check out a new trail with me (with only minimal whining) though I know they would rather be spinning along the trails of the southern Appalachian mountains, our home turf. I particularly want to thank my friend, Joel McCollough, for riding nearly a dozen rides in Georgia and Florida and providing me with excellent research notes for this guidebook. I am very grateful for his help, as well as the steadfast help from my other friends.

Finally, a special word of thanks goes to my editor, Dennis Coello, for his guidance, patience, and friendship. This series of guidebooks has greatly benefited from his many talents. I can honestly say that of all the editors in the publishing business, Dennis is, without a doubt, the most Italian. All kidding aside, it's been an honor. Thanks, Dennis.

Foreword

Welcome to *America by Mountain Bike,* a 20-book series designed to provide all-terrain bikers with the information they need to find and ride the very best trails everywhere in the mainland United States. Whether you're new to the sport and don't know where to pedal, or an experienced mountain biker who wants to learn the classic trails in another region, this series is for you. Drop a few bucks for the book, spend an hour with the detailed maps and route descriptions, and you're prepared for the finest in off-road cycling.

My role as editor of this series was simple: First, find a mountain biker who knows the area and loves to ride. Second, ask that person to spend a year researching the most popular and very best rides around. And third, have that rider describe each trail in terms of difficulty, scenery, condition, elevation change, and all other categories of information that are important to trail riders. "Pretend you've just completed a ride and met up with fellow mountain bikers at the trailhead," I told each author. "Imagine their questions, be clear in your answers."

As I said, the *editorial* process—that of sending out riders and reading the submitted chapters—is a snap. But the work involved in finding, riding, and writing about each trail is enormous. In some instances our authors' tasks are made easier by the information contributed by local bike shops or cycling clubs, or even by the writers of local "where-to" guides. Credit for these contributions is provided, when appropriate, in each chapter, and our sincere thanks goes to all who have helped.

But the overwhelming majority of trails are discovered and pedaled by our authors themselves, then compared with dozens of other routes to determine if they qualify as "classic"—that area's best in scenery and cycling fun. If you've ever had the experience of pioneering a route from outdated topographic maps, or entering a bike shop to request information from local riders who would much prefer to keep their favorite trails secret, or know how it is to double- and triple-check data to be positive your trail info is correct, then you have an idea of how each of our authors has labored to bring about these books. You and I, and all the mountain bikers of America, are the richer for their efforts.

You'll get more out of this book if you take a moment to read the Introduction explaining how to read the trail listings. The "Topographic Maps" section will help you understand how useful topos will be on a ride, and will also tell you where to get them. And though this is a "where-to," not a "how-to" guide, those of you who have not traveled the backcountry might find the planning and equipment tips in "Hitting the Trail" of particular value.

In addition to the material above, newcomers to mountain biking might want

to spend a minute with the glossary, page 237, so that terms like *hardpack*, *single-track*, and *water bars* won't throw you when you come across them in the text.

Finally, the tips in the Afterword on mountain biking etiquette and the land-use controversy might help us all enjoy the trails a little more.

All the best.

Dennis Coello
Salt Lake City

Preface

The South is easy living, hammocks, cool breezes, sweating glasses of iced tea, and steamy oyster roasts on cold November nights. It is debutante balls, Georgia peaches, patchworks of countryside, and hot boiled peanuts sold at the side of the road. It is Fort Sumter and tales of the Civil War. It is the name of William Tecumseh Sherman being hissed through the clenched teeth of old-timers. It is the ghosts of writers and poets such as Archibald Rutledge, Sidney Lanier, Thomas Wolfe, and Flannery O'Connor. It is the Spoleto Festival, a dance called "the shag," little girls in white bonnets, and plump black ladies weaving sweet-grass baskets. It is orange groves, glistening beaches lapped by warm Gulf waves, shrimp boats, and elegant sabal palm trees.

The South is also mountain biking, believe it or not. And outstanding mountain biking to boot, though not in the literal sense of the word *mountain*. You won't find trails scratching up the sides of imposing, rugged crags like those found in the West. You won't even find trails like the ones in the Appalachians that climb gently rolling hills and then drop into verdant, wildflower-strewn valleys. What you will find is mountain biking Southern style, premium pedaling despite the absence of granny-gear climbs and screaming descents.

There are a number of choices for a day in the saddle, from a civilized setting to the boonies. You may find yourself pedaling a trail that ambles along a subtropical resort island that is laced with fine restaurants and five-star hotels where you can curl up in the lap of luxury after a long ride. Or you may choose a path that will take you on the wild side, railing through sprawling marsh and threading through tangles of dense forest. This guide is a strictly Southern take on mountain biking that may make you forget all about altitude.

At least for a while.

It would be a tough call to decide what the South's biggest draw is for cyclists. Weather, or scenery? In many areas of the country, when winter snows and biting cold make mountain bike rides only distant memories of past seasons, these Southern trails beckon. Temperatures in the 70s and 80s in the late winter months of February and March tend to flush hordes of mountain bikers out of hibernation and into the great outdoors to thaw their frozen muscles. For a non-Southerner, it is a pretty decadent experience to be hitting the trails at this time of year.

But, the aesthetics of the South are impossible to ignore. Blasting through stands of pencil-thin pine trees, meandering past stately antebellum plantation homes decorated with magnolias and azaleas, zipping past marsh areas festooned with the scurry of fiddler crabs, and cycling past limestone sinkholes embellished with lush tropical flora are the range of highlights of mountain bike rides in the South, regardless of the season.

Of all the South's attractions, among the most spectacular would have to be its trees. From evergreens to hardwoods, tall palms to ancient cypress, they are everywhere. One of the most striking and classically Southern, though, is the live oak tree. Arguably the most beautiful, these trees epitomize the charm and grace so often associated with the South. Delicate-looking yet strong limbs gently swoop down to the ground like the graceful arms of a dancer bending at the waist in a humble curtsy. Others curve back up to the sky, towering above narrow avenues and creating telescoping vistas. Brilliant sunlight pierces the evergreen canopy, leaving a shadowed tracing of leaves down below. Dripping with Spanish moss that looks like tangles of gray-green unraveled knitting, some of these trees are hundreds of years old. If only they could talk . . . what stories they could tell!

The rides in this guidebook span the region along the southern Atlantic coastline and the state of Florida. They range in difficulty from easy to strenuous, and in length from just a few miles to nearly 50 miles. Many of the roads and trails fall within national forest property, including South Carolina's Francis Marion National Forest and Florida's Apalachicola, Osceola, and Ocala national forests. There are also rides that afford glimpses of the enigmatic Okefenokee Swamp, the subject of scores of wild tales and stories of things that go bump in the night.

Sprinkled across the nation are unspoiled sanctuaries, pristine pockets of wilderness that serve as a refuge to many animal, plant, and bird species. The

Wooden plank bridges extend across the marsh on Edisto Island's Indian Mound Trail.

South is host to many national wildlife refuges that are laced with dike roads and hard-packed dirt refuge roads that seem custom-made for mountain bikes. Not only is the riding good, but the scenery and abundance of wildlife are excellent. In the Savannah National Wildlife Refuge, you might see a bald eagle soar against a backdrop of a dull gray winter sky. In the St. Marks National Wildlife Refuge, you might hear the splash of an alligator clumsily plunging into a pond. In any of the refuges, you are sure to hear the symphony of birdsong of the hundreds of different species found in any one site. Some of the refuges are located on the Atlantic flyway and, therefore, play the role of host to migrating birds from the North who winter in this area. Many of the creatures are threatened or endangered; within these sanctuaries they are protected from human predation and habitat degradation. It is a privileged cyclist who has the opportunity to come so close to and share nature with animals whose habitat is so quickly vanishing.

Ten rail trails are covered in this book, including South Carolina's Swamp Fox Trail, Georgia's McQueens Island Historic Trail, and Florida's Pinellas Trail. Some of these converted railway corridors are located in remote, backcountry settings while others are right in the heart of the city. There are other trails, also meandering through urban settings, that will appeal to the cyclist looking for a ride that isn't a three-hour drive away. Most of these are insulated from the bustle and hum of the city with woods or dense vegetation, which makes for a pleasant reprieve from the weekday concrete-and-chrome world.

Despite the fact that most mountain bikers prefer forest trails, or dirt roads at the very least, there are a few rides described in this book whose surfaces are paved. They were included because they afford glimpses of exquisite scenery or unique attractions in natural areas (such as the Okefenokee Swamp) that, unfortunately, do not offer designated mountain bike trails or even dirt roads for knobby-tired cycling. So, before shrieking in indignation and flipping immediately to the next chapter when you spot the word *pavement,* try to be open-minded; many of these paved routes make exceptional bicycle rides.

And finally, there are the island trails that often skirt elaborate resorts and wind past breathtaking views of the ocean or the Gulf of Mexico. Many of these paths lead to historic relics, blinking lighthouses, or ancient Indian shell mounds. Others are just plain fun to cycle. Most of these are easy rides of reasonable length, which makes them well suited for a family outing. For vacationing visitors, a bicycle ride is a welcome change of pace from swimming, golfing, and sunbathing.

Whatever your experience, whatever your skill level, memorable mountain bike rides await you. So come on, y'all, and hop on your bikes. You are about to pedal some of the best paths in the South!

Lori Finley

Introduction

TRAIL DESCRIPTION OUTLINE

Information on each trail in this book begins with a general description that includes length, configuration, scenery, highlights, trail conditions, and difficulty. Additional description is contained in eleven individual categories. The following will help you understand all of the information provided.

Trail name: Trail names are as designated on United States Geological Survey (USGS) or Forest Service or other maps, and/or by local custom.

Length: The overall length of a trail is described in miles, unless stated otherwise.

Configuration: This is a description of the shape of each trail—whether the trail is a loop, out-and-back (that is, along the same route), figure eight, trapezoid, isosceles triangle, or if it connects with another trail described in the book.

Difficulty: This provides at a glance a description of the degree of physical exertion required to complete the ride, and the technical skill required to pedal it. Authors were asked to keep in mind the fact that all riders are not equal, and thus to gauge the trail in terms of how the middle-of-the-road rider—someone between the newcomer and Ned Overend—could handle the route. Comments about the trail's length, condition, and elevation change will also assist you in determining the difficulty of any trail relative to your own abilities.

Condition: Trails are described in terms of being paved, unpaved, sandy, hard-packed, washboarded, two- or four-wheel-drive, single-track or double-track. All terms that might be unfamiliar to the first-time mountain biker are defined in the Glossary.

Scenery: Here you will find a general description of the natural surroundings during the seasons most riders pedal the trail, and a suggestion of what is to be found at special times (like great fall foliage or cactus in bloom).

Highlights: Towns, major water crossings, historical sites, etc., are listed.

General location: This category describes where the trail is located in reference to a nearby town or other landmark.

Elevation change: Unless stated otherwise, the figure provided is the total gain and loss of elevation along the trail. In regions where the elevation variation is not extreme, the route is simply described as flat, rolling, or possessing short steep climbs or descents.

Season: This is the best time of year to pedal the route, taking into account trail condition (for example, when it will not be muddy), riding comfort (when the weather is too hot, cold, or wet), and local hunting seasons.

Note: Because the exact opening and closing dates of deer, elk, moose, and antelope seasons often change from year to year, riders should check with the local Fish and Game department, or call a sporting goods store (or any place that sells hunting licenses) in a nearby town before heading out. Wear bright clothes in fall, and don't wear suede jackets while in the saddle. Hunter's-orange tape on the helmet is also a good idea.

Services: This category is of primary importance in guides for paved-road tourers, but is far less crucial to most mountain bike trail descriptions because there are usually no services whatsoever to be found. Authors have noted when water is available on desert or long mountain routes, and have listed the availability of food, lodging, campgrounds, and bike shops. If all these services are present, you will find only the words "All services available in . . ."

Hazards: Special hazards like steep cliffs, great amounts of deadfall, or barbed-wire fences very close to the trail are noted here.

Rescue index: Determining how far one is from help on any particular trail can be difficult due to the backcountry nature of most mountain bike rides. Authors therefore state the proximity of homes or Forest Service outposts, nearby roads where one might hitch a ride, or the likelihood of other bikers being encountered on the trail. Phone numbers of local sheriff departments or hospitals have not been provided because phones are almost never available. If you are able to reach a phone, the local operator will connect you with emergency services.

Land status: This category provides information regarding whether the trail crosses land operated by the Forest Service, Bureau of Land Management, a city, state, or national park, whether it crosses private land whose owner (at the time the author did the research) has allowed mountain bikers right of passage, and so on.

Note: Authors have been extremely careful to offer only those routes that are open to bikers and are legal to ride. However, because land ownership changes over time, and because the land-use controversy created by mountain bikes still has not completely subsided, it is the duty of each cyclist to look for and to heed signs warning against trail use. Don't expect this book to get you off the hook when you're facing some small-town judge for pedaling past a "Biking Prohibited" sign erected the day before. Look for these signs, read them, and heed the advice. And remember there's always another trail.

Maps: The maps in this book have been produced with great care, and, in conjunction with the trail-following suggestions, will help you stay on course. But as every experienced mountain biker knows, things can get tricky in the backcountry. It is therefore strongly suggested that you avail yourself of the detailed information found in the 7.5 minute series USGS (United States Geological Survey) topographic maps. In some cases, authors have found that specific Forest Service or other maps may be more useful than the USGS quads, and tell how to obtain them.

Finding the trail: Detailed information on how to reach the trailhead, and where to park your car is provided here.

Sources of additional information: Here you will find the address and/or phone number of a bike shop, governmental agency, or other source from which trail information can be obtained.

Notes on the trail: This is where you are guided carefully through any portions of the trail that are particularly difficult to follow. The author also may add information about the route that does not fit easily into the other categories. This category will not be present for those rides where the route is easy to follow.

ABBREVIATIONS

The following road-designation abbreviations are used in the *America by Mountain Bike* series:

CR   County Road
FR   Farm Route
FS   Forest Service road
I-   Interstate
IR   Indian Route
US   United States highway

State highways are designated with the appropriate two-letter state abbreviation, followed by the road number. *Example:* UT 6 = Utah State Highway 6.

Postal Service two-letter state codes:

AL	Alabama	KY	Kentucky
AK	Alaska	LA	Louisiana
AZ	Arizona	ME	Maine
AR	Arkansas	MD	Maryland
CA	California	MA	Massachusetts
CO	Colorado	MI	Michigan
CT	Connecticut	MN	Minnesota
DE	Delaware	MS	Mississippi
DC	District of Columbia	MO	Missouri
FL	Florida	MT	Montana
GA	Georgia	NE	Nebraska
HI	Hawaii	NV	Nevada
ID	Idaho	NH	New Hampshire
IL	Illinois	NJ	New Jersey
IN	Indiana	NM	New Mexico
IA	Iowa	NY	New York
KS	Kansas	NC	North Carolina

ND	North Dakota	TX	Texas
OH	Ohio	UT	Utah
OK	Oklahoma	VT	Vermont
OR	Oregon	VA	Virginia
PA	Pennsylvania	WA	Washington
RI	Rhode Island	WV	West Virginia
SC	South Carolina	WI	Wisconsin
SD	South Dakota	WY	Wyoming
TN	Tennessee		

TOPOGRAPHIC MAPS

The maps in this book, when used in conjunction with the route directions present in each chapter, will in most instances be sufficient to get you to the trail and keep you on it. However, you will find superior detail and valuable information in the 7.5 minute series United States Geological Survey (USGS) topographic maps. Recognizing how indispensable these are to bikers and hikers alike, many bike shops and sporting goods stores now carry topos of the local area.

But if you're brand new to mountain biking you might be wondering "What's a topographic map?" In short, these differ from standard "flat" maps in that they indicate not only linear distance, but elevation as well. One glance at a "topo" will show you the difference, for "contour lines" are spread across the map like dozens of intricate spider webs. Each contour line represents a particular elevation, and at the base of each topo a particular "contour interval" designation is given. Yes, it sounds confusing if you're new to the lingo, but it truly is a simple and wonderfully helpful system. Keep reading.

Let's assume that the 7.5 minute series topo before us says "Contour Interval 40 feet," that the short trail we'll be pedaling is two inches in length on the map, and that it crosses five contour lines from its beginning to end. What do we know? Well, because the linear scale of this series is 2,000 feet to the inch (roughly 2¾ inches representing 1 mile), we know our trail is approximately ⅘ of a mile long (2 inches × 2000 feet). But we also know we'll be climbing or descending 200 vertical feet (5 contour lines × 40 feet each) over that distance. And the elevation designations written on occasional contour lines will tell us if we're heading up or down.

The authors of this series warn their readers of upcoming terrain, but only a detailed topo gives you the information you need to pinpoint your position exactly on a map, steer you toward optional trails and roads nearby, plus let you know at a glance if you'll be pedaling hard to take them. It's a lot of information for a very low cost. In fact, the only drawback with topos is their size—several feet square. I've tried rolling them into tubes, folding them carefully, even cutting them into blocks and photocopying the pieces. Any of these systems is a pain, but no matter how you pack the maps you'll be happy they're along. And you'll be even happier if you pack a compass as well.

In addition to local bike shops and sporting goods stores, you'll find topos at major universities and some public libraries, where you might try photocopying the ones you need to avoid the cost of buying them. But if you want your own and can't find them locally, write to:

USGS Map Sales
Box 25286
Denver, CO 80225

Ask for an index while you're at it, plus a price list and a copy of the booklet *Topographic Maps*. In minutes you'll be reading them like a pro.

A second excellent series of maps available to mountain bikers is that put out by the United States Forest Service. If your trail runs through an area designated as a national forest, look in the phone book (white pages) under the United States Government listings, find the Department of Agriculture heading, and then run your finger down that section until you find the Forest Service. Give them a call and they'll provide the address of the regional Forest Service office, from which you can obtain the appropriate map.

TRAIL ETIQUETTE

Pick up almost any mountain bike magazine these days and you'll find articles and letters to the editor about trail conflict. For example, you'll find hikers' tales of being blindsided by speeding mountain bikers, complaints from bikers about being blamed for trail damage that was really caused by horse or cattle traffic, and cries from bikers about those "kamikaze" riders who through their antics threaten to close even more trails to all of us.

The authors of this series have been very careful to guide you to only those trails that are open to mountain biking (or at least were open at the time of their research), and without exception have warned of the damage done to our sport through injudicious riding. My personal views on this matter appear in the Afterword, but all of us can benefit from glancing over the following International Mountain Bicycling Association (IMBA) Rules of the Trail before saddling up.

1. *Ride on open trails only.* Respect trail and road closures (ask if not sure), avoid possible trespass on private land, obtain permits and authorization as may be required. Federal and State wilderness areas are closed to cycling.

2. *Leave no trace.* Be sensitive to the dirt beneath you. Even on open trails, you should not ride under conditions where you will leave evidence of your passing, such as on certain soils shortly after a rain.

Observe the different types of soils and trail construction; practice low-impact cycling. This also means staying on the trail and not creating any new ones. Be sure to pack out at least as much as you pack in.

3. *Control your bicycle!* Inattention for even a second can cause disaster. Excessive speed can maim and threaten people; there is no excuse for it!

4. *Always yield the trail.* Make known your approach well in advance. A friendly greeting (or a bell) is considerate and works well; startling someone may cause loss of trail access. Show your respect when passing others by slowing to a walk or even stopping. Anticipate that other trail users may be around corners or in blind spots.

5. *Never spook animals.* All animals are startled by an unannounced approach, a sudden movement, or a loud noise. This can be dangerous for you, for others, and for the animals. Give animals extra room and time to adjust to you. In passing, use special care and follow the directions of horseback riders (ask if uncertain). Running cattle and disturbing wild animals is a serious offense. Leave gates as you found them, or as marked.

6. *Plan ahead.* Know your equipment, your ability, and the area in which you are riding—and prepare accordingly. Be self-sufficient at all times. Wear a helmet, keep your machine in good condition, and carry necessary supplies for changes in weather or other conditions. A well-executed trip is a satisfaction to you and not a burden or offense to others.

For more information, contact IMBA, P.O. Box 412043, Los Angeles, CA 90041, (818) 792-8830.

HITTING THE TRAIL

Once again, because this is a "where-to," not a "how-to" guide, the following will be brief. If you're a veteran trail rider these suggestions might serve to remind you of something you've forgotten to pack. If you're a newcomer, they might convince you to think twice before hitting the backcountry unprepared.

Water: I've heard the questions dozens of times. "How much is enough? One bottle? Two? Three?! But think of all that extra weight!" Well, one simple physiological fact should convince you to err on the side of excess when it comes to deciding how much water to pack: a human working hard in 90-degree temperature needs approximately ten quarts of fluids every day. Ten quarts. That's two and a half gallons—*12* large water bottles, or *16* small ones. And, with water weighing in at approximately 8 pounds per gallon, a one-day supply comes to a whopping 20 pounds.

In other words, pack along two or three bottles even for short rides. And make sure you can purify the water found along the trail on longer routes. When writing of those routes where this could be of critical importance, each author has provided information on where water can be found near the trail—if it can be found at all. But drink it untreated and you run the risk of disease. (See *Giardia* in the Glossary.)

One sure way to kill both the bacteria and viruses in water is to boil it for ten minutes, plus one minute more for each 1,000 feet of elevation above sea level. Right. That's just how you want to spend your time on a bike ride. Besides, who wants to carry a stove, or denude the countryside stoking bonfires to boil water?

Luckily, there is a better way. Many riders pack along the effective, inexpensive, and only slightly distasteful tetraglycine hydroperiodide tablets (sold under the names Potable Aqua, Globaline, and Coughlan's, among others). Some invest in portable, lightweight purifiers that filter out the crud. Yes, purifying water with tablets or filters is a bother. But catch a case of Giardia sometime and you'll understand why it's worth the trouble.

Tools: Ever since my first cross-country tour in 1965 I've been kidded about the number of tools I pack on the trail. And so I will exit entirely from this discussion by providing a list compiled by two mechanic (and mountain biker) friends of mine. After all, since they make their livings fixing bikes, and get their kicks by riding them, who could be a better source?

These two suggest the following as an absolute minimum:

tire levers
spare tube and patch kit
air pump
allen wrenches (3, 4, 5, and 6 mm)
six-inch crescent (adjustable-end) wrench
small flat-blade screwdriver
chain rivet tool
spoke wrench

But, while they're on the trail, their personal tool pouches contain these additional items:

channel locks (small)
air gauge
tire valve cap (the metal kind, with a valve-stem remover)
baling wire (ten or so inches, for temporary repairs)
duct tape (small roll for temporary repairs or tire boot)
boot material (small piece of old tire or a large tube patch)
spare chain link

> rear derailleur pulley
> spare nuts and bolts
> paper towel and tube of waterless hand cleaner

First-Aid Kit: My personal kit contains the following, sealed inside double Ziploc bags:

> sunscreen
> aspirin
> butterfly-closure bandages
> Band-Aids
> gauze compress pads (a half-dozen 4″ × 4″)
> gauze (one roll)
> ace bandages or Spenco joint wraps
> Benadryl (an antihistamine, in case of allergic reactions)
> water purification tablets
> Moleskin/Spenco "Second Skin"
> hydrogen peroxide, iodine, or Mercurochrome (some kind of antiseptic)
> snakebite kit

Final Considerations: The authors of this series have done a good job in suggesting that specific items be packed for certain trails—raingear in particular seasons, a hat and gloves for mountain passes, or shades for desert jaunts. Heed their warnings, and think ahead. Good luck.

Dennis Coello
Salt Lake City

COASTAL SOUTH CAROLINA

Coastal South Carolina is a place where I have spent some of the best days of my life. For me and many others, this region of the Palmetto State has an appeal that is hard to define. It is a sensual place, with languid ways and steady rhythms. It is the lowcountry . . . steeped in history and washed in beauty.

This is also prime outdoors country with pristine national forests and state parks, such as Francis Marion and Hunting Island, that rank with any of their kind in the world. Up and down the coast are diverse, beautiful areas gilded with ribbons of trails and winding forest roads. These are places where mountain bikes fit perfectly. You will cycle across green marshes, with your tires making a wake of the tall grasses and flushing hundreds of birds from their feeding grounds. You will cycle deep into woods that are dimly lit, aromatic, full of sounds, yet full of silences. You will pedal sun-splattered, narrow trails that are bordered with stiff palmettos that noisily rustle as you blast by. And while there may be no mountains or waterfalls, you won't find the scenery lacking. This is just about as good as it gets.

The first few rides described in this guidebook begin near the town of Georgetown, the third oldest city in South Carolina. This quaint coastal town presents an interesting juxtaposition of a historic district dating back to pre–Revolutionary War days and towering industrial complexes. On a weekend research trip to Georgetown (my first visit since childhood), we drove into town very late on a Friday night. Through tired, blurred eyes I looked across the Sampit River to see a stunning display of lights. For a moment, I thought we had missed a turn; the lighted sight across the water looked like a large, metropolitan city. This wasn't at all the Georgetown I remembered from my youth. Actually, the lights were those of the International Paper Company, a sprawling structure that has been rooted in Georgetown for years, but one that I had never seen before at night.

The historic city of Charleston lies south of Georgetown, and between the two is a lush area of wooded, undeveloped country that is veined with the waters of the Santee River. It is in this area that General Francis Marion effectively employed his extensive knowledge of the terrain and nuances of the forest to hide himself and his troops after harassing British soldiers during the Revolutionary War. This sneaky general became a thorn in the side of the British and earned the name *Swamp Fox* for his clever backwoods tactics. The huge Francis Marion National Forest situated in this corridor between Georgetown and Charleston is a paradise to local mountain bikers. Seven favorite rides are described and will have you traversing mile after mile of backcountry, while skirting swamps and inlets and crossing marshes and pine forests. My personal favorite is the sly one's namesake—the Swamp Fox Trail.

The rides in this coastal wilderness range through a number of habitats, including stands of loblolly pine, grassy clearings, and swamp areas replete with eerie, black water and the buttressed trunks of ancient cypress trees. You will have a chance to see Carolina bays, elliptical depressions in the earth believed to

Sweet-grass baskets woven by native Charlestonians are sold along roadsides and in Charleston's downtown area.

have been created by meteors. You will also get an up-close look at the damage a hurricane can wreak.

Though years have passed since Hurricane Hugo roared through Francis Marion in 1989, its disastrous effects are still evident. Splintered trunks are all that remain of the many tall, mature trees that snapped like matchsticks during the storm. Some of the oaks whose trunks were able to withstand the force of the winds were stripped of all their branches. They now stand in the forest like forlorn amputees. In a matter of only a few hours, this incredibly powerful storm destroyed more timber in South Carolina than any other natural disaster recorded in the history of America. These damaged areas of the forest are a sobering reminder of Mother Nature's occasional angry moods. Though time is lending its healing touches to the landscape, it is still difficult to refrain from telling a visitor, "If you think it's pretty now, you should have seen it before Hugo."

As you drive south toward Charleston on Highway 17, there will be dozens of wooden stands that dot the shoulder of the road, bearing greenish-blonde baskets for sale. These are sweet-grass baskets made by black women in the Charleston area, employing basket-weaving techniques brought over by the first

African slaves. We stopped by one of the stands after cycling the trail at the Santee Coastal Reserve and met one of the basket weavers, a lovely, middle-aged woman named Lillian whose face was as dark as coal. Looking at her, I thought of the late Archibald Rutledge's remark about his friend, Old Gabe, with whom he hunted for 43 years. Rutledge wrote, "He is so black that when he leans against a burnt pine, you can't see him." (Archibald Rutledge's former home, Hampton Plantation, is right up the road from Lillian's stand.)

Lillian never rose from her seat while we made our selection, but continued her work on a partially woven basket. She would reach for a loose strand of grass from a recycled Kellogg's Cornflakes carton that rested beside her chair and would then weave it into the growing basket in her lap. She would occasionally chuckle at our spirited conversation and cheerfully answered our questions. Her speech was a beautiful Southern drawl laced with a hint of Gullah. This lowcountry dialect is English modified with African words, construction, and rhythm, combined with some Elizabethan words. This dialect is spoken predominantly by blacks living on the remote barrier islands. Though Gullah may be difficult for most of us to understand, its lyric beauty is indisputable.

These basket ladies are also seen in the city of Charleston at the City Market and on the corner of Broad and Meeting streets, shadowed by the steeple of St. Michael's Church. The church, similar in design to London's St. Martin's-in-the-Field, claims the title of Charleston's oldest church and looms above the historic downtown area. Nearby is St. Philips Church (built circa 1800) whose main graveyard spaces were reserved only for native Charlestonians. Visitors and nonnatives were buried in a graveyard across the street. So serious were they about this tradition that the remains of John C. Calhoun, former vice president of the United States of America, were moved from this burial site in the main graveyard to a spot "across the street" when it was discovered that he had been born elsewhere in the state. Ah . . . the rules of propriety. And they are enforced in the South as in no other place.

Florence King writes about Southern etiquette, manners, and rules in her book *Confessions of a Failed Southern Lady*. She talks about her grandmother's attempts to mold her into a fine Southern woman and being taken to task when she did not live up to those strict ideals. "But," she writes in her defense, "no matter which sex I went to bed with, I never smoked on the street."

Four of the South Carolina rides are located in Charleston proper. Two are rail trails; the West Ashley Greenway is an especially worthwhile mountain bike ride with its respectable round-trip length of 16 miles and scenic lowcountry surroundings. The two other rides—Charles Towne Landing and Magnolia Wildlife Trail—are located in historical settings and offer easy, interesting tours.

The ride at Charles Towne Landing, site of the first permanent English settlement in South Carolina, offers cyclists a number of highlights, including a reconstructed seventeenth-century period village showing visitors what the colonist's daily life was like. There is also a 20-acre zoo exhibiting in a natural setting animals indigenous to South Carolina in the late 1600s.

The ride on the grounds of Magnolia Plantation claims the oldest man-made attraction in America—the 300-year-old ancestral home of the Drayton family. This is an especially beautiful ride during the spring season when the gardens are in bloom. Camellia bushes the size of trees, a horticultural maze, an eighteenth-century herb garden, a Biblical garden, and the Audubon Swamp Garden draw hordes of visitors to this enchanting Charleston estate.

The last four rides described in this section of the guidebook are located on Edisto Island or in the Beaufort and Hilton Head Island areas. The spectacular scenery is the main draw for these rides, for the conditions turn wild and wooly after leaving the city of Charleston. This southern tip of the South Carolina coast, so inviting to mountain bikers, is also inviting to filmmakers. *The Big Chill* and *Prince of Tides* were both filmed in the Beaufort area.

The exceptional beauty of coastal South Carolina and the myriad attractions and highlights of the area are a big drawing card to movie moguls and many others. After pedaling the mountain bike trails and roads, it will be easy to understand why this region is also appealing to cyclists.

Georgetown Area

RIDE 1   *SANTEE COASTAL RESERVE HIKE / BIKE TRAIL*

South of the historic city of Georgetown lies the Santee Coastal Reserve, a sprawling mix of more than 23,000 acres of marsh, maritime forest, pine flatwoods, savannahs, bald cypress swamps, Carolina bays, and miles of beach frontage along the Atlantic Ocean. Sandwiched between the Santee River, the Cape Romain National Forest, and the Francis Marion National Forest, this area was originally inhabited by Santee Indians in the 1600s. Later, this fertile land was dotted with prosperous rice plantations and cotton fields.

Today, the rich soil of the reserve supports a variety of vegetation, providing an excellent food source for a variety of wildlife. White-tailed deer, opossum, bobcat, feral hogs, and fox roam the area, as do snakes and alligators. Loggerhead sea turtles come to the reserve to nest and can be seen along the beaches. It is believed that every species of Atlantic shorebirds can be found here during certain times of the year.

Within the reserve are several trails, including a 7.2-mile, single-track trail that is a favorite of local mountain bikers. This loop rolls through a range of different habitats of the reserve and parallels the Intracoastal Waterway. It is a moderately easy ride requiring some spotty technical maneuvering over exposed tree roots and deadfall in the trail.

The first time I cycled the trail, my friends and I commented on the beauty of the drive into the reserve toward the trailhead. A white, hard-packed sand road cut a straight path through a dense stand of tall, pencil-thin longleaf pine trees; it was really quite lovely. The scenery changed after a few miles and we found ourselves driving down a beautiful avenue of live oaks. A wild turkey hen darted in front of our car, scampered down the center of the road for a few feet, and then made a quick dash for the cover of the woods. We later decided that she must have been trying to outrun a roving pack of wild mosquitoes.

When we arrived at the parking area for the trail, we were surprised to find it empty. Where, we wondered, were all the people on such a pretty summer Saturday? We discovered the answer as soon as we stepped out of the car to unload our bikes and were attacked by swarms of ravaging mosquitoes. With cries and yelps and sounds of skin being slapped, we scurried for the safety of the car and the bottle of Skin-So-Soft. (This Avon product has proven to be one of the most effective insect repellents that coastal residents have found. You

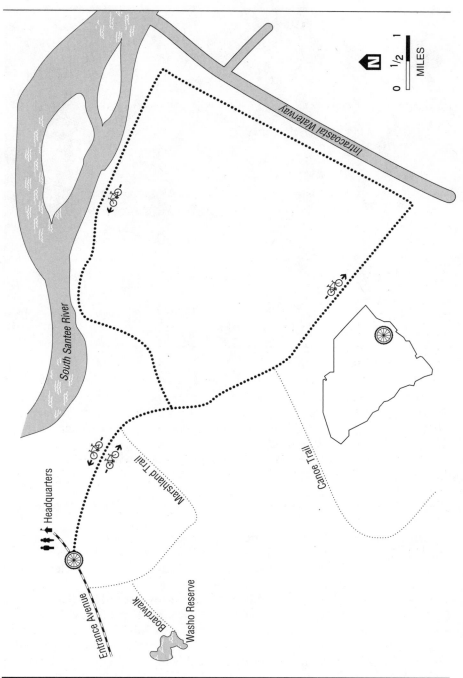

Live oak trees grace the drive in Santee Coastal Reserve.

can even find small bottles for sale in lowcountry convenience stores.) Wiping blood from the bites on our exposed limbs, we watched from the closed car windows as black clouds of ninja mosquitoes enveloped us; their high-pitched, angry whines could have muffled the sound of a jet passing overhead. Obviously Hitchcock never visited the coastal Carolinas in the summer. A thriller based on these bloodsuckers would have made *The Birds* seem as benign as a Disney film.

General location: This ride is located off US 17, between McClellanville and Georgetown.

Elevation change: There is no appreciable change in elevation.

Season: Mid- to late-summer rides often come complete with 100-degree temperatures, high humidity, and Mosquitoes from Hell. Choosing a cooler time of the year will make your mountain bike ride much more enjoyable.

Services: Some services are available in the nearby towns of McClellanville and Georgetown, while all services are found in Charleston. There are good primitive campgrounds in the nearby Francis Marion National Forest.

Hazards: Poisonous snakes such as rattlesnakes, cottonmouths, copperheads, and coral snakes do live in this area, so you should keep an eye out for them.

Also, there are alligators who call the reserve home; if you spot one, maintain a safe distance from it.

Rescue index: In the event of an emergency, help could be obtained fairly quickly since the trail is not too long. A manned headquarters office is located near the trailhead.

Land status: South Carolina Wildlife and Marine Resources Department.

Maps: Since the reserve is bounded on its western side by a corner of the Francis Marion National Forest, part of the reserve can be found on the Francis Marion National Forest map, which is available from the ranger station. The trail is shown in more detail on three USGS 7.5 minute quadrangles: Santee, Minim Island, and Cape Romain.

Finding the trail: From the intersection of US 17 and Service Road 857 a few miles north of McClellanville, turn onto SR 857, also known as South Santee Road. There is a small, green sign for the Santee Coastal Reserve. The turnoff to Hampton Pinckney State Park is across US 17 from the road to the reserve. Proceed on SR 857 for 1.5 miles to the turnoff to the reserve. You will see a small, white church on the left, adjacent to the dirt road leading into the reserve; turn left here. At 1.7 miles, the Nature Trail is on the left. (This out-and-back hiking trail follows a grass roadbed for a round-trip of 1.2 miles.) Continue straight until reaching the reserve parking area at 2.7 miles. At the fork just past the reserve parking area, you can reach the Visitor Information Center and Big Game Check Station by bearing left. Park in the designated parking area and follow the posted signs for the bike/hike trailhead.

Sources of additional information:

Santee Coastal Reserve
S.C. Wildlife and Marine Resources Department
P. O. Box 37
McClellanville, SC 29458
(803) 546-8665

Easy Rider Bikes
1039 Johnnie Dodds Blvd. (Anna Knapp Plaza)
Mount Pleasant, SC 29464
(803) 881-0222

Notes on the trail: The Santee Coastal Reserve is open to visitors from February 1 through October 31. Monday through Saturday, it is open from 8 A.M. to 5 P.M. and on Sundays it is open from 1 P.M. to 5 P.M. However, there was one occasion when I drove to the reserve to ride the trail during the posted hours, only to find it closed. You might wish to telephone the headquarters office when planning a trip to be certain that the trail will be open. (See "Sources of additional information" for the address and telephone number for the Santee Coastal Reserve.)

Francis Marion National Forest

RIDE 2   HAMPTON PLANTATION LOOP

This loop of nearly 16 miles offers a moderately difficult mountain bike ride through beautiful coastal scenery and past areas steeped in history and human record. Most of the miles extend over dirt Forest Service roads, though there are a few short legs of paved road. There are a few sandy sections of road that will test some riders' bike-handling skills, but most of the ride is easy from a technical standpoint.

The ride begins at Hampton Plantation State Park, on whose grounds sits the Hampton mansion, a National Historic Landmark. First built in the mid-1700s, the mansion began modestly as a six-room farmhouse that later expanded with the addition of a grand ballroom and other wings. Members of the Horry family, part of the French Protestants called Huguenots who had emigrated to South Carolina to escape persecution in their native land, were the original owners of the mansion. Through marriage, the plantation and its mansion later graced the hands of two more of South Carolina's most socially and politically prominent families—the Pinckneys and the Rutledges.

Dignitaries such as Lafayette, Francis Marion, and George Washington have walked through the welcoming columns of the Hampton mansion. In fact, a huge live oak tree standing in front of the house has been the subject of a story about Washington that was passed down through generations. It is told that Harriot Pinckney Horry commented to Washington during a visit that she intended to move the tree because it blocked the view of the house. The President disagreed and advised her to leave the tree be, "as no man could make an oak." She followed his advice and the "Washington Oak," now hundreds of years old, still rests in the front lawn of the mansion today.

Hampton Plantation was one of the most prosperous agricultural enterprises in the United States prior to the Civil War. Its glory days were realized from an extensive, profitable rice culture; an estimated 250,000 pounds of rice were produced at Hampton Plantation during 1850 alone. The owner during this period of time, Henry Middleton Rutledge, left Hampton at the beginning of the Civil War to serve as a Confederate officer but returned in 1865 to a much different situation. The war created lean economic conditions that greatly affected the productivity of the plantation. A trade blockade along the Southern coastline during the war vastly disrupted the export of rice. The emancipation of the slaves

RIDE 2 *HAMPTON PLANTATION LOOP*

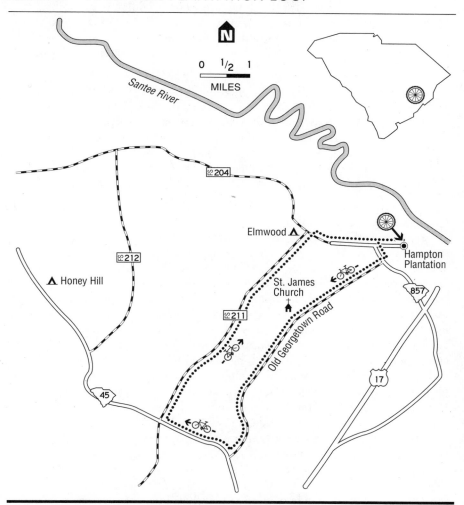

after the war drastically reduced the plantation owners' labor force. After only a short time, the South Carolina rice planters realized they could not compete with the more technologically advanced rice producers in states such as Louisiana, Arkansas, and Texas. Devastating hurricanes that hit the South Carolina coast in the late 1800s and early 1900s finally sealed the fate of commercial rice production in the state.

The last resident of the Hampton mansion was Henry Middleton Rutledge's son, Archibald, South Carolina's beloved first poet laureate. He grew up on this plantation along the delta of the Santee River and fostered a deep love for the area. Archibald Rutledge spent the majority of his adult life in Pennsylvania teaching English, but retired to this, his ancestral home, in 1937. He spent the rest of his life on the plantation writing and produced a number of books, including *Home by the River*. In this book about Hampton Plantation, Rutledge wrote:

> Sometimes when I stand on the porch in the moonlight, I imagine that I can see the Santee Indians flitting from oak to oak; then Tarleton's Redcoats thundering up the avenue; then Francis Marion and his partisans stealing in by the back door to devour the "leavings" of a plantation dinner; then the chariot of General Washington, coming up in state, somewhat creaky for need of axle grease. And I realize that I, too, am but a visitor here in this stately home. I am, therefore, trying to be a considerate guest.

Archibald Rutledge died in 1973 and was buried in the family graveyard near the house that he so dearly loved.

As you leave the park, you will soon turn onto Old Georgetown Road to continue on the ride. After cycling several miles on this easy dirt road, you will pass another historic edifice: St. James–Santee Episcopal Church. This early Georgian ecclesiastical-style church is referred to as the "Brick Church" by locals because of its brick sides and rounded brick columns out front. Shuttered windows and a low-pitched roof give this church a classic lowcountry look. It is listed on the National Register of Historic Places for "possessing exceptional value in commemorating or illustrating the history of the United States." Weathered tombstones mark the final resting places of a number of church members and area residents, including such dignitaries as Daniel Huger, one of the earliest settlers in the Santee River delta. Daniel was the son of John Huger, a French Huguenot who fled to South Carolina to escape the persecution by Louis XIV following the revocation of the Edict of Nance in 1685. In the church graveyard, a barely legible monument, whose engraved words have been worn smooth from years of exposure to the elements, briefly tells the story of their family.

The ride continues on Mill Branch Road, also known as Forest Service Road (FS) 211, which is flanked by quiet forest on its winding path back toward the state park. Along each side of the road, slender longleaf pine trees spring up from a wind-rippled sea of verdant ferns. The trunks rise without interruption for 80 to 100 feet before sprouting heads of branches and swaying green tresses. The bare, silver, needlelike trunks look like thousands of exclamation points shocking the landscape.

During summer, be sure to notice the profusion of pink wildflowers springing forth from the bed of ferns. There are also common cattails decorating the freshwater marsh areas with their characteristic yellowish-brown, velvety spikes and slender, long, green leaves. An edible plant, the immature flower spike can be boiled and eaten like corn on the cob. Adjacent to the Forest Service roads

The St. James-Santee Episcopal Church is also known as the "Brick Church."

and interspersed throughout the forest are rye-filled clearings used for attracting wildlife, particularly white-tailed deer.

General location: This ride is located in the eastern quadrant of the Francis Marion National Forest, which is located between Charleston and Georgetown.
Elevation change: There is no appreciable change in elevation.
Season: This ride is open year-round to mountain bikes. The temperate winter in South Carolina is one of the favorite seasons for cycling these open, dirt roads. Though the trails are still ridden in the shimmering heat of summer, the high temperatures and humidity during that time of the year can be oppressive.

Services: Most services are available in the nearby towns of McClellanville and Georgetown. All services are available in Charleston, located south of the national forest. A number of campgrounds are located nearby and are managed by the Forest Service.

Hazards: The chief hazard on this ride is biting insects. Watch for snakes when you stop at the St. James–Santee Episcopal Church, especially in the parts of the churchyard and graveyard that are overgrown with weeds.

Rescue index: The rescue index is good, especially during the fall hunting season when you are more likely to see a passing vehicle on the roads.

Land status: The Hampton Plantation State Park is owned and managed by the South Carolina Department of Parks, Recreation, and Tourism. The remainder of the ride falls within the boundaries of the national forest and is managed by the U.S. Forest Service.

Maps: A Forest Service map of the Francis Marion National Forest is available from the ranger station. The ride is also detailed on the USGS 7.5 minute quadrangle for Santee.

Finding the trail: From the intersection of US 17 and Rutledge Road, also known as Service Road 857, north of McClellanville, turn onto Rutledge Road. Drive for 1.9 miles to the entrance of the Hampton Pinckney State Park, which will be on the right. Park here.

Sources of additional information:

Wambaw Ranger District
P. O. Box 788
McClellanville, SC 29458
(803) 887-3257

Hampton Plantation State Park
1950 Rutledge Road
McClellanville, SC 29458
(803) 546-9361

Easy Rider Bikes
1039 Johnnie Dodds Blvd. (Anna Knapp Plaza)
Mount Pleasant, SC 29464
(803) 881-0222

RIDE 3 *GUILLIARD LAKE LOOP*

This ride begins at Francis Marion National Forest's Guilliard Lake Recreation Area, the site of the former town of Jamestown. This 925-acre scenic area located along the south side of the Santee River embraces a landscape rich with ancient

RIDE 3 *GUILLIARD LAKE LOOP*

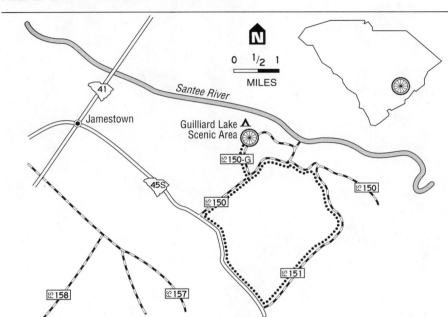

cypress trees. Twists of thick, sturdy vines wrapped around the branches and up the trunks of pines, live oaks, and other trees lend a junglelike appearance to the forest.

Summer days can be so thick with humidity that the air itself tends to be reminiscent of a jungle as well. It's pretty bad when you can almost refill your water bottles by simply opening the tops and sweeping them through the air. But don't be deterred by my tales of oppressive humidity, for days like that are the exception rather than the rule.

This moderate ride leads mountain bikers along a beautiful loop of wide, nontechnical dirt roads for about 13.5 miles of outstanding pedaling. Sandy, chalk-white roads bend through the forest leading you on a tour of beautiful lowcountry that will cause you to return time and time again. During the winter, this is an especially good route to cycle; the openness of the road and lack of shade from tree canopy overhead allow the sun's rays to warm your back.

General location: The ride begins along the northcentral boundary of the Francis Marion National Forest, which is located between Charleston and Georgetown.

Elevation change: There is no appreciable change in elevation.

Flat, non-technical dirt roads are perfect for children on mountain bikes.

Season: The route can be cycled year-round, but the hot days of summer can verge on becoming unbearable for any outdoor recreation, including bicycling. Though the trails in the forest are prone to flooding after rainy periods, the dirt roads of this loop trail are rarely affected and can be cycled far sooner than single-track trails during wet weather.

Services: Most services are available in McClellanville or Georgetown. Charleston and Mount Pleasant are farther away, but do offer more services, including bike shops. There are several campgrounds in Francis Marion National Forest, including one at the Guilliard Lake Recreation Area, the starting point of this ride.

Hazards: Mosquitoes and other biting insects can make your ride miserable, if not impossible, if you have not doused your skin with bug repellant. There are poisonous snakes in the forest, but you are unlikely to see any if you stay on the dirt roads.

Rescue index: The rescue index is fairly good as the route stays on ungated Forest Service roads that are open to vehicles. It is possible that a car could happen along and be flagged down in case of an emergency. Don't count on it, though. Be prepared with a first-aid kit and a tool kit, and know how to use them.

Land status: National forest.

Maps: A Forest Service map of the Francis Marion National Forest is available from the ranger station. The ride is also found on two USGS 7.5 minute quadrangles: Cedar Creek and Honey Hill.

Finding the trail: From the intersection of US 17 and SC 45 near McClellanville, drive northwest on SC 45 for approximately 17 miles to the intersection with Forest Service Road 150. Turn right onto FS 150 and drive 1.6 miles to FS 150-G. You will see a sign for Guilliard Lake Recreation Area. Turn left onto FS 150-G and drive for 1.5 miles to the parking area.

Sources of additional information:

Wambaw Ranger District
P. O. Box 788
McClellanville, SC 29458
(803) 887-3257

Easy Rider Bikes
1039 Johnnie Dodds Blvd. (Anna Knapp Plaza)
Mount Pleasant, SC 29464
(803) 881-0222

RIDE 4   *WAMBAW CREEK WILDERNESS LOOP*

Along South Carolina's coast lies McClellanville, a sleepy village highlighted with historic old churches and streets canopied with the latticed branches of live oak trees. The town's major industry is fishing, which keeps the Intracoastal Waterway busy with boats gliding in from sea that seem to be webbed with the erratic, swooping flights of raucous birds squawking for some discarded morsel of fish. Most of the shrimpers and fishermen were born and raised on this coast and have never breathed any air other than the moist air of the salt marsh and sea into their lungs. Their shoulders, permanently inked in a deep Carolina gold, ripple with the muscles earned from years of pulling lines and hoisting filled shrimp nets. Some are eager to strike up a friendly conversation, while others, more curmudgeonly, prefer to grumble quietly as they attend to their on-deck tasks. Their countenances, lined with the deep grooves of wrinkles from years of exposure to the elements, are worthy of a photograph.

This 18-mile moderate loop ride begins about 3 miles north of McClellan-

RIDE 4 *WAMBAW CREEK WILDERNESS LOOP*

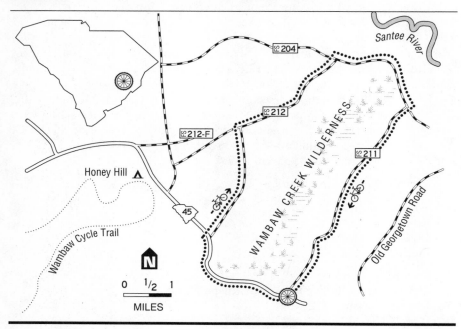

ville. It follows sparsely traveled, hard-packed dirt roads that circle the wilderness area. Wambaw Creek is lined with typical swamp flora such as tupelo, cypress, and saw palmettos; its black water is sprinkled with flowering water lilies. You may wish to take one of the side roads to get a closer look at the creek, but remember that mountain bikes are prohibited in all designated wilderness areas. Stay on the Forest Service roads.

General location: The ride begins approximately 3 miles north of McClellanville and approximately 40 miles north of Charleston.

Elevation change: There is no appreciable change in elevation.

Season: This loop of dirt roads can be ridden year-round. Summer is a hot, humid, buggy season and can be uncomfortable for those reasons. Rainy weather does not affect the condition of these dirt roads nearly as much as it affects single-track trails, so this loop can be cycled sooner than some other rides after a period of heavy rain.

Services: While many services are available in McClellanville and Georgetown, they are small towns; Charleston offers more.

Hazards: Biting insects are a problem during the warm months; bring bug repellant. There are alligators in the swampy areas near the creek, but you shouldn't

South Carolina's state tree—the Palmetto.

have a problem if you keep your bike on the road. And, of course, there are poisonous snakes all over the lowcountry—this ride is no exception.

Rescue index: The rescue index is good, with help available in nearby McClellanville. The loop follows ungated Forest Service roads the entire time, so you are less vulnerable than you would be on a remote single-track deep in the forest.

Land status: National forest.

Maps: The Francis Marion National Forest map is available from the ranger station for a small fee. The ride is also detailed on the USGS 7.5 minute quadrangle for Santee.

Finding the trail: From McClellanville, drive north on SC 45 for approximately

3 miles to an intersection with Forest Service Road 211. Park at any road pulloff near this intersection.

Sources of additional information:

Wambaw Ranger District
P. O. Box 788
McClellanville, SC 29458
(803) 887-3257

Easy Rider Bikes
1039 Johnnie Dodds Blvd. (Anna Knapp Plaza)
Mount Pleasant, SC 29464
(803) 881-0222

RIDE 5 *SWAMP FOX TRAIL*

Tucked away within the 250,000-acre Francis Marion National Forest lies a 21-mile-long scenic single-track trail (42 miles long as an out-and-back) where a mountain bike fits perfectly. Cyclists can explore the backcountry of the forest, slip into the swamplands, and blast through open stands of pines. More than 200 years ago, this area was the haunt of General Francis Marion, who was notorious during the American Revolution for attacking and tormenting the more powerful British troops and then hiding out with his men in the low-lying, dense swamp forests. Known as the *Swamp Fox* for his clandestine tactics, this Revolutionary War hero earned a place in American history. When asked to describe the sly old general, a fellow officer was quoted as saying, "the devil himself could not catch him."

This moderately difficult ride is one of South Carolina's favorite rail trails. The trail, built over old logging lines, begins by rolling along well-drained ridges that penetrate low-lying, boggy areas shaded with water oaks. It then plunges through drier pine forests before threading through the dark, cypress swamp areas. There are sections of this hard-packed single-track that offer some technical challenge, but most of the trail is fairly straightforward. Several portions of the trail seem to have a hard time ever drying out completely, so expect to return to your car with mud-painted shins. The trail can be ridden in its entirety by setting up a shuttle or ridden, in part, as an out-and-back by starting at one terminus and riding as far as you wish.

A few sections of the trail somberly wind through stands of forest that were ravaged by Hurricane Hugo during the middle of the night on September 21, 1989. Splintered trunks of battered trees stand silently like weather-beaten tombstones as a testament to the fury of the storm. As we cycled through the now-

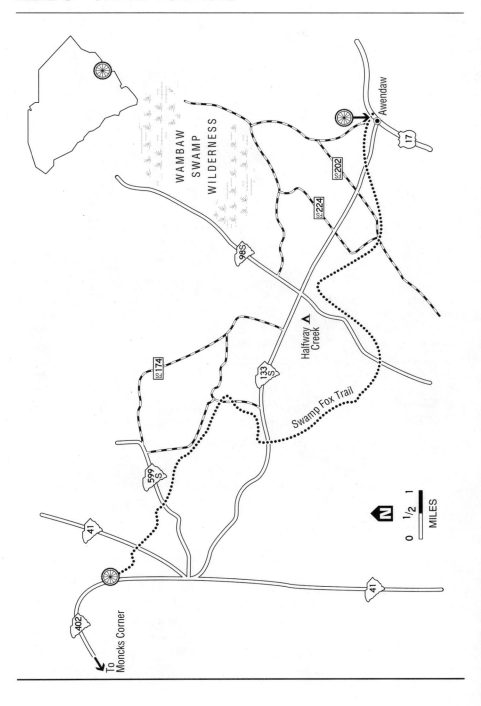

Zipping past hurricane-ravaged trees in Francis Marion National Forest.
Photo by Bob Finley

peaceful forest, I remembered the stories of the few people who had not evacuated from the coastal towns and who were forced to listen to the raging voice of the storm. Many of these folks described the sound of the hurricane-force winds as "the wailing of hundreds of trains." They could feel the ground shake with the thud of falling trees but could not hear the snapping and crashing of hundred-year-old tree trunks because of the deafening roar of the winds. The devastating ruin left by those winds has been likened to the blast sites of atomic bombs, the ruins of Beirut, even the path of Sherman's March across the South. As you cycle through these sections of recovering forest, you will see a macabre reminder that nothing is eternal, nothing is permanent in the forest.

Though 70% of the lumber-quality trees of Francis Marion National Forest was destroyed, the recovery is already evident. Fortunately, excellent forest management programs were in effect prior to the storm, and many immature stands of hardwoods and pines came through the hurricane unscathed. These younger trees that survived the powerful wrath of the storm have become the nucleus of the new forest.

General location: This trail is located about 40 miles north of Charleston.

Elevation change: There is no appreciable change in elevation.

Season: Springtime is probably the best season for cycling because of pleasant temperatures and the lack of mosquitoes, though it is often fairly wet. The trail can be cycled year-round, however.

Services: All services are available in nearby Charleston, while some services are available in Georgetown and Moncks Corner.

Hazards: Intense heat and biting insects are to be expected during the summer; you should bring plenty of water, sunscreen, and bug repellant. Poisonous snakes such as water moccasins, copperheads, and rattlesnakes do live in this forest but it is unlikely that you will encounter them. Hunting is permitted in the forest; wearing some bright, unnatural color during hunting season is advised. Check with the ranger station for the exact dates when hunting is allowed. You may wish to avoid this trail on opening day.

Rescue index: The rescue index is poor because the trail winds for miles away from access roads. In addition, the trailhead is several miles from a city offering emergency assistance. For these reasons, you should bring a tool kit and a first-aid kit with you on the trail.

Land status: National forest.

Maps: The Francis Marion National Forest map is available from the ranger station for a nominal fee. The trail is also detailed on three USGS 7.5 minute quadrangles: Awendaw, Ocean Bay, and Huger.

Finding the trail: The eastern trailhead is located on US 17 at the town of Awendaw, about 40 miles north of Charleston. The western terminus of the trail is located on SC 41 near the town of Huger.

Sources of additional information:

Wambaw Ranger District
P. O. Box 788
McClellanville, SC 29458
(803) 887-3257

Easy Rider Bikes
1039 Johnnie Dodds Blvd. (Anna Knapp Plaza)

Mount Pleasant, SC 29464
(803) 881-0222

Notes on the trail: At .2 miles from the eastern trailhead at Awendaw, be sure to notice the chair carved into a huge tree trunk by a chain saw—wielding workman during the clean-up efforts following Hurricane Hugo.

RIDE 6   *WAMBAW CYCLE TRAIL*

Located in the sandhills area of the Francis Marion National Forest is a moderately strenuous mountain bike ride that is a favorite of serious cyclists. Since it is nearly 40 miles long, you might begin to think that you have crossed several time zones before you finally return, bedraggled, to your waiting vehicle. Technically challenging in sections, the trail blasts straight through sand pits that will cause your rear wheel to fishtail if you have not geared down. Catching air on the numerous whoop-de-doos is another of the many perks that draw the local hammerheads.

Wambaw Cycle Trail is actually two loops of single-track trail that can be ridden separately for shorter, easier rides. The eastern loop, approximately 12 miles long, crosses under power utility towers and then plunges through a dense pine forest, offering cyclists a fun and easy ride. The western loop meanders for about 24 miles through deciduous stands of oak, dogwood, and hickory as well as through conifer stands of loblolly and pond pine. It also skirts the shores of Round Pond, a haven for water birds and other water-loving creatures.

Unfortunately, this trail is also open to motorized vehicles such as motorcycles, three-wheelers, and four-wheelers. I arrived at the trailhead one Saturday morning only to find it teeming with motorcyclists, trailers loaded with motorcycles, and pickup trucks loaded with entire families. The high-pitched whine of engines had already begun to fill the forest. One particularly rough-looking fellow slowly sauntered toward me and then stopped at my car. Pointing to my mountain bike still resting in the Yakima rack, he unscrewed a Camel from the corner of his mouth and dryly remarked, "Looks like your 'motorsickle' ain't grown up yet." Lord. On pretty, warm weather weekends, you might want to surrender this trail to the motorcyclists and save this otherwise excellent ride for a weekday.

General location: This trail is located within the Francis Marion National Forest, about 40 miles north of Charleston and about 8 miles northwest of McClellanville.

Elevation change: There is no appreciable change in elevation.

Season: This loop is open to mountain bikes year-round. Summers are hot and

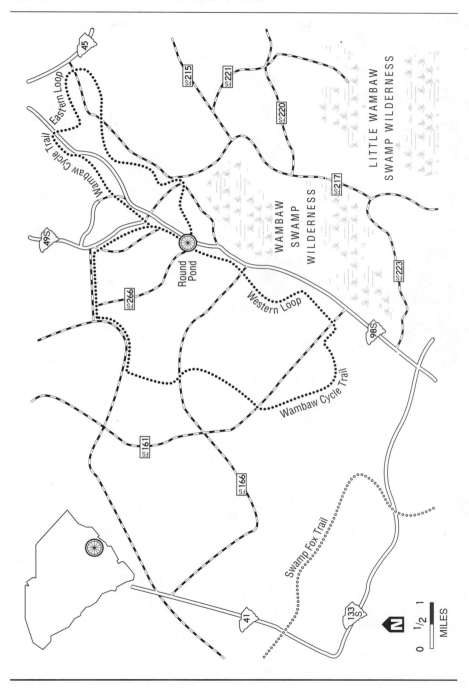

Rounding a bend on the Wambaw Cycle Trail.

muggy; the cooler months of fall and winter are more pleasant for mountain biking. Hunting is permitted at certain times of the year in the forest, so check with the ranger station for specific dates. Since the opening day of hunting season is generally a zoo, you might consider planning your ride for another day.

Services: All services are available in Charleston. The ranger station can provide you with a list of campgrounds located within the forest and their amenities.

Hazards: There are poisonous snakes in the forest, but they are not often spotted on this heavily-used trail. During the hunting season, you should wear bright, unnatural colors. Mosquitoes, ticks, and red bugs are always happy to see you—keep them at bay with an ample dousing of bug dope on any exposed skin.

Rescue index: The rescue index is fairly good since the trail is heavily used. Help is available in nearby McClellanville and also in Charleston.

Land status: National forest.

Maps: The Francis Marion National Forest map is available from the ranger station for a couple of bucks. The trail is also detailed on three USGS 7.5 minute quadrangles: Honey Hill, Shulerville, and Ocean Bay.

Finding the trail: From Awendaw (south of McClellanville), drive west on SC 133S for approximately 3.5 miles to the intersection with SC 98S. Drive for about

6 miles to the Round Pond trailhead, which will be on the left. Park in the large parking area.

Sources of additional information:

Wambaw Ranger District
P. O. Box 788
McClellanville, SC 29458
(803) 887-3257

Easy Rider Bikes
1039 Johnnie Dodds Blvd. (Anna Knapp Plaza)
Mount Pleasant, SC 29464
(803) 881-0222

RIDE 7 *JERICHO LOOP*

After a period of heavy rain, this trail offers excellent opportunities for cyclists to observe animals searching for an arklike wooden ship and then pairing off for 40 days and 40 nights. *Wet* is not a watery enough word to describe this ride. You might want to consider saving this trail for a dry day unless you derive some perverse pleasure from emerging from the woods looking like a mud-covered Arnold Schwarzenegger trying to hide from *The Predator*. Trail damage aside, let's face it—it is not much fun cycling through mud so thick and deep that your bike remains standing despite the fact that you have no forward momentum and your feet are still clipped into the pedals. This lowcountry mud is serious, wheel-sucking stuff. But don't miss the Jericho Trail—it is a great mountain bike ride after a drought of six or seven years.

During dry weather, this moderately difficult 20-mile loop trail becomes a superb mountain bike ride. Really. Unlike some of the coastal trails that blaze a straight monotonous path through the woods, this trail twists through the forest, leading cyclists to interesting highlights. It dips and curves down to swamps decorated with rounded cypress knees, blasts across open meadows that are feeding grounds for white-tailed deer in the early evening, and crosses a number of different creeks. Wild azaleas, dogwoods, and wildflowers color this long path during the spring and summer months.

General location: This ride is located in Francis Marion National Forest near Moncks Corner, about 40 miles north of Charleston.

Elevation change: There is no appreciable change in elevation.

Season: Winter and spring are generally wet seasons, but before installing outriggers and a winch on your mountain bike, check with the ranger station for

RIDE 7 *JERICHO LOOP*

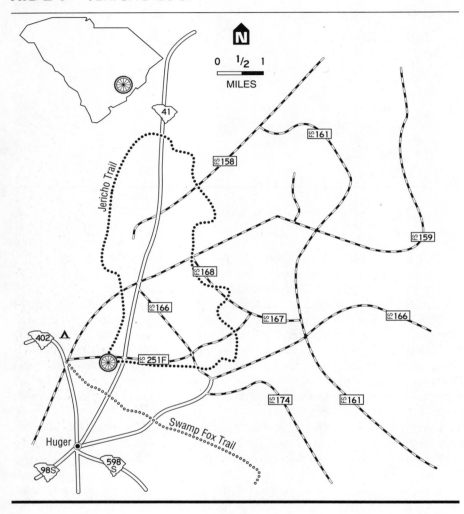

current trail conditions. Summer comes complete with blazing sun and biting insects. Be sure to bring sunscreen, insect repellant, and several filled water bottles.

Services: All services are available in nearby Mount Pleasant and Charleston, while some are available in Moncks Corner. There are several campgrounds located within the national forest near the trailhead.

Hazards: During the summer, biting mosquitoes and chiggers are little more

Equestrians also use many of the trails designated for mountain bike use. *Photo by Owen Riley, Jr.*

than a nuisance, but ticks offer additional problems. Some carry Lyme disease and Rocky Mountain spotted fever, so be sure to check for any stowaways after you ride. Many reptiles call this forest home, including the poisonous rattlesnake, copperhead, and water moccasin. Most snakes will make a gallant effort to avoid you, but the water moccasin has a reputation for being somewhat aggressive. Be particularly observant and careful in the swamp areas.

Rescue index: The rescue index is marginal. Though the trail intersects a number of Forest Service access roads, they are lightly traveled. In addition, the nearest city offering emergency medical assistance is miles away. For these reasons, be certain to bring along a tool kit and a well-appointed first-aid kit.

Land status: National forest.

Maps: The Francis Marion National Forest map is available from the ranger station for a nominal fee. The trail is also detailed on four USGS 7.5 minute quadrangles: Shulerville, Ocean Bay, Bethera, and Huger.

Finding the trail: The trailhead is located on SC 41 at the intersection with Forest Service Road 251-F. This is near the town of Huger, approximately 1 mile north of the Swamp Fox Trail's western trailhead.

Sources of additional information:

Witherbee Ranger District
P. O. Box 1532
Moncks Corner, SC 29461
(803) 336-3248

Easy Rider Bikes
1039 Johnnie Dodds Blvd. (Anna Knapp Plaza)
Mount Pleasant, SC 29464
(803) 881-0222

RIDE 8   *HELL HOLE BAY WILDERNESS RIDE*

Long ribbons of hard-packed dirt roads skirt the Hell Hole Bay Wilderness, appearing to veteran thrill-seekers as an inviting opportunity for "jamming in the big ring." These cyclists will tell you that nirvana can be found right here in coastal South Carolina's national forest.

For those more interested in a leisurely tour than an endorphin rush, this moderately difficult 17-mile loop also provides scenic surroundings and a chance to glimpse a variety of wildlife. White-tailed deer, wild turkey, rabbits, dove, quail, raccoon, and squirrel all thrive in this forest and are hunted during certain seasons. There are also bobcat, fox, and more than 250 species of birds. You might even spot the infamous opossum, South Carolina's semiofficial state "road kill." Southerners rarely have an opportunity to observe opossum alive and scampering through the woods; generally we only see these furry black-and-white critters after they have become flattened fauna.

Observant cyclists may also see the endangered red-cockaded woodpecker, about the size of a bluebird. The bird's head and back are black with small white spots that are arranged in rows on the back, giving it a ladder-back appearance. With the exception of a small red dot above the male's cheek, the males and

RIDE 8 *HELL HOLE BAY WILDERNESS RIDE*

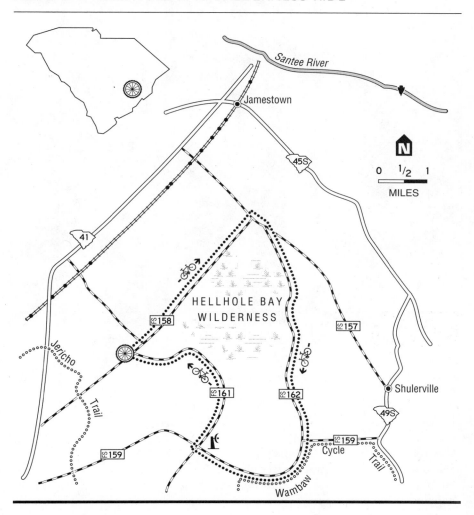

females look alike. Living in a clan of two to six birds, they roost in a colony of living pine trees with rotting cavities. The woodpeckers nest in holes that often take them a year or more to excavate. After Hurricane Hugo destroyed most of the woodpeckers' nesting trees in 1989, forestry technicians drilled over 500 nesting holes in some of the remaining pines in an attempt to help this endangered species. These woodpeckers have the unusual habit of boring additional holes adjacent to their nests, creating an ooze of pine resin. This flowing pitch

The buttressed trunks of cypress trees are a common sight in the South's swamps.

makes the nesting trees look like candles and is usually a telltale sign of the woodpecker's presence.

General location: This ride is located within Francis Marion National Forest, about 40 miles north of Charleston.

Elevation change: There is no appreciable change in elevation.

Season: Late fall and winter are the most temperate seasons for mountain biking. Summer temperatures and humidity can be almost unbearable at times; accompanying biting insects increase the misery index.

Services: All services are available in Mount Pleasant and Charleston. There is a gas station and convenience store in Huger. A number of campgrounds are available year-round in the national forest.

Hazards: Aside from the annoyance of mosquitoes and other toothy insects, there are no true hazards to avoid on this ride.

Rescue index: The ride sticks to open Forest Service roads for its entire length; therefore the rescue index is good. Help can be found in nearby Moncks Corner, Mount Pleasant, and Charleston.

Land status: National forest.

Maps: The Francis Marion National Forest map is available from the ranger station. This loop of Forest Service roads is also found on two USGS 7.5 minute quadrangles: Shulerville and Jamestown.

Finding the trail: From the town of Huger, proceed north on SC 41 for approximately 5 miles to the intersection with Forest Service Road 158. Turn right onto FS 158 and drive for 2.9 miles to the intersection with FS 161. Park at any road pulloff near this intersection.

Sources of additional information:

Wambaw Ranger District
P. O. Box 788
McClellanville, SC 29458
(803) 887-3257

Witherbee Ranger District
P. O. Box 1532
Moncks Corner, SC 29461
(803) 336-3248

Easy Rider Bikes
1039 Johnnie Dodds Blvd. (Anna Knapp Plaza)
Mount Pleasant, SC 29464
(803) 881-0222

Notes on the trail: This ride passes sections of forest that will afford cyclists an up-close view of the path of destruction made by Hurricane Hugo in September 1989.

Charleston

RIDE 9   *WEST ASHLEY GREENWAY*

It is hard to imagine that a quiet mountain bike trail stems from such a noisy urban setting of honking car horns and screeching brakes. But it does. This 16-mile (round-trip) out-and-back rail trail begins along a congested section of road cacophonous with the din of traffic. But soon after boarding your mountain bike, you will find yourself pedaling along a green grassy corridor which, in the not so distant past, was laced with crossties and rails.

The noise of Charleston quickly fades as the trail winds past backyards of a quiet, modest neighborhood. Small, well-tended vegetable gardens flank the trail during summer, while azaleas planted along back fences color the path with vivid pinks and reds during spring. Fragrant, deep purple wisteria blossoms hang from vines that climb up tall tree trunks and braid through their branches like a young girl's satin ribbons.

The day that we mountain biked this route, I cycled ahead of my group and was the first to arrive at a section of trail that left the heavily wooded area to thread through scenic lowcountry marsh. As I waited for the rest of the cyclists to catch up, the pungent smell of the marsh—salty and fecund—bathed my nose with each passing breeze. I took in long, deep breaths as I watched laughing gulls pirouette through the air and then suddenly dive to strike the surface of the salty creek to nab a small fish for dinner. Their loud, high-pitched *ha-ha-ha-ha-haah-haah-haah-haah* cries made their name seem perfectly appropriate. Their interesting voices and swirling aerial acrobatics entertained me for quite some time until I noticed a flock of double-crested cormorants perched upright on the roof of a nearby dock house. This goose-sized, dark bird is common in the Charleston marsh areas. Its name comes from the Latin word *corvus marinus*, meaning "sea crow."

Charleston's Water Commission acquired this abandoned railroad corridor back in the mid-1980s. The commission contacted the City Parks Department and proposed that the Parks Department develop the surface of the corridor as a trail while the Commission continued to use the subsurface. The two entities struck a deal that made everyone happy. The Parks Department gained a public trail without expending any precious budget funds and the Water Commission avoided the cost of maintenance and landscaping of their property.

This Seaboard Coast Line railroad right-of-way was once the path of chugging

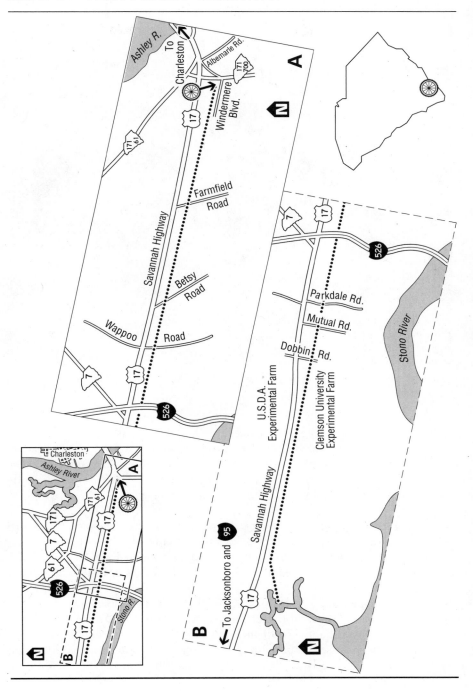

After several miles of cycling away from the city on West Ashley Greenway, the natural scenery becomes especially beautiful.

locomotives that delivered cotton and other goods from the Charleston area to other parts of the Southeast. Now the trees lining this path no longer hear the wail of the steam whistle, only the spin of bicycle wheels and the sound of cheerful voices. The railway equipment has been removed; all that remains are the ghosts of a bygone era and an inviting trail for bicyclists.

General location: This ride begins, as the name implies, west of the Ashley River, west of Charleston's historic downtown peninsula. It actually begins at Albemarle Road, though many cyclists choose to begin at Folly Road (SC 171) to avoid crossing this busy highway on bicycles. This shortens the ride by about .5 miles.

Elevation change: There is no appreciable change in elevation.

Season: Because of the mild winters in Charleston, this trail can be ridden year-round. Spring is probably one of the most pleasant seasons, temperature-wise, and one of the most scenic because of flowering plants and trees. Midday rides in late summer and early autumn are fairly miserable because of the humidity and heat. At that time of the year, an early morning or late afternoon ride would be more enjoyable.

Services: All services are available in Charleston.

Hazards: There are a few sections of trail that are littered with broken glass—proof positive that rednecks exist even in the beautiful, aristocratic city of Charleston. Biting insects and heat should be expected during the summer months; bring along bug dope, sunscreen, and plenty of water.

Rescue index: The trail parallels US 17 for its entire distance, so help can easily be obtained in case of an emergency.

Land status: The trail is managed by the Charleston's Department of Parks.

Maps: Maps can be obtained from the Department of Parks in Charleston. The trail can also be found on two USGS 7.5 minute quadrangles: Charleston and Johns Island.

Finding the trail: From downtown Charleston, drive over the Ashley River on US 17 toward the area of Charleston known as "West of the Ashley." Just before reaching the intersection of US 17 and SC 61, you will see a sign directing you to Albemarle Road. Turn left onto Albemarle Road. Proceed for .2 mile to a parking lot on the right marking the Albemarle Road terminus for the trail.

Sources of additional information:

Department of Parks
30 Mary Murray Drive
Charleston, SC 29403
(803) 724-7321

Palmetto Cyclery
1319 Savannah Highway
Charleston, SC 29407
(803) 571-1211

Notes on the trail: At the time of this writing, the trail had been developed to an endpoint at the Clemson Experimental Station for 7.6 miles of cycling. You can ride an additional (very scenic) mile past this point to a dilapidated wooden trestle. The Department of Parks ultimately plans to replace this trestle with a safe wooden bridge, which will allow the trail to extend all the way to Johns Island.

If you begin the ride from a point on Folly Road, you can avoid crossing the busy highway. This is an especially good option if you have young children in your group. To reach this starting point, cross the Ashley River on US 17 from Charleston. You will almost immediately come to an intersection of US 17 and SC 61; bear left on US 17. You will then reach another intersection of roads; proceed on SC 171 to Windermere Shopping Center. There is a sign for the West Ashley Greenway at the edge of this strip of shops. Park on the right behind the shops.

RIDE 10 *WEST ASHLEY BIKEWAY*

Mountain bike rides just don't get much easier than this four-mile-long (round-trip) out-and-back. The paved surface, flat terrain, and lack of technical challenges provide a good introductory ride for beginners and young children. Though this trail may be too short to draw serious mountain bikers, its location within the city of Charleston makes it attractive to many.

Once a Seaboard Coast Line rail route, the corridor was abandoned in 1976 and soon became an inner city dumping ground for refuse. Overgrown with weeds, rodents, rusting appliances, and discarded mattresses, the area was finally targeted for cleanup by local residents, who gained financial assistance from federal and state agencies. Today, this section of railway corridor has been converted to an attractive multi-use trail for cyclists, joggers, and walkers. It also serves as a testament to what can be done through the combined efforts of government and active citizens with a set-jaw resolve.

General location: This ride is located west of the Ashley River and west of Charleston's historic downtown area.

Elevation change: There is no appreciable change in elevation.

Season: This trail can be ridden year-round. The temperature and humidity become quite uncomfortable in the late summer and early fall months; you may wish to avoid bicycling during the middle of the day at those times of the year.

Services: All services are available in Charleston.

Hazards: Biting insects and heat during summer months are the only real inconveniences on this short trail.

Rescue index: The trail's length and proximity to well-traveled roads make the rescue index good.

Land status: The trail is managed by Charleston's Department of Parks.

Maps: Maps of the trail are available from Charleston's Department of Parks. The trail is also found on the USGS 7.5 minute quadrangle for Johns Island.

Finding the trail: From downtown Charleston, drive over the Ashley River on US 17. You will almost immediately come to an intersection with SC 61; bear left to continue on US 17. Drive for approximately 3.6 miles to Wappoo Road; turn right. The Wappoo Road terminus for this rail trail will be on the right. The trail extends for 2 miles to St. Andrews Boulevard near SC 61.

Sources of additional information:

Department of Parks
30 Mary Murray Drive
Charleston, SC 29403
(803) 724-7321

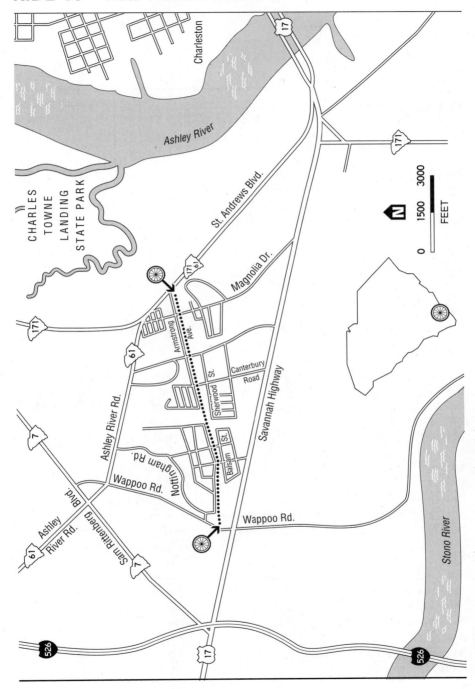

Palmetto Cyclery
1319 Savannah Highway
Charleston, SC 29407
(803) 571-1211

RIDE 11   *CHARLES TOWNE LANDING LOOP*

Though certainly not much of an aerobic workout, this easy ride at the site of the first permanent English settlement in South Carolina offers an ideal day of cycling to families and beginners. A loop of about four miles of paved pathway and some single-track trail will lead you through 80 acres of beautiful gardens inside Charles Towne Landing State Park. History seems to waft through the Spanish moss dripping from the gnarled limbs of stately oaks—you almost expect to glimpse the diaphanous figure of the ghost of an early colonial settler gliding by.

There are a number of interesting highlights that will entice you to stop along the ride. A reconstruction of a seventeenth-century period village, complete with a smithery, woodworker's shop, and print shop, offers visitors an example of the early colonist's daily life. In an experimental garden, rice, indigo, sugarcane, cotton, and other crops are grown just as they were in 1670. Floating at the wharf is the *Adventure,* a full-scale replica of a 53-foot trading vessel that was sailed during the seventeenth century. It reminds visitors of the critical importance that trading by sea had in the early development of the colony. There is also a 20-acre zoo featuring animals indigenous to coastal South Carolina in the late 1600s. Bison, puma, elk, alligator, bobcat, white-tailed deer, wolves, and bear are some of the animals that can be observed in this natural-habitat zoo.

General location: Charles Towne Landing State Park is located in the city of Charleston.

Elevation change: There is no appreciable change in elevation.

Season: This park is open year-round, though the more pleasant times of the year to ride are during the winter and spring months.

Services: All services are available in Charleston. There is a bike rental shelter located in the park. There is also a snack bar in the park, offering hot dogs, sandwiches, and ice cream. Water and rest rooms are available here as well.

Hazards: Scorching sun during the summer months can threaten tender, pale skin; bring sunscreen. Biting bugs can be a real nuisance during hot weather. Watch out for people walking along these trails and be sure to slow down as you pass them.

Rescue index: Park personnel are readily available to help at all times.

Land status: State park.

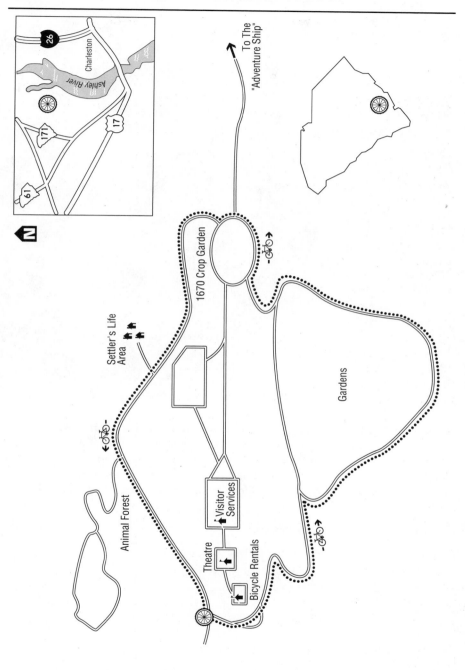

Live oak trees mirrored in the still waters of one of Charles Towne Landing's ponds.

Maps: Park maps are provided at the admission booth. This area is also found on the USGS 7.5 minute quadrangle for Charleston.

Finding the trail: From Charleston, cross the Ashley River on US 17. You will almost immediately come to a fork in the road. Take the right fork, which is SC 61. Proceed for approximately 3 miles to the park entrance, which will be on the right.

Sources of additional information:

Charles Towne Landing State Park
1500 Old Towne Road
Charleston, SC 29407
(803) 556-4450

Charleston Visitor Center
P. O. Box 975
Charleston, SC 29402
(803) 853-8000

Palmetto Cyclery
1319 Savannah Highway
Charleston, SC 29407
(803) 571-1211

Notes on the trail: Most bicycle types are suitable for these pathways: all-terrain bicycles, cruisers, etc. A full-fledged mountain bike can certainly be ridden along these paths, but is not necessary.

A modest admission fee is charged at the entrance booth.

RIDE 12   *MAGNOLIA WILDLIFE LOOP*

This is another easy ride that is graced by stunning scenery and is chock-full of interesting highlights. Five miles long, this loop is not a single-track trail but a combination of dirt and dike roads that wind along the fringes of the beautiful Audubon Swamp. Because it gently meanders along flat terrain and poses no significant technical challenge, this is a perfect ride for beginners and children. However, more experienced and better conditioned cyclists will still find the ride appealing, with its natural wonders and historical strolls back in time.

Once used as a freshwater reservoir for Magnolia Plantation's rice fields, these 60 acres of brackish swampland have since become an oasis for tupelo, cypress, and water oak. Though it provides sanctuary for many varieties of wildlife attracted to wetlands, the Audubon Swamp is probably best known for its amazing number and variety of waterfowl. Over 100 years ago, John J. Audubon visited this marshland to obtain specimens of water birds, including the stately anhinga. You can still commonly hear along this trail the low grunts from this blackish "snakebird," so called because of its appearance when swimming: the only visible parts of its submerged body are its long, slender neck and head. The bird lacks oil glands to aid it in preening, so it must perch with its wings half-open to dry them in the sun. You may wish to climb the wildlife observation tower to try to spot this odd-looking water bird, as well as the 223 other types of birds that have been sighted and observed in these rice fields, lakes, and natural swamps.

And, as you might expect, alligators flourish in the black waters of this swamp. Normally, they are seen mostly during the summer season, but you can expect an appearance on any day bathed with warm, continuous shafts of sunlight. On one early spring mountain bike ride, we were surprised to see so many alligators out so early in the season. They must have had spring fever as badly as we did, out enjoying the unseasonably warm March day. One keen-eyed cyclist in our group spotted the first, a juvenile gator who had suspended his small body over a floating log. He looked like a child playfully draped across a rubber raft with limbs dangling into a swimming pool. Farther along the path, we spotted

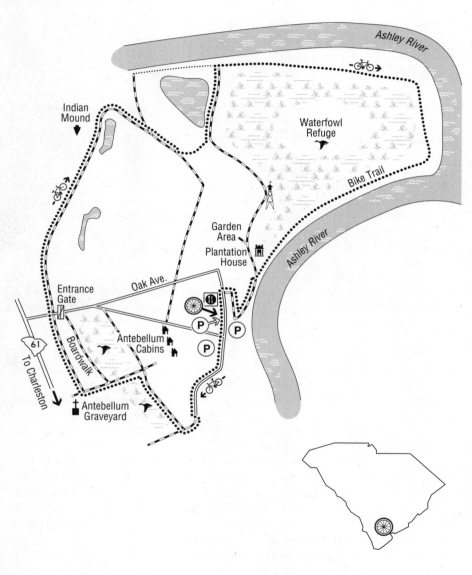

Young cyclists on one of Charleston's many rides.

a much larger alligator, about seven feet long, hovering motionless in the still, eerie, black water. Being so close to such a large and potentially dangerous animal tends to make me a little uneasy. We did not linger for long at the edge of the swamp.

In addition to alligators, birds, and other wildlife, many additional attractions can be glimpsed on this ride. The largest prehistoric Indian burial ground on the East Coast is located along this route, marked as the *Indian Mound*. The Smithsonian Institution displays artifacts from this burial site. Colorful wildflowers now blanket this final resting place of Indians. You will also cycle past an area known as "the Street," which is a row of the last remaining antebellum slave cabins which once dotted the plantation. Some of the cabins are inhabited today by the descendants of some of those slaves.

The simple woodland graveyard where Adam Bennett is buried can also be seen from the bike trail. Bennett was the dear friend and chief slave of Reverend John G. Drayton. Together, these two men redesigned Magnolia Plantation's oldest formal garden from its original Louis XIV French style to its present informal English style. During the Civil War, General Sherman's Union troops were advised that Bennett knew where the Drayton family silver had been buried to protect it from the looting soldiers. In 1865, the troops tied a rope around Bennett's neck and dangled him from a limb of one of the great oaks in the plantation garden. The soldiers fired shots about Bennett's feet and gradually tightened the rope in an attempt to force him to reveal the secret burial site. Though faced with death, Bennett did not tell and, finally, the soldiers grew tired and disgusted and released him. Afterward, to advise his former master of the soldiers' actions, Bennett walked 250 miles to the North Carolina retreat where John Drayton had fled during the war. Together, they returned to Charleston to continue their work on the plantation. Ironically, the coveted family silver was buried beneath the same oak tree the Union soldiers used to threaten Adam Bennett with death by hanging.

This bicycle trail is located on the grounds of Magnolia Plantation, which is now listed in the National Register of Historic Places. The natural beauty of the swamp is an interesting contrast to the manicured gardens of this plantation along the Ashley River. Begun in the late 1600s as a plantation estate garden, Magnolia Gardens blooms year-round and is considered among the world's most beautiful. Magnolia Plantation, the 300-year-old ancestral mansion of the Drayton family, is also open to the public and is regarded as the oldest man-made attraction in America.

General location: Magnolia Plantation and Audubon Swamp Garden is located 11 miles northwest of Charleston.

Elevation change: There is no appreciable change in elevation.

Season: The trail can be ridden year-round. An early spring ride offers a good opportunity to see the incredible stands of nearly 300 varieties of azaleas and more than 900 varieties of camellias. The temperatures are more moderate at that time of the year as well.

Services: All services are available in nearby Charleston and Summerville. Bikes can be rented at the concession stand on the grounds of the plantation. There are snacks, water, and rest rooms available on site.

Hazards: Alligators are plentiful in this area, as are several kinds of poisonous snakes. Stay on the roads and keep your distance from alligators. Scorching sun and biting insects in spring and summer will threaten to spoil your day, so come armed with sunscreen and insect repellant.

Rescue index: Help is readily available in this popular tourist attraction.

Land status: This property is privately owned and managed as a nonprofit, charitable foundation. It has been open to the public since 1870. There is a small admission fee.

Maps: Maps are provided at the admission booth when you enter the plantation. The trail can also be found on two USGS 7.5 minute quadrangles: Johns Island and Ladson.

Finding the trail: From downtown Charleston, drive across the Ashley River on US 17. You will almost immediately come to a fork in the road; take the right fork, which will be SC 61. Follow this state highway for approximately 11 miles. The entrance to Magnolia Plantation and the Audubon Swamp Garden will be on the right.

Sources of additional information:

Magnolia Plantation and Audubon Swamp Gardens
Route 4, Highway 61
Charleston, SC 29414
(803) 571-1266

Charleston Visitor Center
P. O. Box 975
Charleston, SC 29402
(803) 853-8000

Notes on the trail: Full-fledged mountain bikes are not necessary on these trails. All-terrain bicycles, beach cruisers, etc. would fare perfectly well on these level, well-surfaced roads and trails.

From the parking lot, you will begin by cycling away from the entrance to the gardens. The bike trail is clearly marked and begins on a narrow, paved pathway that quickly changes over to a hard-packed, wide single-track trail. After about a mile, the trail seems to end on the main road near the entrance booth. The bulk of the ride follows, on established dirt and dike roads.

Edisto Island

RIDE 13 *EDISTO ISLAND BIKE PATH*

It is difficult for me to write objectively about a place that I love so. Superlatives gush from my pen when I describe Edisto Island, for it was on this enchanting island that I summered each year as a young girl. And it was on this island that I returned as an adult, with children of my own, to spend countless summer days beside crashing Atlantic waves. It was on Edisto's glistening beaches that I watched as my towheaded toddler scooped up pale sand in her dimpled hands, while my infant daughter napped peacefully on a blanket in the shade. My spirit feasts on this island.

Let me offer a word of warning. Guard yourself as you cycle this beautiful island—like a charming lover, Edisto will steal your heart.

There is something decidedly seductive and alluring about the island seascape, but Edisto's charm doesn't stop there. It is an unpretentious place where folks clad in T-shirts, shorts, and flip-flops are the norm. It is a place where a big night on the town involves hitting one of the local seafood joints for some fried shrimp, hushpuppies, and a bottle of cold beer. Nightlife starts with slow walks along the beach to watch the dying orange embers of the sun slowly dissolve into the blue waters of the inlet. Then a little later, if you are really looking for excitement, you can go on a guided beach walk to try to observe loggerhead turtles that nest here. And that's about it, folks. Even if the turtles don't show up for the entertainment portion of the moonlit show, you will experience the delicious sensation of the warm Atlantic waves licking your ankles as you walk barefoot along the ocean's edge.

Returning year after year, you will find few things changed. It is that constancy and reluctance to change that seems to invite tradition and roots. Perhaps it is the sense of peacefulness and calm that blankets the island that appeals to most of us. My father always joked that each time he drove across the drawbridge and onto the island, he could hear my mother's blood pressure drop with an audible "thunk."

Even before arriving on Edisto, you will be captivated by its spell. As you drive along SC 174 (a designated scenic highway) toward the island, you will be surrounded by beautiful, 100-year-old live oak trees. The highway is bordered by these huge trees draped with Spanish moss and, in some places, their intertwined branches form a canopy overhead. It looks like the limbs from both sides of the

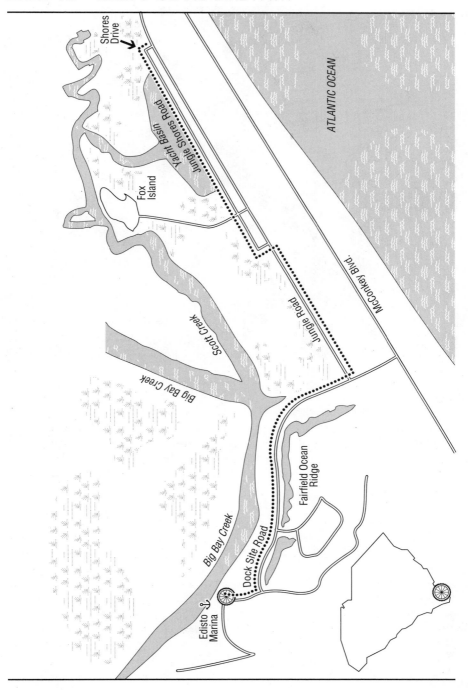

Miles of marsh on Edisto Island.

road have strained to reach across the road and then tightly grabbed hold of one another. These evergreens are especially beautiful in winter, when contrasted against the bare branches of surrounding deciduous trees. From a distance, their romantic silhouettes are unmistakable, and with their leaves like verdant petticoats and their delicately curving branches, they are decidedly the most feminine of all trees.

This easy bike path will lead you on a five-mile tour of part of the island. This ten-mile out-and-back ride on flat terrain can be easily cycled on almost any type of bicycle, from a beach cruiser to a mountain bike. Though the trail surface is paved, portions of the path are buckled or broken, which makes it unsuitable for thin-tired road bikes. The ride begins near the marina and then curves around the lagoons of Fairfield Plantation before turning onto Jungle Road. Appropriately, the road is bordered by tangles of junglelike woods shrouded in mystery; you half expect to see a colorful toucan perched on a tree branch. The air is thick with the ever-present chirping of crickets, and though this high-pitched trill seems deafening when you first arrive on the island, it quickly melds with the background to become pleasant white noise.

General location: The trail is located on Edisto Island, between Beaufort and Charleston.

Elevation change: There is no appreciable change in elevation.

Season: This route can be ridden year-round.

Services: With the exception of a bike shop and hospital, all services are available on the island. There are two grocery stores, restaurants, and campsites and cabins at the Edisto Beach State Park. There is no motel on Edisto but there are houses, villas, and condominiums available for rent through several rental agencies on the island.

Hazards: Be sure to watch for traffic at the road crossings, especially on the Jungle Shores Road leg of the bike route.

Rescue index: The route parallels well-traveled roads from which help could easily be flagged down.

Land status: The path is maintained by the town of Edisto Beach.

Maps: The route can be found on two USGS 7.5 minute quadrangles: Edisto Beach and Edisto Island.

Finding the trail: After driving into the town of Edisto on SC 174, turn right onto Jungle Road. (Follow the signs to Fairfield Ocean Ridge.) Drive 2.7 miles to a stop sign. Turn right here and proceed an additional 1.1 miles to a large parking area for the marina just past Fairfield Ocean Ridge. Park here.

Sources of additional information:

Edisto Chamber of Commerce
P. O. Box 206
Edisto Island, SC 29438
(803) 869-3867

Palmetto Cyclery
1319 Savannah Highway
Charleston, SC 29407
(803) 571-1211
(Alana Bell is the owner of this bike shop and will go out of her way to help you.)

Notes on the trail: There will be signs marked "Bike Route" at the beginning of the ride and at all of the turns. After cycling 1.7 miles, you will turn left onto Jungle Road for an additional .6 mile of cycling. By turning left onto Dawoo Street, you will continue on this path. It quickly merges into Jungle Shores Road, which is the final leg of the bike route.

RIDE 14 *INDIAN MOUND TRAIL*

Possibly one of the prettiest single-track trails along the coast of South Carolina, this easy, four-mile-long (round-trip), out-and-back single-track trail also offers a glimpse of an unusual feature. As the name suggests, the trail leads to a bend in Big Bay Creek where ancient Indian shell mounds rest. Believed to be more than 4,000 years old, these mounds sit on cliffs overlooking the creek. They serve as evidence of the early presence of Indians on the island, though it is not known why this bend on a lowcountry creek was used for so many years. Though the abundant shellfish was undoubtedly important to them, it is believed that there was some ceremonial or social significance to the site.

Some of the locals won't go near the shell midden, claiming that Indian spirits still drift among the huge piles of weather-beaten shells. Interestingly, my younger daughter, a fearless eight-year-old, was oddly spooked when cycling the trail with me, even though she did not know the history or the lore of the area.

The path begins by zipping through a maritime forest that features some of the tallest palmetto trees in the state. The graceful branches of live oak trees, garnished with drapes of Spanish moss, lend an air of gentility to the surroundings. The trail peeks out of the dense, lush forest several times, crossing a marsh on a wooden boardwalk and clinging to the open bank of Scott Creek. The drone of tree frogs and the higher-pitched song of crickets complement this classic lowcountry scenery.

General location: The trail is located on Edisto Island, which is between Beaufort and Charleston.

Elevation change: There is no appreciable change in elevation.

Season: The trail can be ridden year-round, though some summer rides can be miserably hot, humid, and plagued with annoying insects.

Services: This trail is located within the Edisto Beach State Park, which offers campsites as well as rustic cabins for rent. Restaurants (Salty Mike's, which overlooks the Edisto marina, is my favorite eatery on the island), grocery stores, and gas stations are located on Edisto Island. However, for a bike shop, pharmacy, or medical treatment facility, you will need to drive to Charleston, about 40 miles away.

Hazards: Poisonous snakes do slither and slink about this trail; keep a watchful eye out for them. There are also sections of trail with exposed tree roots that should be negotiated with some degree of caution, especially after a rain when they are slippery and wet. Flying over your handlebars from having your front wheel tweaked by a root is certainly grand entertainment for the rest of your pedaling party, but it greatly increases the probability of returning home with a fractured clavicle or shattered wrist. Ouch!

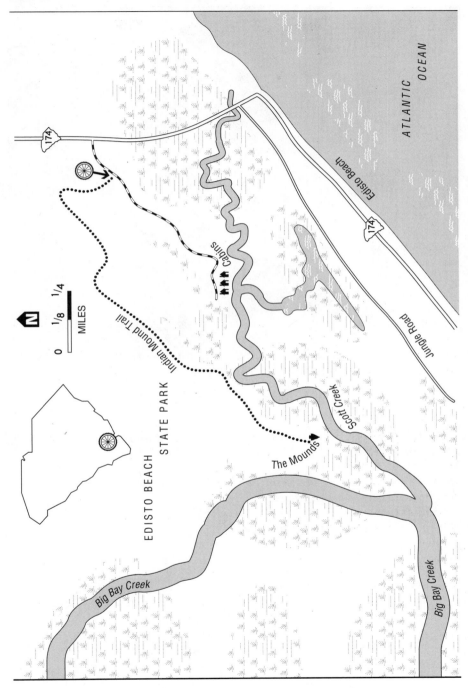

ATLANTIC OCEAN

Edisto Beach

174

174

Jungle Road

Cabins

Scott Creek

Indian Mound Trail

N

MILES

0   1/8   1/4

EDISTO BEACH STATE PARK

The Mounds

Big Bay Creek

Big Bay Creek

Narrow, fun single-track of Edisto Island's Indian Mound Trail. *Photo by Elizabeth Finley*

Rescue index: The rescue index is fair. Though you are on single-track trail away from any roads carrying traffic, the trail is short.

Land status: State park.

Maps: The trail can be found on two USGS 7.5 minute quadrangles: Edisto Beach and Edisto Island.

Finding the trail: Edisto Island can be reached by driving in on SC 174 and following the road signs. Just before the road ends, there will be a sign on the right for the Edisto Beach State Park. Turn right toward the cabins. At .2 miles, there will be a trailhead sign and a dirt parking area on the right. Park here.

Sources of additional information:

Edisto Beach State Park
8377 State Cabin Road
Edisto Island, SC 29438
(803) 869-2156

Palmetto Cyclery
1319 Savannah Highway
Charleston, SC 29407
(803) 571-1211

Beaufort / Hilton Head

RIDE 15   *HUNTING ISLAND LOOP*

Hunting Island State Park, on Hunting Island, offers mountain bikers one of the most "tropical" settings found on the South Carolina coast. Although the inexorable forces of wind and wave have carved a great deal of shore from this important barrier island, this erosion has brought the lush forest into startlingly close proximity to the crashing ocean. The best place to see the dramatic effects of this ongoing process is the long inlet lagoon slicing behind the south beach of the island. A single-track trail passing through the high sea oats and salt marsh cordgrass follows the crumbling contours of the lagoon, providing an almost constant view of the waterway with its banks overhung by precariously tilting palmettos. A wide variety of bird life—including brown pelicans, herons, egrets, and terns—can be observed from the lagoon trail. This narrow path of sand sometimes ducks back into a dense rampart of cabbage palmettos to bypass areas of standing water, but eventually returns to the fragile bluff above the lagoon beach.

This six-mile loop of fire roads, single-track trail, and beach riding offers a beautiful and somewhat challenging ride to mountain bikers. The route between Sea Island Parkway and the inlet lagoon parallels the park's beaches, giving cyclists a good taste of the beauty of coastal South Carolina.

The fire roads and nature trails maintained by park personnel are relatively straight, gently rolling, and slightly rutted. Though not technical, the surface of sand and loose earth requires some attention. The single-track trails, developed by local fat-tire fanatics, are more challenging, with a series of roller-coaster dips, wraparound turns between tree trunks, and several log hops. The narrow trail running alongside the lagoon presents steep drop-offs beachside, and a deep litter of palm fronds that sometimes makes the going difficult and noisy. These short but demanding sections of single-track are sure to satisfy hard-core riders interested in honing their bike-handling skills.

The less challenging (actually easy) nature trail cuts southwest through a mysterious maritime forest of oaks, slash pine, and palmetto. Saw palmettos spread broad, green fans into the trail, and riders noisily rustle the leaf stalks as they fly by. Several short side trails spill out onto the fine white sands of the park's beaches, offering stunning views of the Atlantic Ocean.

RIDE 15 *HUNTING ISLAND LOOP*

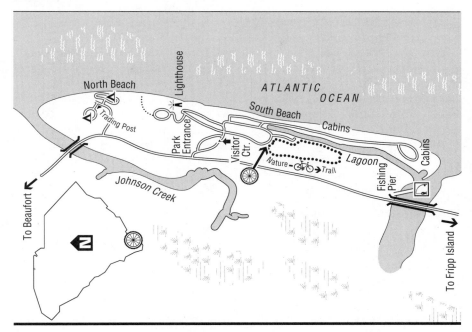

General location: East of Beaufort.

Elevation change: Although there are portions of the trail that are rolling, with some steep dips and rises, there is no appreciable change in elevation.

Season: The trail is located within Hunting Island State Park, which is open 7 days a week, year-round. The best seasons for riding are late fall through early spring. During that time, the heat and humidity associated with these subtropical woods have abated and opportunities for observing wildlife are greater.

Services: All services are available in Beaufort. In addition, the park itself offers the essentials during peak operating season. The Trading Post, located in the park's camping area, sells groceries and camping supplies. The park's 200-site camping area is equipped with individual water and electrical hook-ups, heated rest rooms, and showers. These are pretty fancy offerings for folks (like me) accustomed to primitive sites with no amenities. For a really decadent camping experience, there are 15 rental cabins available.

Hazards: Poisonous snakes and biting insects, including the irritating sand gnat, are potential hazards during periods of hot weather. Ticks are plentiful in the brush of the wooded areas of the island. Abrupt, eroded drop-offs adjacent to the inlet lagoon present a danger to cyclists traveling at high speeds through this section. There are alligators roaming this island; keep your distance if you spot one of these powerful reptiles.

Rescue index: The trail is never more than a mile or two from the park's Visitor Center or the Sea Island Parkway.

Land status: State park.

Maps: The park provides a free pamphlet that features a map of Hunting Island. Also, the ride is shown on two USGS 7.5 minute quadrangles: Fripps Inlet and St. Helena Sound.

Finding the trail: From Interstate 95 South, take Exit 38 to US 21 South/Alt. 17. Follow US 21 South and follow the signs to Beaufort and on to Hunting Island. The main entrance to the state park will be on the left side of the highway (Sea Island Parkway) approximately 50 miles after leaving I-95. Turn into the state park and follow the signs toward South Beach. Park in the parking area provided for the beach. You will find the nature trail (dirt jeep track/fire road) to the left of the paved road shortly after leaving the parking area.

Sources of additional information:

Hunting Island State Park
1775 Sea Island Parkway
St. Helena Sound, SC 29920
(803) 838-2011

Beaufort Bike Shop
2731 Highway 21
Beaufort, SC 29902
(803) 524-2453

Notes on the trail: Park personnel are committed to making the nature trails good routes for hikers and bikers, and local bicyclists assist in this effort. The development and maintenance of the single-track trails is primarily a project of the local bike shop in Beaufort. Work continues to increase the length of the loop and the number of trail connectors for the single-track and nature trails on Hunting Island. After the ride you may wish to visit the state park's excellent Visitor Center, whose displays identify the denizens of the coast and explain the natural forces constantly changing the island. The center's boardwalk crosses a small pond complete with fountain and alligators. Bear in mind that these alligators are in no way contained within the pond area.

You shouldn't leave the island without stopping by the famous lighthouse, perhaps the most prominent feature of this 5,000-acre park. Built in 1875, this 136-foot, striped lighthouse once served as a beacon for ships entering St. Helena Sound. Deactivated on June 16, 1933, this historic lighthouse is one of the last remaining lighthouses on the Atlantic coast.

Nearby Fripp Island is reached via Hunting Island Road and is worth a visit if you have the time. This island has retained much of its natural beauty and has somehow avoided the commercialization monster that has eaten up so many of

Views of the inlet lagoon from the path on Hunting Island. *Photo by Joel McCollough*

these idyllic islands. Understated, relaxed, and natural are the key words here. The pace is slow, with white-tailed deer freely roaming about. There are no Doo-Drop-Inns or El Cheapo Lodges advertised with blinking neon signs, but there are vacation homes and villas available for rent. Golf and fishing seem to be the favorite sports on Fripp Island, though swimming and bicycling are also enjoyed.

RIDE 16 *PINCKNEY ISLAND NATIONAL WILDLIFE REFUGE*

This easy, eight-mile (round-trip), out-and-back mountain bike ride offers beautiful vistas of pine forests, freshwater ponds, and broad Carolina salt marshes. Though it is not a technically challenging ride, the excellent surface and outstanding scenery make it appealing to most cyclists. It runs along the entire length of Pinckney Island, from the parking area near Last End Point to the northern tip at White Point. Counting the grassy side trails, there are over 14 miles of nature trails available for hiking and bicycling. Two of these trails lead out to the island's eastern shore at Shell Point and Bull Point. From the shoreline you

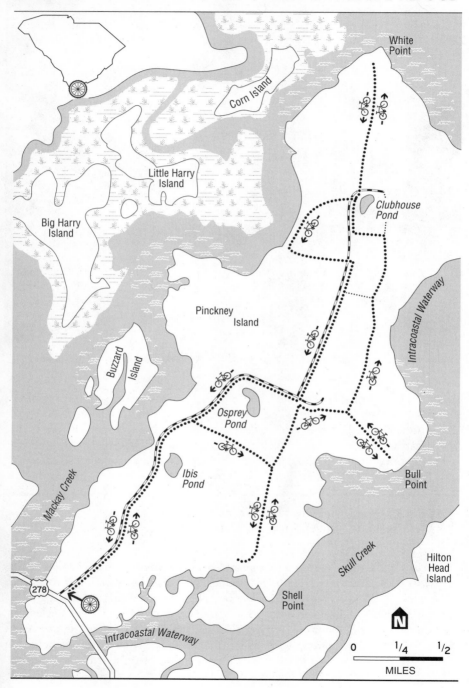

can see the marinas at Hilton Head Island across Skull Creek (the Intracoastal Waterway). The main ride follows a road of pale dirt and gravel that beckons mountain bikers to come along and see the sights of the refuge. And what sights there are to see!

Nearly 70% of this lowcountry refuge is salt marsh or tidal hammocks, which are actually just small islands. Tall marsh cordgrass gently sways in sea breezes that blow across the marsh. Sea ox-eye gives the landscape some color with its burrlike, yellow flowers. In autumn, marsh elder dresses up the causeways with its greenish-white blossoms. During high tide, notice the salt marsh snails that cling to the stalks of these marsh plants; these air breathers would drown if they were covered by water for more than one hour. At low tide, the mudflats and shallow creeks create a smorgasbord for wading and shore birds. Just a few of the birds that you might find dining in the salt marsh are oystercatchers, terns, sandpipers, herons, snowy egrets, ibises, willets, and gulls. Excellent points from which to view the marshes as you ride include the tenuous isthmus of roadbed between the parking area and Ibis Pond, as well as a tidal creek crossing on the trail to White Point.

Hilton Head Island protects the refuge from destructive sea storms, thus creating a safe sanctuary for resident animals and migratory birds. This pristine habitat is a mecca for wildlife. Four species of animals federally listed as threatened or endangered have been recorded within the refuge boundaries: the Southern bald eagle, peregrine falcon, wood stork, and American alligator. The refuge personnel work diligently to preserve their habitat from degradation and to protect them from human predation. There are other animals in the refuge that are also given a little man-made help. As you cycle along, look for nesting boxes that have been erected throughout some of the ponds for wood ducks. Near the salt marsh, you will see nesting platforms provided for roosting osprey. You are bound to notice the V-shaped hoofprints of white-tailed deer in the white sand; these wary creatures are prolific on the island. The refuge personnel maintain the deer herd by scheduling hunts as needed on a yearly basis, rather than establishing a hunting schedule and season in advance.

Pinckney Island has an undeniably rich natural history, but it is as interesting to historians as it is to naturalists. Archaeologists believe that prehistoric inhabitants—cavemen, if you will—lived on the island as long ago as 10,000 B.C. Coastal Indians later inhabited the island until the mid-1700s, when the Pinckney family acquired it. Charles Cotesworth Pinckney retired to the island and built a home near White Point, which was subsequently destroyed in 1824. As a Revolutionary War commander, signer of the U.S. Constitution, and candidate for president in the 1804 election, Pinckney was considered to be quite an accomplished fellow. He went on to develop a prosperous cotton plantation on 297 acres of Pinckney Island. Though he died in 1825, the plantation continued to thrive until 1861, when the island was invaded by Union troops during the Civil War. In 1862, South Carolina troops attacked the Third New Hampshire Infantry here, killing four Federal soldiers. The Pinckney property changed

Easy dirt roads lead cyclists through the wildlife refuge.

hands a few more times before it was finally donated in 1975 to the U.S. Fish and Wildlife Service to be used as a nature and wildlife preserve.

General location: The refuge is near Hilton Head Island.
Elevation change: There is no appreciable change in elevation.
Season: The refuge and its trails are open to the public year-round during daylight hours. The refuge is occasionally closed for periods of prescribed burning of underbrush in stands of southern pines, usually during winter months.

The period from late fall through early spring offers the best rides due to mild temperatures, low humidity, absence of biting insects, and the presence of vast numbers of migratory waterfowl.

Services: All services are available on Hilton Head Island. Bring plenty of bags of gold with you, though, because this is an expensive resort island. There is an RV campground on Hilton Head and tent camping sites in the towns of Hardeeville and Pritchardville.

Hazards: The graveled road is well maintained, but is overgrown with grass during summer months. This overgrowth can conceal snakes, some of which may be poisonous. Summer also comes complete with poison ivy, stinging insects, and those burrowing annoyances, chiggers and ticks. Occasionally, alligators may be encountered near Clubhouse Pond. This refuge is not a petting zoo; stay away from the animals, especially those burly gators. You should also be cautious of loose gravel, potholes, and puddles in the trails and road.

Rescue index: The main road is only a few miles long, so a member of your group should be able to obtain help fairly quickly. Try to be self-sufficient, however, and bring along a first-aid kit and a tool kit. To prevent the need for rescue in the first place, make an effort to exercise your common sense. A little does seem to go a long way.

Land status: National wildlife refuge.

Maps: The ride is featured in the brochure for Pinckney Island National Wildlife Refuge, with a map detailing the trail network. You can also use the refuge map from the U.S. Fish and Wildlife Service for Pinckney Island. The refuge is shown on two USGS 7.5 minute quadrangles: Bluffton and Spring Island.

Finding the trail: From Interstate 95, take Exit 5 at Hardeeville to reach SC 46. Drive east on SC 46 toward Bluffton and Hilton Head Island. Turn onto US 278 and drive east for about 5 miles to the refuge entrance, which will be on the left.

Sources of additional information:

U.S. Fish and Wildlife Service
Savannah Coastal Refuges Office
P. O. Box 8487
Savannah, GA 31412
(912) 652-4415

Cycle Center
115 Pineland Mall
Hilton Head, SC 29928
(803) 681-7450

Outdoor RV Resort
P. O. Box 21585
Hilton Head, SC 29925
(803) 681-3256 or 1-800-845-9560

Gateway Campground
P. O. Box 720
Hardeeville, SC 29927
(803) 784-2267

Stoney Crest Plantation
Highway 46
Pritchardville, SC 29910
(803) 757-3249

Notes on the trail: Water is not available at the refuge so be sure to fill your water bottles before you arrive on the island.

COASTAL GEORGIA

Whether you are a city slicker or a backwoods purist, coastal Georgia has a mountain bike ride for you. The beauty of the area will leave a lasting impression, as will the delicious sampling of different types of rides offered along this stretch of coastline. You will be able to choose from pristine wilderness rides in scenic national wildlife refuges, or historic city tours along quaint cobblestone streets.

Five of the rides are found in the Savannah area; five others are located on barrier islands and in or near the enigmatic Okefenokee Swamp. Many of the trails and dirt roads along the coast are flanked by gorgeous lowcountry scenery that makes Southerners proud and others envious.

From the South Carolina state line, you can throw a rock toward the city of Savannah and, chances are, it will land close to the trailhead of an excellent mountain bike ride. This historic city, which moves at a nineteenth-century gait, has been hailed as a city of poetry. Even the name Savannah has a poetic ring to it. Pronounced slowly, the syllables roll from the tongue like honey from a turned spoon.

Thoughts of this charming old Southern city evoke many images. Saying the name may make you think of the Spanish moss hanging from the gnarled branches of oaks like tinsel from a Christmas tree, or wrought-iron balconies colored with tumbling flowers, or even the scent of fragrant purple wisteria hitching a ride on an occasional spring breeze.

For cyclists, it also evokes images of excellent trails and rides within the city itself, in the nearby Savannah and Harris Neck National Wildlife refuges, and on Skidaway and Tybee islands.

Tybee is the beginning of a chain of 13 barrier islands, also known as "the Golden Isles," which may be the most notable feature of the Georgia coastal region. While some of these islands are fully developed, offering five-star amenities and full-scale pampering, others remain pristine and virtually untouched by the hands of commercial developers. Included in this guide are descriptions of bicycle rides on the luxurious resort islands of St. Simons and Jekyll, the oldest in the string of barrier islands. On the Golden Isles you will find the riding good, the scenery great, and the history extraordinary.

The last rides in Georgia lie near or within the alluring Okefenokee Swamp. Prehistoric cypress trees command the stage with branches adorned with dead-still moss that is mirrored by the sluggish black water of the swamp. For thousands of years, this mysterious "land of the trembling earth" has fascinated explorers, including the Indians as early as 2000 B.C. The nineteenth century saw the advent of white explorers who drove out the Timucuan Indians and established settlements along the periphery of the swamp. Today, the only explorers you might see on the roads and nearby trails of the Okefenokee Swamp are the ones armed with maps and guidebooks, on foot and in canoe and on mountain bike.

Savannah

RIDE 17 *LAUREL HILL WILDLIFE RIDE*

For mountain bikers interested in nature and not simply in hammering out the miles, this peaceful site in the Savannah National Wildlife Refuge will seem as much a refuge as it does for the wild creatures protected here. In fact, the refuge's short distance from Savannah and Hilton Head make this an ideal ride for cyclists longing to get away from the mayhem of congested city life. The contrast between industry and wilderness is especially remarkable at the beginning of the ride. Towering steel complexes of the Savannah Ports Industry clash harshly with the natural vistas of flowing river and the scenic beauty of marshland that seems to unfurl for miles until finally smudging the horizon.

Six miles of easy riding along a well-maintained road of crushed limestone and earth provide a good, nontechnical ride that is especially inviting to inexperienced riders or families with small children. Experienced cyclists can make this short loop ride more exciting with the inclusion of some of the miles of grassy dike roads that spin off the main road. These dike roads appeal to the hammerheads because they are not open to vehicles and have a bumpy, more technical surface. Though cruisers and all-terrain bicycles would fare quite well on the main road, full-fledged mountain bikes afford the greatest degree of control and comfort on the grassy dike roads.

The ride varies from offering pleasant shade as it zips through a tunnel of tightly woven live oak branches to being wide open and sunny as it barrels across dike-laced marshland. During the middle of the summer, the Southern heat becomes almost unbearable in these shadeless sections. There are days when you can actually see the heat as it hangs oppressively over the road in quivering suspension. Though these are days that most humans don't care for, the alligators of the refuge seem to revel in the heat. On one occasion, as we slowly wheeled across the sun-baked road next to the causeway, we were jolted out of our heat-induced anesthetic state by an explosion of water and sand just ten feet below us. Unknowingly, we had apparently gotten a little too close to a huge alligator sunning himself. The sounds we heard were that of his violent leave-taking as he abandoned his spot in the sun and dumped his huge body into the pool below.

In addition to the gators in the refuge, there are also white-tailed deer, bobcat, opossum, raccoon, and feral hogs dwelling in the large stands of cypress and tupelo found here. You might even catch sight of an otter slipping about the

RIDE 17 *LAUREL HILL WILDLIFE RIDE*

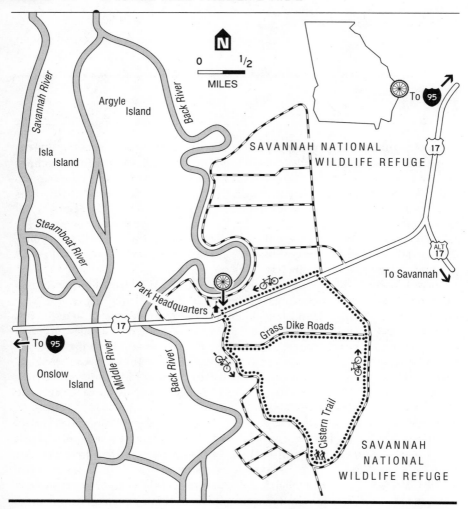

edges of a pond coated with water lilies. The birds, though, may be the most notable highlight in this lowcountry wilderness. In fact, this area serves as a key sanctuary in the Atlantic Flyway. Each year an estimated 20,000 migratory ducks winter here from November through February. In addition, the swallow-tailed kite, purple gallinule, wood stork, heron, ibis, endangered bald eagle, and others can be found in the refuge at certain times of the year. All months of the year offer birders ample sightings, though the period from October through April is regarded as best because of the mild temperatures and the presence of additional species of wintering birds not normally found in the refuge during the summer. The melodic trill of the bird songs and calls has an amazing effect of soothing the soul. With closed eyes and open ears, you might find the natural symphony of birdsong more beautiful than any orchestral aria.

In addition to the natural highlights, there are also historical highlights to interest cyclists along this ride. The 3,000 acres of freshwater impoundments that are managed for migratory waterfowl were once the rice fields of working Savannah plantations. Most of these dikes enclosing the pools were built by slaves back in the mid- to late-1700s. There is also an example of a rice field "trunk" that was used for the cultivation of this grain back in the nineteenth century. This "trunk" is actually a wooden culvert (hollowed tree trunks were used years ago) with flap gates that were raised or lowered, through tidal action, to control the level of water in the impoundment pools. Another reminder of the rice plantation past is an old brick cistern located in a maritime forest of cabbage palmetto, live oak, and mulberry. This brick water reservoir gives a name to the short footpath—the Cistern Trail—that skirts the marsh and offers a look at the varied terrain of the forest.

General location: This ride lies within the boundaries of the Savannah National Wildlife Refuge, which straddles the Georgia–South Carolina state line north of Savannah. Laurel Hill Wildlife Ride is actually located in Jasper County, South Carolina, but the ride begins in Georgia.

Elevation change: There is no appreciable change in elevation.

Season: Rides during the winter months are often the most pleasant due to cooler temperatures, lack of humidity, and absence of annoying gnawing insects. Birdwatching is at its peak from October through April when many species of wintering birds have migrated to the refuge and are nesting. But summer months claim unique perks, as well. For cyclists interested in spotting alligators, the warm months of late spring and summer are ideal times to mountain bike. Expect heat, humidity, and swarms of thirsty mosquitoes, though. During special hunts, the refuge is closed to the general public. When planning a ride, check ahead with the refuge office to be certain that the refuge is open on the day that you plan to cycle, and to get gate-closing times.

Services: All services are available in Savannah and the nearby towns of Port Wentworth and Garden City. Commercial camping is available at Gateway Campground in Hardeeville, South Carolina, and Stoney Crest Plantation in Pritchardville, South Carolina.

Hazards: This ride includes a 1-mile stretch along US 17, which carries high-speed traffic. Cyclists should exercise extreme caution on this brief leg of the ride. There is also light traffic on Laurel Hill Wildlife Drive, though it is not much of a concern with the posted speed limit of 20 miles per hour and one-way (counterclockwise) traffic. There are poisonous snakes and alligators in the refuge, but if you keep your distance from them, they will most likely reciprocate the favor. Posted signs along the way remind visitors that it is a violation of

Single-track trail found along South Carolina's coast. *Photo by Joel McCollough*

federal law to harass alligators in any way. Watch out for occasional chuckholes that will seize front tires and cause great embarrassment and possible injury to the unsuspecting cyclist left sprawled out in the road.

Rescue index: The main loop shares the Laurel Hill Wildlife Drive with automobiles, so help could be flagged down from a motorist willing to render assistance or go for help.

Land status: National wildlife refuge.

Maps: The ride can be found on the U.S. Fish and Wildlife Service map, Savannah National Wildlife Refuge. Maps and leaflets are available at the exhibit shelter to the left of the parking area. The ride is also finely detailed on the USGS 7.5 minute quadrangle for Limehouse. (Wilderness Outfitters has a good supply of quad maps, as well as other maps and information.)

Finding the trail: From Interstate 95, take Exit 5 to US 17 at Hardeeville, South Carolina. Drive on US 17 for approximately 2 miles to the refuge entrance, which will be on the left.

Sources of additional information:

U.S. Fish and Wildlife Service
Savannah Coastal Refuges Office
P. O. Box 8487
Savannah, GA 31412
(912) 652-4415

Wilderness Outfitters, Inc.
103 East Montgomery Cross Road
Savannah, GA 31406
(912) 927-2071

Cycle Center
7064 Hodgson Memorial Drive
Savannah, GA 31406
(912) 355-4771

Gateway Campground
P. O. Box 720
Hardeeville, SC 29927
(803) 784-2267

Stoney Crest Plantation
Highway 46
Pritchardville, SC 29910
(803) 757-3249

RIDE 18   *SAVANNAH HISTORIC DISTRICT BIKEWAY*

Cobblestone streets, 100-year-old oak trees, historic old Southern homes, fragrant azalea blossoms . . . all yours to be appreciated from the open seat of a bicycle. This three-mile loop of bikeway is an easy ride that meanders along narrow streets through Savannah's beautiful historic downtown district. The cobblestone streets, made from the cast-off ballast of ships, makes a mountain bike the ideal touring vehicle for this area. A good all-terrain bicycle would also work well, but cyclists on skinny-tired road bikes would have a difficult time. This is a short metropolitan ride that is quite easy, although the bumpy, sometimes buckled, road conditions require some bike-handling ability.

The first mile of this route corrects any misconceptions that Savannah's historic district (one of the nation's largest historic landmark districts) is merely two square miles crammed full of a bunch of dusty old homes and buildings. Certainly there are thousands of individual structures—some exhibiting magnificently restored architecture—of historical significance: grand old family mansions, dignified row houses, and huge churches with tall steeples reaching for the heavens. However, there is much more. Due, in part, to the eighteenth-century civic planning of General James Oglethorpe, downtown Savannah's architectural weight is both balanced and accented by numerous small, gardenlike squares and extensive parks.

The historic district incorporates over a dozen of these green cells as it follows Barnard, Gordon, and Lincoln streets before angling around Colonial Park Cemetery. Stately old trees shade these squares, and brick-paved walks divide manicured lawns to converge on graceful fountains and monuments. Even though the ride is easy and you may not need a rest, you ought to spend a few peaceful moments in one of these leafy sanctums to appreciate fully the unique atmosphere found here in historic Savannah.

Following spring's flowering azaleas, summer is alive with color from crepe myrtles, oleanders, and blooming annuals in the gardens and covered balconies of residents. River Street offers color as well with its bright awnings and placards announcing art galleries, restaurants, shops, and taverns. This plaza area along the Savannah River plays host to numerous festivals throughout the year, but is most famous for its St. Patrick's Day celebration.

You will begin this historical sojourn at the Visitor Center, which is actually the old Central Georgia Railroad Station, circa 1860. It is fitting that the station acts as a gateway to the route since it was one of the first to benefit from the preservation efforts of the Historic Savannah Foundation. A stunning house on West Gordon, built between 1860 and 1869 for Noble A. Hardee, extends the antebellum style into the postwar decades. Gordon Street showcases some of Savannah's finest residential architecture and a wealth of wrought iron. Wesley

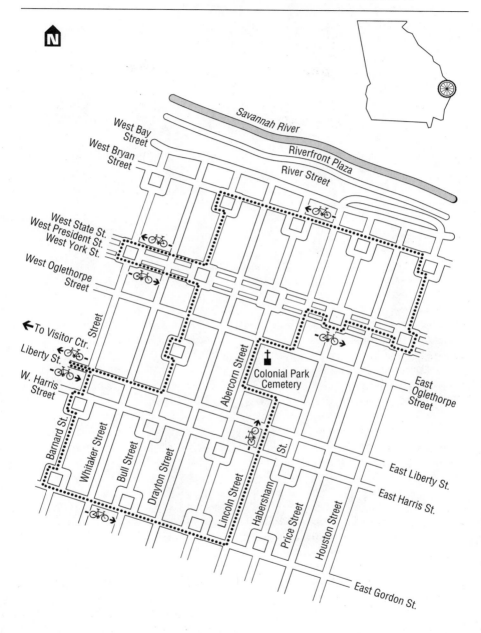

One of the many impressive churches found in Savannah's historic district. *Photo by Joel McCollough*

Monument United Methodist Church, circa 1890, dominates Calhoun Square with its double steeples.

The bike route turns onto Lincoln Street to head north toward Colonial Park Cemetery, which served as an early burial ground for Georgia's colonists. The bikeway then rounds Greene Square and proceeds toward Washington Square. Nearby, on East St. Julian Street, a house built for Hampton Lillibridge is rumored to be haunted. The bikeway continues through the picturesque streets, passing additional historic structures and areas, until it finally returns you to the Visitor Center, which marks the end of a visually stunning bicycle ride.

General location: Savannah, Georgia.
Elevation change: Aside from the slight descent to the river, there is no significant change in elevation.
Season: This bikeway can be ridden year-round because of mild winters along the coast. Spring rides are especially popular when azaleas, dogwoods, and daffodils are in glorious bloom. Color continues into summer months, however, with the deep pink blossoms of crepe myrtle trees and fragrant oleander bushes.
Services: All services are available in the city, many within close range in the downtown district.
Hazards: Heavy automobile traffic in narrow streets poses the chief hazard. The numerous city squares along the bike route should be negotiated cautiously since motorists entering these squares may fail to yield to cyclists. (I cycled a 400-mile road tour one year that ended in Savannah and, on that final push into the city, was exposed to some Savannah drivers who felt compelled to prove to us that rednecks do exist outside of Hazard County. There was one driver, whose pickup truck bed was littered with dozens of empty beer cans, who seemed to be particularly enraged at the sight of the tandem bicycle team in our group. He angrily laid on his horn and tried to run them off the road, but they were cool and just waved at him. The female on the bike was especially cool—she just waved one finger.) The vast majority of the motorists are courteous, but there are a few out there who don't understand the "Share the Road" concept. Watch out for them—they are dangerous.
Rescue index: This is an urban bike route, so the rescue index is excellent.
Land status: City of Savannah.
Maps: The Savannah Downtown Area Map and Legend is available at the Visitor Center and includes a key describing the highlights of the historic district. Also available is a separate map showing the current bicycle corridors through the area.
Finding the trail: From Interstate 95, take Exit 17 to Interstate 16 East toward the Savannah Historic District. Follow the Savannah Visitor Center signs. Traveling east on I-16, take the Louisville Road exit and turn right onto Louisville Road. At the first light, turn left onto West Boundary Street and then turn right onto Turner Boulevard. The Savannah Visitor Center and History Museum complex will be on the right, with public parking provided. You will begin the ride from the Visitor Center, using the Liberty Street connector.

Sources of additional information:

Savannah Visitor Center
P. O. Box 1628

Savannah, GA 31402-1628
(912) 944-0456

Cycle Center
7064 Hodgson Memorial Drive
Savannah, GA 31406
(912) 355-4771

Notes on the trail: There is additional mileage to pedal along River Street. Proposed bike routes include a north-south corridor, possibly along Habersham Street.

RIDE 19   *SKIDAWAY ISLAND TRAIL*

The six short miles of trail through this maritime forest give an excellent example of the diverse flora indigenous to coastal Georgia. At the beginning of the 12-mile out-and-back, you will see a freshwater slough to the left where a variety of shorebirds and wading birds such as herons and egrets form nesting colonies. By contrast, to the right is a view of tidal creeks and salt marsh, festooned with the scurry of fiddler crabs. Tall cabbage palms and oleander bushes line this sunny section of trail. Farther along, the trail enters a shady forest of live oak trees whose gnarled, twisted limbs are adorned with Spanish moss. This "moss" that looks like tangles of gray-green unraveled knitting is actually a bromeliad related to the pineapple. Fanlike saw palmettos and winding grapevines are the few plants growing below the live oaks as the dense canopy of the leaves blocks out direct sunlight and discourages understory growth. These plants contribute to the beauty of this forest and enhance this classic lowcountry scenery.

In addition to the beautiful coastal scenery on this island, there is a profusion of wildlife. A cyclist will be most rewarded with wildlife glimpses on an early morning or late afternoon ride. On one sunset ride, I saw several white-tailed deer, feral hogs, and rabbits. There were also wild turkey tracks in the sand and tracks of that infamous coastal scavenger, the raccoon. Alex Haley's *Roots* was filmed on this island; you will ride past cleared areas where African villages were built for the movie set.

The trail begins as a hard-packed single-track blanketed by layers of fallen live oak leaves. After a few miles, the trail spills into a grassy clearing and is replaced by a sandy, unpaved, single-lane road. Though an easy trail, it contains sandy sections of jeep roads that require some technical skill to keep you from bogging down and falling. Because of the lack of connecting trails or roads to form a loop, this trail must be ridden as an out-and-back. The main trail is about six miles long one-way, but this distance can be increased to eight or nine miles by riding the numerous side trails that dead-end at the edge of the marsh. Also,

RIDE 19   *SKIDAWAY ISLAND TRAIL*

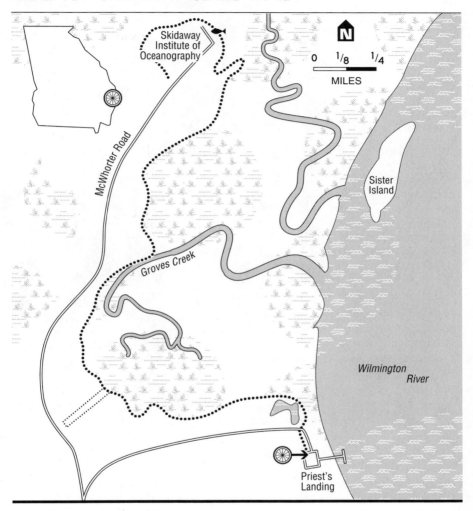

an optional excursion to the Aquarium of the University of Georgia's Marine Extension Center will lengthen this ride by another mile.

General location: The trail is located near Savannah, Georgia.
Elevation change: There is no remarkable change in elevation.
Season: This trail can be ridden year-round, but becomes unpleasant during the months of July, August, and September because of heat, humidity, and biting

Live oaks tower over Skidaway Island's single-track trail.

insects. An early spring ride will offer an opportunity to see the Cherokee rose, Georgia's state flower, in bloom.

Services: All services are available in Savannah.

Hazards: Ticks are a problem if you get off the trail and into the underbrush. There are poisonous snakes on the island, though it is unlikely that you will encounter any if you stay on the trail.

Rescue index: The trail is never far from McWhorter Drive or O.S.C.A. Road. From these roads, passing cars could easily be flagged down to obtain assistance.

Land status: State wildlife refuge.

Maps: The trail can be found on the Savannah/Chatham County map and is also found on the USGS 7.5 minute quadrangle for Isle of Hope.

Finding the trail: Skidaway Island is located near Savannah and can be reached from Interstate 95 by exiting at Exit 16. Proceed 12 miles toward Savannah. Turn right onto Montgomery Cross Road and proceed 1.4 miles to Whitfield Avenue. Turn right onto Whitfield (which becomes Diamond Causeway) and proceed 6 miles to the end of the road. Turn left at the stop sign onto McWhorter Drive and proceed 2 miles to a fork in the road. Take the right fork and continue for 1 mile to Priest's Landing. Park here. The trailhead is on the left.

Sources of additional information:

Cycle Center
7064 Hodgson Memorial Drive
Savannah, GA 31406
(912) 355-4771

Wilderness Outfitters, Inc.
103 East Montgomery Cross Road
Savannah, GA 31406
(912) 927-2071

Notes on the trail: The Olympic Village for the 1996 sailing competition will be constructed at Priest's Landing.

RIDE 20 *McQUEENS ISLAND HISTORIC TRAIL*

Formerly a route of the Old Savannah–Tybee Railroad, this scenic rail trail hugs the shoreline of the Savannah River for a distance of a little less than six miles. Ridden as an out-and-back, a total distance of 11.3 picturesque miles can be cycled. The entrance to the path is through a gate that actually bisects the trail into two separate rides. Both portions of the trail display distinctly different personalities in terms of riding difficulty. The six miles (round-trip) of trail to the left of the gate offer easy pedaling along a surface of crushed limestone, with a few bumpy sections even though all of the crossties have been removed. The leg of trail to the right of the gate is shorter than the western portion but is more technical due to its less improved surface and numerous tidal creek crossings. It is intermittently surfaced with crushed limestone, though most portions consist of raw earth and matted grass. Within a mile and a half, this former railway corridor narrows to a virtual single-track trail with some obstacles to negotiate.

After discovering this mountain biking find a while back, I suggested the ride to my friend, Joel, who was visiting relatives on the coast. Grateful for an excuse to tear himself away from the joys of a family reunion, he hopped on his mountain bike to check out the trail for himself. A few weeks later, I received a letter from him thanking me for the tip. He described the trail beautifully as he wrote:

RIDE 20 *McQUEENS ISLAND HISTORIC TRAIL*

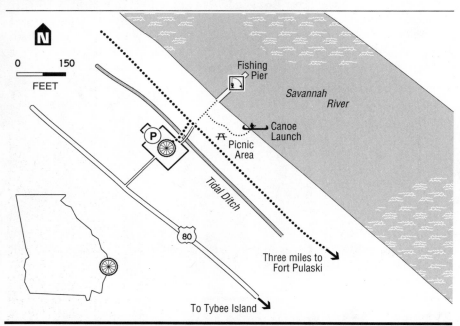

On a foggy morning ride, I seemed to be pedaling page-by-page though a living field guide of impressive coastal birds. An immature bald eagle rose at my shoulder and rowed lazily across the channel. Harriers and a merlin arced like meteors over the trail while snowy egrets waded through the shallow tidal pools between the trail and the highway. Mockingbirds rocketed from the dense shrubbery and swooped screaming ahead of me. As I approached the eastern end of the trail, flotillas of seabirds maneuvered nervously on the channel. As I neared the road bridge and gate house to Fort Pulaski National Monument, the palms took over and I felt like a lonely sojourner in the tropics, until the next semi roared by 40 yards away on US 80.

Had William Bartram, the naturalist, been a cyclist, he might have been duly impressed by the ride and written similar words.

General location: This rail trail is located in Savannah, Georgia.
Elevation change: There is no appreciable change in elevation.
Season: This trail can be ridden year-round. However, it is located on a marsh along the South Channel of the Savannah River and is therefore affected by ex-

A misty morning on the McQueens Island Historic Trail. *Photo by Joel McCollough*

tremely high tides. The unpleasant side effects of summer's biting insects, heat, and humidity have a tendency to wilt even the sturdiest of mountain bikers.

Services: All services are available in Savannah and on nearby Tybee Island.

Hazards: There are signs posted along the way that warn trail users to watch out for snakes. Be alert for abrupt drop-offs at the creek crossings. You will need to exercise caution on the double-track bridges; they are built with crossties that are sometimes slippery when wet. You may wish to dismount and walk your bike across them.

Rescue index: The trail is never more than 50 yards from US 80, from which help could be flagged down.

Land status: County park.

Maps: The trail is found on the Savannah/Chatham County map and is also found on the USGS 7.5 minute quadrangle for Fort Pulaski.

Finding the trail: From Interstate 95, take Exit 16 to GA 204 East. Drive 14.7 miles into Savannah to the intersection with US 80. Turn right onto US 80 and proceed east for 9 miles toward Tybee Island. After crossing Bull River, continue driving .3 miles to a roadside parking area on the left. Park here.

Sources of additional information:

Chatham County Department of Parks and Recreation
P. O. Box 1746
Savannah, GA 31402
(912) 352-0032

Wilderness Outfitters, Inc.
103 East Montgomery Cross Road
Savannah, GA 31406
(912) 927-2071

Cycle Center
7064 Hodgson Memorial Drive
Savannah, GA 31406
(912) 355-4771

Notes on the trail: Children in your group will be able to cycle most of this trail very easily. There are numerous pieces of playground equipment provided along the more developed eastern portion of the trail. Also, picnic tables are placed at frequent intervals along the trail.

RIDE 21   *SAVANNAH–OGEECHEE CANAL TRAIL*

These few miles of old towpath winding through pretty countryside tend to transport cyclists back in time. As the highway disappears and the traffic noise diminishes, it is easy to imagine the days back in the antebellum South with its less efficient but more picturesque forms of commercial transportation. The mind conjures up images of freight-laden barges being slowly towed by mules or horses plodding alongside the canal toward the lock. You can almost hear the bellowing echoes of the ghosts of barge men calling to one another across the water.

The towpath is undergoing restoration at the time of this writing; coordinators of the effort plan to lengthen the rideable trail to a total one-way distance of 16 miles. Currently, the segments of towpath that are open to bicycles provide a moderately difficult seven-mile round-trip, out-and-back ride. An all-terrain bicycle or full-fledged mountain bike is essential for riding this bumpy single-track and hard-packed dirt roadbed. There are also patches of deep sand in a few sections of the trail that must be negotiated with some technical know-how. When the restoration of the entire canal route is completed, there will be gentler sections of trail with a better-groomed surface, in addition to these more technical portions of towpath.

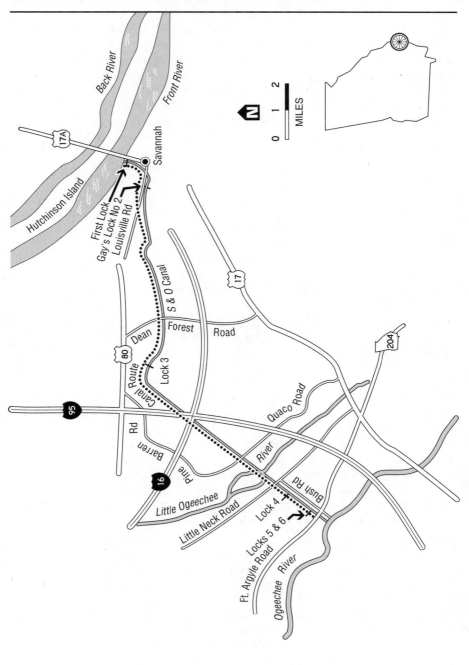

This 3.5-mile section of trail is fairly wide and clear as it carves a lazy curve through the lush lowcountry woodlands and swamps. On both sides of the path, still green water creates a sense of serenity between the massive trunks of cypress trees. Colonnades of pale sunlight pierce the canopy of tree branches to spotlight turtles resting on logs. The calm is shattered by the sound of a large creature splashing into water somewhere off in the distance. Suddenly, every floating log becomes a menacing alligator. Though the pastoral scenery tends to lull you away from reality, occasional glimpses of businesses and residences along the way will jolt you into remembering that you must return to civilization at the end of the ride.

Though the scenery—not unlike that of a primeval swamp—is enough to draw mountain bikers to this trail, there are other highlights along this old tow-path. History buffs will have the chance to study the construction of one of the old locks that once served the canal. Although disuse has allowed fallen leaves, limbs, and other debris to choke the lock, it still offers a chance to observe closely the early nineteenth-century canal engineering.

General location: This trail is located in Savannah, Georgia.

Elevation change: There is only a slight change in elevation along the 3.5 miles of canal you'll be riding.

Season: The path can be cycled year-round, though summer rides are often hot and sultry. Fall and winter rides are generally more pleasant, with cooler temperatures and lower humidity.

Services: All services are available in Savannah.

Hazards: You should watch out for poisonous snakes during warm months or even in the winter during periods of strong sunlight. Alligators are present in this area and could pose a hazard. Narrow bridges and steep-sided creeks should be crossed carefully, after dismounting. Watch for strands of barbed wire from old downed fences where the canal route passes pasture. Last of all, exercise caution at the access point, which carries high-speed vehicular traffic.

Rescue index: Major traffic arteries intersect the canal route at various points; help could be obtained from passing motorists. There are also a number of businesses adjacent to the canal land whose employees would probably allow you to use their telephones to call 911 for help.

Land status: City of Savannah and Chatham County property.

Maps: This towpath is shown on the Savannah–Ogeechee Canal Society hand-drawn map. It is also shown on the Savannah/Chatham County map. (The Savannah–Ogeechee Canal is perpendicular to GA 204 at Bush Road.)

Finding the trail: The towpath is currently under development and restoration, with different sections being opened or closed due to the work. For current trail information and access, contact Bill Stemwell, the coordinator of the Savannah–Ogeechee Canal Society, listed below. He is a nice fellow who will be happy to provide you with any information you might need before riding the trail.

Southeastern wildlife refuges are a haven for alligators.

Sources of additional information:

Bill Stemwell, Coordinator
Savannah–Ogeechee Canal Society
(912) 232-8685

Wilderness Outfitters, Inc.
103 East Montgomery Cross Road
Savannah, GA 31406
(912) 927-2071

Cycle Center
7064 Hodgson Memorial Drive
Savannah, GA 31406
(912) 355-4771

Notes on the trail: The featured 3.5-mile section of trail lies between Dean Forest Road (GA 307) and the interchange of Interstate 95 and I-16.

The Savannah–Ogeechee Canal Society, which is restoring the canal and its adjacent towpath, is an all-volunteer group. The good condition of the sections of the trail described in this chapter is a tribute to the hard work, dedication, and enthusiasm of these folks. Their goal is to restore this historic canal to a fully operational waterway, which will be used for recreation by canoeists and kayakers. The path running parallel to the canal will be completely restored for use by bikers, hikers, joggers, and naturalists. Local cyclists interested in donating some time and elbow grease to this effort should contact the coordinator of this project, Bill Stemwell, at the above-listed telephone number.

Barrier Islands

RIDE 22 *HARRIS NECK NATIONAL WILDLIFE REFUGE*

Cycling between the long reaches of grassland and marsh and into verdant tunnels of moss-covered oaks will give mountain bikers a good taste of the diverse lowcountry habitats contained within this refuge. This easy, six-mile paved loop offers a good mountain bike ride for families with young children or inexperienced cyclists. The ride begins with a short connector of soft dirt which quickly merges into a paved road. Since there are no technical single-track trails to negotiate, this ride provides a good introduction to mountain biking without unduly challenging fledgling cyclists.

As in so many of these coastal refuges, the birds steal the show. More than 200 different species of birds have been identified, including Canada geese, great egret, widgeon, teal, night heron, the endangered bald eagle, and many others. While many are year-round residents, others are winter migratory visitors. Photographers and birders delight in the opportunity to spot these winged creatures, as do cyclists with a naturalist slant.

Historically, this site was occupied in the mid-1700s by a plantation on the banks of the South Newport River. It was later used as an Air Force training center during World War II—in fact, deserted army airfield runways are still in existence. The old ribbons of runways seem to disappear into the distance, swallowed up by grass. Clumps of prickly pear, brightly festooned with colorful blossoms in May and June, seem to mock the ghostlike, tattered runways of the past.

General location: The refuge is located approximately 50 miles south of Savannah.

Elevation change: There is no appreciable change in elevation.

Season: The refuge is open year-round for use during daylight hours, though most of the refuge is closed to the public on weekends. The cooler months of late fall through early spring are the best times to cycle this loop. These months also offer greater chances for observing the profusion of birds during their migratory period.

Services: All services are available in Savannah and convenience stores are available between the city and the refuge. Water is not available at the refuge, so be sure to fill water bottles before your arrival. There are rest rooms at the Harris

RIDE 22 *HARRIS NECK NATIONAL WILDLIFE REFUGE*

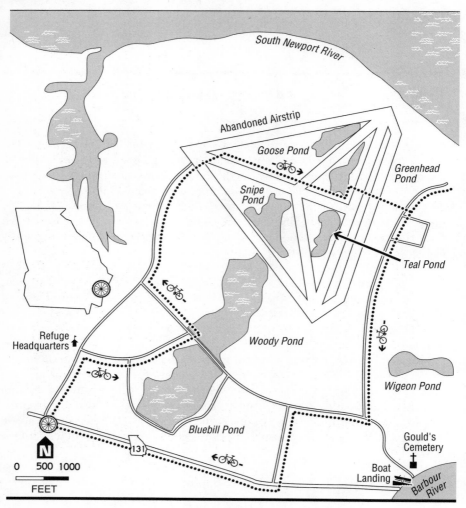

Neck Recreation Area, near the entrance to the refuge. Camping is available at the Belle Bluff Campground in Townsend, Georgia, and at the Pinewood Lake Campground in Riceboro, Georgia.

Hazards: Poisonous snakes and alligators are found in substantial numbers all over the refuge; watch for them as you cycle, particularly on warm, sunny days. Large rattlesnakes have been reported along the cycling route. If you get off the main loop, you should be aware that the woods and brush harbor ticks. Check yourself carefully for any that managed to jump aboard after your ride. Biting,

The exceptional scenery of oak-lined dirt roads draws cyclists of diverse abilities to the mountain bike rides along the coast.

stinging insects are a real nuisance during the dog days of summer; an ample dousing of insect repellant will greatly improve the quality of your ride. Watch for potholes in the road and for traffic.

Rescue index: The ride follows a lightly traveled, paved path the entire distance, from which help could be flagged down.

Land status: National wildlife refuge.

Maps: The ride can be found on the U.S. Fish and Wildlife Service map, Harris Neck National Wildlife Refuge. The ride is also detailed on the USGS 7.5 minute quadrangle for Saint Catherine's Sound.

Finding the trail: From Interstate 95, take Exit 12 to US 17. Drive south on US 17 for approximately 1 mile to the intersection with GA 131. Turn left and drive east for 7 miles to the refuge entrance, which will be on the left.

Sources of additional information:

U.S. Fish and Wildlife Service
Savannah Coastal Refuges Office
P. O. Box 8487
Savannah, GA 31412
(912) 652-4412

Wilderness Outfitters, Inc.
103 East Montgomery Cross Road
Savannah, GA 31406
(912) 927-2071

Cycle Center
7064 Hodgson Memorial Drive
Savannah, GA 31406
(912) 355-4771

Belle Bluff Campground
Route 2
Townsend, GA 31331
(912) 832-5323

Pinewood Lake Campground
Route 2
Riceboro, GA 31323
(912) 832-5407

RIDE 23 *ST. SIMONS ISLAND BIKE PATH*

This 12.5-mile loop offers bicyclists of all ages and all levels of experience an easy, enjoyable ride. No technical skill is needed on this asphalt bike path and almost any kind of bicycle—from a full-fledged mountain bike to a beach cruiser—will feel perfectly at home on this path.

As you begin the ride along Frederica Road, you will pass the well-manicured greens of the Sea Palms Golf and Tennis Resort on the left. Here the bike path gently sashays around the mammoth trunks of towering live oaks. The natural scenery then dissipates as the path enters the downtown area, passing small shops and well-kept residences. On Ocean Boulevard, you will pass the Coast Guard Station at East Beach with its array of flags snapping in the stiff ocean

RIDE 23 *ST. SIMONS ISLAND BIKE PATH*

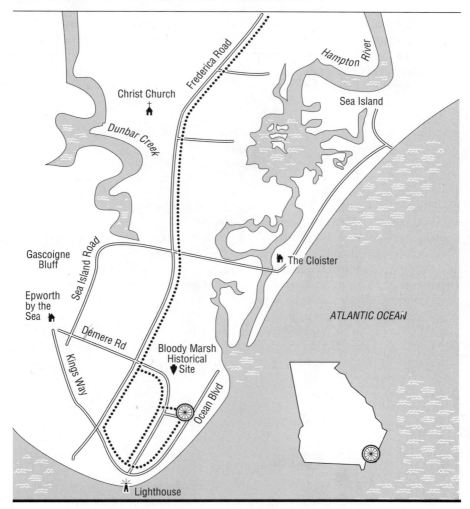

breezes. As you continue, you will be treated to a panoramic vista of salt marsh stretching northward at East Beach Causeway. About a mile farther, a similar view is offered at the Bloody Marsh Historical Site, where the most significant colonial battle on the Georgia coast was fought.

This site is as alluring to naturalists as it is to historians, with its bustling armies of hermit crabs. They almost seem to be reenacting, in miniature, the 1742 Battle of Bloody Marsh between the Spanish and the British. During this surprise attack, the British, whose troops were girded by Creek Indians and hundreds of Scottish Highlanders, defeated the Spanish, thereby deciding the future of this entire colonial region. The Spaniards returned to St. Augustine after the battle and peace was restored on the island.

After finishing the bike ride, you may wish to continue your historical explorations on foot. Even during the middle of summer, the gentle semitropical breezes wafting through palm fronds offer a cooling touch. Cooling you even more as you walk will be the shady canopy from the laced branches of live oak trees that border many of the narrow roads of this colonial island. They stand tall and proud like genteel Southern women greeting visitors from a columned cottage porch.

Before leaving the island, be sure to visit St. Simons Lighthouse, one of only two lighthouses on the Georgia coast open to the public. If you did not get your heart rate up on the flat bike path, you are sure to be panting by the time you climb the 129 stairs to the top. What little breath you have remaining will be quickly taken away when you gaze from the observation platform out at the splendid view over the island and out to sea. If you look toward the south, you will be able to see Jekyll Island across the sound. This lighthouse has been standing since 1872 and continues to serve as a navigational beacon to boats at sea. The original lighthouse on this site operated before that date but was burned during the Civil War by Confederate forces who chose to sacrifice it rather than risk its use by those nasty Yankees, er . . . I mean, the Union troops.

Close to the north side causeway entrance to the island is the site of Hamilton Plantation, now known as Epworth-by-the-Sea. This was one of the largest plantations in Georgia during the antebellum period. Old slave cabins still sit on the plantation grounds as a reminder of that era in Southern history. Nearby is Gascoigne Bluff, named for Captain James Gascoigne, who escorted the ships of the first English settlers to this island back in 1736. Some of the live oak timbers from the bluff were used in the construction of the Brooklyn Bridge.

On a more reverent note, you might also wish to visit Christ Church, the second oldest Episcopal church in Georgia and the third oldest church in the state. It stands near the site of a huge oak tree where Charles and John Wesley preached their first sermon to the Indians. Planters built the original square church but it was destroyed during the Civil War. Reverend Anson Green Phelps Dodge, Jr., built the current church as a memorial to his wife. (Dodge became the main character in author Eugenia Price's trilogy of books on St. Simons Island.) The all-wood interior is beautifully punctuated with a mosaic of stained-glass windows depicting early colonial scenes of St. Simons. One shows General Oglethorpe bartering with an Indian chief and another shows Charles and John Wesley preaching to the Indians under the old oak tree. Don't leave without taking a stroll through the old graveyard, where many of the early settlers are buried.

General location: This ride is on St. Simons Island, located on the southern Georgia coast.

The ride on St. Simons Island offers beautiful ocean views. *Photo by Joel McCollough*

Elevation change: There is no appreciable change in elevation.

Season: The bike path is open year-round to cyclists. The traditional summer vacation months are a less desirable time of year to ride because of heavy traffic at the road intersections. Oppressive heat and humidity during that time of year also tend to put a damper on a ride. However, there is often a refreshing sea breeze to temper the conditions.

Services: Most services are available on the island. Nearby Brunswick, Georgia, offers additional services that may not be found on St. Simons Island.

Hazards: Traffic at road crossings is the main hazard of this ride; exercise caution at all crossings. The crossings at Demere Road and Mallery Street can be especially hazardous.

Rescue index: All portions of the bike path parallel major roads, from which help could be flagged down.

Land status: State of Georgia property.

Maps: St. Simons Island Chamber of Commerce and Visitor Center offers a color map showing the bike path, major arteries, and principal attractions. A detailed bike path map is also available from Benjy's Bike Shop.

Finding the trail: From Interstate 95, take Exit 8 and drive approximately 4 miles on GA 25 to the intersection with US 17. Turn onto US 17 and drive an additional 1.5 miles before turning left onto Torras Causeway, which leads to the island. Once on the island, follow Kings Way to Ocean Boulevard. Turn onto Ocean Boulevard and drive to Massengale Park, which will be on the right. The bike path is across the street from the park entrance.

Sources of additional information:

St. Simons Island Chamber of Commerce and Visitor Center
530-B Beachview Drive
St. Simons Island, GA 31522
(912) 638-9014
or 1-800-525-8678

Benjy's Bike Shop
238 Retreat Village
St. Simons Island, GA 31522
(912) 638-6766

Notes on the trail: The typical circuit of the bike path begins from its northern terminus on Frederica Road, then south to Kings Way, curving east onto Ocean Boulevard, and then back to Frederica Road via East Beach Causeway and Demere Road. More mileage is possible along Kings Way toward the Island Club and on Demere Road. (There is a dirt trail running from Frederica Road west to the marshes. However, this is an equestrian corridor and mountain bikers are advised to keep out.)

RIDE 24 *JEKYLL ISLAND BICYCLE PATH*

What a pleasure it is to arrive at a place where bicycles are not only welcome, but are the recommended vehicle for visitors who wish to get a true taste of the area. Perhaps I shouldn't be so surprised, but after seeing more "Bikes Prohibited" signs on public trails than I care to count, the welcome on Jekyll Island was well received. To say the least!

Twenty miles of paved bicycle paths circumnavigate this seven-mile long barrier island, from St. Simons Sound in the north to Jekyll Point in the south. There is a short unpaved section of trail between Ben Fortson Parkway and the historic district, but the vast majority of the path is smooth asphalt. Almost any type of bike would travel well on this surface, from a beach cruiser to a fat-tired mountain bike. This well-marked, 20-mile path is actually a loop, though it can certainly be ridden in part as an out-and-back. Additional mileage can be pedaled by exploring the forested areas at the island's northern and southern

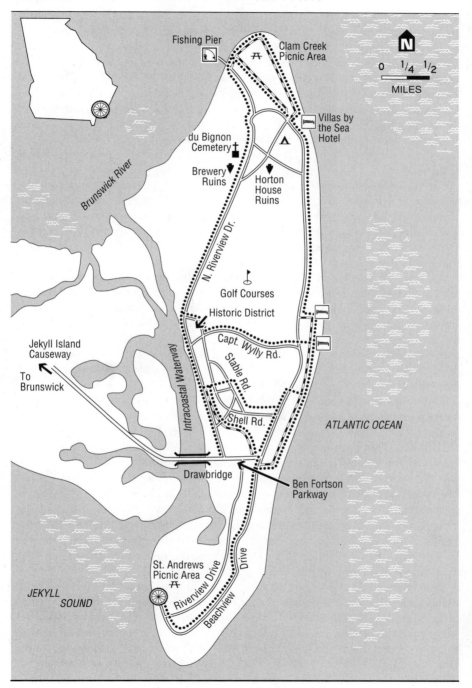

N

0   1/4   1/2
MILES

Fishing Pier

Clam Creek
Picnic Area

Villas by
the Sea
Hotel

du Bignon
Cemetery

Brewery
Ruins

Horton
House
Ruins

Brunswick River

N. Riverview Dr.

Golf Courses

Historic District

Capt. Wylly Rd.

Stable Rd.

Shell Rd.

Intracoastal Waterway

Jekyll Island
Causeway

To
Brunswick

ATLANTIC OCEAN

Drawbridge

Ben Fortson
Parkway

St. Andrews
Picnic Area

Riverview Drive

Beachview
Drive

JEKYLL
SOUND

points. Virtually no technical skill is required to cycle this gently winding path, making it an ideal bicycle ride for families. (Hard-core mountain bikers should not despair, however. Unpaved roads and trails are also present.)

This extensive system of bicycle routes takes you to almost every point of interest on the island. For about three miles along North Riverview Drive, the path winds through the landscaped grounds of a seaside resort. You will then come upon the ruins of the historic Horton House and the family cemetery of the du Bignons. You will also pass the ruins of the old brewery established in the eighteenth century by Oglethorpe to supply Savannah with local beer. This was Georgia's first brewery; it utilized locally grown grain and hops in production of the suds.

The trail cleaves a wilderness area on Clam Creek before shooting past the beachfront strip of restaurants, shopping centers, and hotels on the northern tip of the island. This good-sized forested area spreads southeast of the campground toward the golf courses and will thrill the hard-core cyclists in your group. The area's network of unpaved roads and trails offers adventurous mountain bikers a welcome respite from the blacktop.

To continue on a naturalist's sojourn, you should bear north toward the fishing pier, where you will pedal past a striking natural sculpture of sun-bleached, wind-sculpted live oak trees standing in the salt marsh. Fiddler crabs scurry across the path, while snowy egrets stalk their next meal. Near the entrance to the pier, you may opt for the undeveloped single-track trail that penetrates a maritime forest choked with oaks and palmettos. This wild path is not included on the bike path maps, but is a good option for a backwoods mountain bike experience.

The northern and southern points of the island offer cyclists the best opportunities for observing wildlife. White-tailed deer are present, as are raccoon and mink. A favorite path for bird-watching lies between Ben Fortson Parkway and Shell Road. This path passes through maritime forest, marsh areas, and tidal creeks before turning north through a mixed forest of hardwood and pine. You will finally wind up at Stable Road near the historic district. On sunset rides, keep your eyes open for the ghost of a white stallion. Legend has it that, during the colonial days, a great white stallion led a herd of wild horses on the island. When a posse tried to capture him and had him trapped on the north end of the island, he jumped into the churning sea rather than allow himself to be captured by these men. Now islanders talk of the diaphanous figure of the horse roaming about the island from time to time.

This barrier island's human habitation began with the Guale Indians, who hunted and fished for years until Spanish soldiers ran them off in the sixteenth century. About 200 years later, General Oglethorpe laid claim to this and other islands for the British. Jekyll Island changed hands again when Christopher du Bignon, a Frenchman who fought in the Revolution, bought the island after the war. His family sold it in 1886 for $125,000 to a group of affluent Northerners who wanted a seaside retreat where they could relax in a more casual atmo-

Beautiful, well-groomed trails are found on Georgia's coast.

sphere than was offered in the popular retreats found along the coast of Rhode Island.

Wealthy men such as William Rockefeller, Joseph Pulitzer, J. P. Morgan, and Marshall Field formed the Jekyll Island Club. These "Who's Who's" among notables and their families used this spot as their private winter resort for years. Though their aim was to achieve a casual atmosphere, the end result would hardly fall into our contemporary definition of casual. Some of these families arrived on private yachts, each family with 15 to 20 trunks brimming with tuxedos for men and elegant evening gowns for women. These people would have drawn back in horror at the thought of arriving at a casual supper in T-shirts, shorts, and Tevas. Huge "cottages" began to spring up; some had as many as 30 rooms and one paltry shack had 17 bathrooms. They even brought along personal attendants: nannies, cooks, butlers, chauffeurs, and maids. If this was less formal than what they had tired of in the north, I shudder to think of how proper and stuffy their formal vacation resorts were.

Though Jekyll Island was a vacation hideaway, these millionaires couldn't divorce themselves entirely from business. There is a historical marker on the island commemorating the origination of the first experimental transcontinental telephone call in 1915 from Jekyll Island. This occurred while Theodore N. Vail, president of AT&T, convalesced at the Jekyll Island Club. It is also believed that the secret meetings that resulted in the Federal Reserve Act of 1915 took place here on Jekyll Island. Thrilling, huh?

Finally, the Depression years began and this playground for the rich and famous began to show signs of strain. By the time World War II broke out, the island was nearly deserted. The state of Georgia bought the island in 1947 and developed it into a state park. Though it is an extensively developed resort community, the Jekyll Island Authority has worked diligently to preserve the island's historic sites and relics. The "cottages" of the wealthy former club members are open for tours and have visitors commenting on the apparent misnomer for these elaborate mansions.

General location: Jekyll Island is one of southern Georgia's barrier islands and is located between St. Simons and Cumberland islands.

Elevation change: There is no appreciable change in elevation.

Season: Jekyll Island's semitropical climate makes for year-round bicycling. Winters are mild with occasional freezes while cooling sea breezes temper summer's heat. Even with the breezes, though, you should expect to be hot during the middle of summer.

Services: All services are available on the island or in Brunswick, Georgia, which is located 10 miles to the north. There are a number of bike rental facilities, so you're in luck if you chose not to bring your own wheels from home.

Hazards: The wilderness areas of the island are infested with ticks, as well as poisonous snakes. There are also alligators on the island. Alligators that stroll into someone's yard or onto the beach are quickly trapped by Jekyll Island Authority personnel and transported away from the island. You should also be alert to the few blind curves along North Riverview Drive; these should be taken slowly.

Rescue index: The rescue index is excellent since the bike path rarely flows more than a short distance from well-traveled roads. The only exceptions are the loop around Clam Creek Picnic Area and a wooded area between Ben Fortson Parkway and Shell Road.

Land status: State of Georgia property.

Maps: Good maps delineating the bike paths are available at the welcome center located on the Jekyll Island Causeway. The island is also found on the USGS 7.5 minute quadrangle for Jekyll Island.

Finding the trail: From Interstate 95, take Exit 8. Drive approximately 4 miles on GA 25 to the intersection with US 17. Drive south on US 17 through Brunswick and cross the Sidney Lanier Bridge to the Jekyll Island Causeway (GA 520). A parking fee is charged at the collection station at the entrance to the island.

Sources of additional information:

Jekyll Island Authority
Convention and Visitors Bureau
One Beachview Drive
P. O. Box 3186
Jekyll Island, GA 31527
(912) 635-3636
or 1-800-342-1042 (within Georgia)
or 1-800-841-6586 (out-of-state)

Okefenokee Swamp

RIDE 25 *BIG CREEK NATURE TRAIL*

Situated in "Okefenokee Country," this easy ride is located within Laura S. Walker State Park. This short loop of single-track trail begins in a sun-drenched pine forest and continues for 1.2 miles. A layer of pine needles and oak leaves makes for a quiet ride and gives the trail a neat, groomed appearance. Though too short to attract riders interested only in mountain biking, this is a pleasant ride for park visitors interested in enjoying the other outdoor activities offered here in addition to mountain biking. It is also an excellent ride for kiddos.

This park was created during the Depression years as part of a federal program designed to protect natural resources. It was named for Laura Singleton Walker, one of the early conservation pioneers. In fact, it is one of the few parks in Georgia named for a woman. Long before it was in vogue to do so, she was actively involved in the protection of trees and other natural treasures. The beautiful forest flanking the Big Creek Nature Trail can be enjoyed today, largely because of these preservation and protection measures taken years ago.

You will begin pedaling through a pine plantation planted in 1989; blackberries and huckleberries flavor this part of the forest. The trail then swings south to shoot between tall yucca and saw palmettos in a beautiful sandhill forest habitat, common in southern Georgia. Here, pines and oaks hold sway while offering welcome shade during the heat of summer. After a pleasant run through the forest, the trail bends to the right toward Big Creek and crosses several swampy patches on wide boardwalks. The pines and oaks of the sandhill forest disappear and are replaced by swamp vegetation of cypress, magnolia, birch, and bay.

The white rays of strong sun are filtered through myriad leaves, creating dancing coins of light on the brown water of Big Creek. Tannic acid gives the creek its rich tea color, which is characteristic of freshwater streams throughout the Okefenokee Swamp. A narrow, unmarked footpath follows the creek toward the highway and the lake. Lines of creamy yellow foam from the spillway at the nearby dam float on the surface of Big Creek. Finally, the roar of powerboats crisscrossing the lake heralds the end of this brief but beautiful ride.

General location: This trail is located in Laura S. Walker State Park in Waycross, Georgia.
Elevation change: There is no appreciable change in elevation.

RIDE 25 *BIG CREEK NATURE TRAIL*

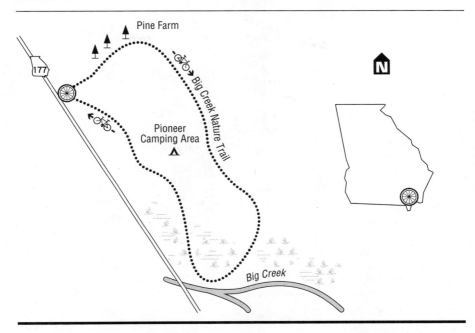

Season: The trail is rideable during all seasons, but should be avoided after heavy rains because of boggy, impassable sections. During summer, hosts of biting insects join the old familiar misery makers, heat and humidity. The park is open 7 days a week; there is a nominal admission charge at the main entrance.

Services: All services are available in Waycross, which is 10 miles away. The park offers camping facilities, as well as drinking water and vending machines for snacks.

Hazards: There are poisonous snakes in the forest, so watch where you step when you are off your bike. Also, there are ticks clinging to the underbrush; stay on the trail to keep them from clinging to you. Bear in mind that this is primarily a walking trail; be alert for hikers and yield to them in all situations. The boardwalks and footbridge are slippery when wet; you might want to dismount and walk.

Rescue index: The short length of this trail makes the rescue index excellent. The trail generally runs parallel to GA 177 and the park's Visitor Center is within sight of the trailhead.

Land status: State park.

Maps: A map of the trail is available at the Visitor Center. The trail is also detailed on the USGS 7.5 minute quadrangle for Hoboken West.

"Cat-face" scars mark the trees harvested for the pine sap used in turpentine production. *Photo by Joel McCollough*

Finding the trail: From Interstate 95, take Exit 6 and proceed on US 86 West for approximately 33 miles. Turn left onto GA 177 (Laura Walker Road) and drive 2 miles south to the park entrance, which will be on the right. The Big Creek Nature Trail begins on the opposite side of the road from the park entrance.

Sources of additional information:

Laura S. Walker State Park
5653 Laura Walker Road
Waycross, GA 31501
(912) 287-4900

Georgia Department of Natural Resources
Laura S. Walker State Park
Route 6, Box 205
Waycross, GA 31501
(912) 283-4424

Georgia State Parks and Historic Sites
205 Butler Street, Suite 1258 East
Atlanta, GA 30334
(404) 656-3530

Notes on the trail: There are a number of benches situated along the trail. Near the first bench, notice the pine tree trunk that bears a long "cat-face" scar. This is evidence of the area's widespread harvesting of pine sap used in the production of turpentine.

RIDE 26 *SWAMP ISLAND WILDLIFE RIDE*

Cyclists pedaling this nine-mile (total), out-and-back ride on the eastern edge of the enigmatic, mysterious Okefenokee Swamp are in for a real treat. This easy ride is on a paved road, so cyclists of diverse abilities and experience can enjoy the allure of these surroundings. The road is actually located in the Suwannee Canal Recreation Area, a land of extensive prairies as well as open waters, forests, and dark swampland.

The hallowed sanctuary of wilderness known as the Okefenokee Swamp has appeared forbidding and mythical to its visitors and nearby inhabitants for centuries. It is a land of mirrored lakes, grand reaches of cypress, and early mornings shrouded with billows of fog that have settled over the sluggish black water during the night. It is a land of legend and curiosity with its floating islands that tremble and quake. It is a land of fascination and fear with stories of the glowing eyes of alligators that slip through the night waters, of cougars screaming in the moonlight, and of black bears crashing through the trees. But by the calming light of day, the swamp is simply a storehouse of treasures, a place of beauty and tranquility. And though the stories of things that go bump in the night do raise the hair on the back of your neck, they are only stories of animals doing what comes naturally.

The Indian name "Okefenokee" means trembling earth, an apt term for the way the ground feels under your feet in places. This natural phenomenon is caused by decomposition of layers of peat, which produces methane gas. This gas forces great masses of peat to break away from the floor of the swamp and float to the surface. Vegetation and even trees grow on these chunks of peat,

RIDE 26 *SWAMP ISLAND WILDLIFE RIDE*

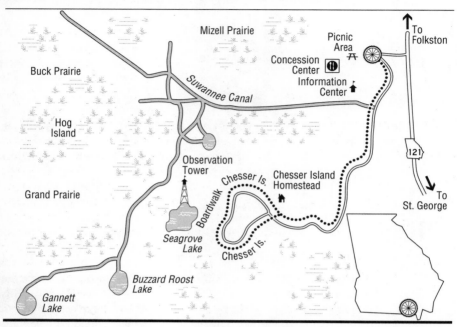

giving them the appearance of islands. Though slightly anchored by roots, these islands still shake when stepped on, hence the appellation "trembling earth."

Of all the early settlers along the periphery of the Okefenokee Swamp, perhaps the most colorful and interesting was a six-foot-tall woman named Lydia Stone. This tough, spunky, hard-working lass shrewdly acquired 30,000 acres of land and became the wealthiest of all pioneers. When she was 63 years old, she married her second husband, a man named Milton Crews (but known as "Baby Doll" to Lydia), who was barely 21 years old.

As you begin the ride along the Swamp Island Wildlife Drive, the scenery may seem slightly monotonous at first, but you will quickly discover the breathtaking expanses and teeming details that give it a unique beauty. Acres of vivid green saw palmettos stretch away among thousands of fire-blackened pines. Pausing in the grassy shoulder of the road in certain seasons, you will see tiny blooming wildflowers. Several miles into the ride, the road parallels a placid channel of water whose inky surface mirrors the buttressed trunks of towering cypress trees. Other trees seem diminutive and cowering in the presence of the cypress, the patriarch of the swamp.

A ride in late June proved especially rewarding for us with the appearance of a female alligator tending at least a dozen young. The kids may have been late hatchlings from the previous year; in any case, they still displayed their distinctive yellow bands and high-pitched bark. Such perks are best appreciated from the saddle of a bicycle, rather than from the sterile confines of an automobile.

Further exploration of the area's natural beauty can be made on several miles of hiking trails branching from this main drive. If you have the time to observe the beautiful mosaic of flora along these trails, dismount and park your bike. The first of these footpaths is the Canal Diggers Trail, which loops through the course of an abandoned waterway. An observation tower on the Deerstand Trail affords sweeping vistas of Chesser Prairie, whose beautifully mysterious hammocks of tupelo, cypress, maple, and bay serve as shelter to many swamp denizens.

Though these paths are all scenic and popular, the 1.5-mile Swamp Walk is undoubtedly Suwannee's sterling experience. This well-maintained boardwalk juts into the midst of the vast prairies and lakes that characterize the recreation area. From the parking area, the boardwalk angles through tangles of dense hammocks and undergrowth. At times, a tunnel effect is created by the closely spaced tree trunks and intertwining vines. Observation shelters are strategically located at points frequented by wildlife. Quite large (and surprisingly old) box turtles can be seen sunning on islands of peat surrounded by small ponds patrolled by palm-sized dragonflies. Tiny birds, often exotically colored, flit across the boardwalk to vanish into the dark wall of vegetation. Large animals can be heard moving off unseen as the boards creak underfoot. Two walks to the right lead to ideally situated, enclosed blinds built for the benefit of photographers and bird-watchers.

An observation tower located at the end of the main boardwalk allows unobstructed views over Seagrove Lake toward Grand Prairie. Though this box-seat view of an azure lake strewn with deep green islets is impressive, the sounds emanating from this patchwork of water and foliage may be the most intriguing thing about it. Birdcalls and occasional reptilian bellows rise in discordant chorus, while just below the tower some small furry animal scuttles through the grass of the lakeshore, leaving a wavering wake.

General location: This ride is located along the eastern edge of the Okefenokee Swamp, about 11 miles southwest of Folkston, Georgia.

Elevation change: There is no appreciable change in elevation.

Season: This ride can be pedaled year-round, but is less enjoyable during summer months because of high humidity, merciless heat, and tormenting swarms of biting insects.

Services: Some services, such as bike rentals, snacks, etc., are provided by the on-site concessionaire. There are full-service campgrounds located at nearby state parks. The closest campground to the Suwannee Canal is at Traders Hill Recreation Area, but it has limited facilities. Other services are found in nearby Folkston, Georgia.

Hazards: Although normally quite shy, there are alligators by the truckloads in

Though prohibited to bicycles, Okefenokee's Swamp Walk is an interesting hiking highlight after your ride. *Photo by Joel McCollough*

this swamp. You will probably see at least one on your ride and, when you do, you should keep your distance and avoid agitating it. There are about 40 different types of snakes in this area, including a number of poisonous snakes such as the eastern coral, eastern diamondback rattlesnake, canebrake rattlesnake, and cottonmouth. Like the alligators, the snakes will not seek you out, but you must watch where you step, sit, and place your hands. Though rarely seen, black bear roam throughout the refuge. Unlike the aggressive black bear in the Great Smoky Mountains, a swamp bear is loath to attack, unless she finds you between her and her cubs.

Rescue index: The rescue index is good since the ride is along a lightly traveled, paved road. Help can be obtained at the Richard S. Bolt Visitor Center at the entrance to the drive.

Land status: National wildlife refuge.

Maps: There are maps available at the Visitor Center and at the concession. The ride is also found on the USGS 7.5 minute quadrangle for Chesser Island.

Finding the trail: From Interstate 95, take Exit 2. Drive west on GA 40 to Folkston. Turn onto GA 23/121 and drive south for 7 miles. Turn right onto Spur 121 and drive an additional 4 miles to the recreation area.

Sources of additional information:

U.S. Fish and Wildlife Service
Suwannee Canal Recreation Area
Route 2, Box 338
Folkston, GA 31537
(912) 496-3331

Concessionaire
Suwannee Canal Recreation Area
Route 2, Box 338
Folkston, GA 31537
(912) 496-7156

Traders Hill Recreation Area
Charlton County Court House
Folkston, GA 31537
(912) 496-3392, Extension 7660

Notes on the trail: Before taking the Swamp Walk, you may wish to dismount, park your bikes, and stroll out to the Chesser Island Homestead. This is a step back in time to the early 1900s.

FLORIDA

Thoughts of cycling in Florida are certain to conjure up many images—swaying palm trees, glistening beaches lined with the bronzed bodies of sun worshipers, rolling ocean waves—even Mickey Mouse. This is the glitter-and-glitz Florida that we have come to expect from slick brochures and television commercials. But the advertisers have failed to tell us about the dense wilderness and remote backcountry where the surroundings are wild and wooly. It's true . . . even Florida has areas that we mountain bikers know as the "boonies."

When I first began the research for trails in Florida, I have to admit that I arrived in the state with a certain degree of skepticism. I envisioned heavily commercialized and densely populated areas such as Miami and wondered how there could possibly be any mountain bike rides of merit in America's southernmost state. But, local cyclists and Forest Service personnel pointed me in the right direction and, in no time, I was pedaling beautiful and sometimes challenging rides that quickly altered my perception about cycling in the Sunshine State.

Fortunately for mountain bikers, most of Florida's tourists blast down Interstate 95 from Georgia to parts far south without so much as a sidelong glance at the beautiful countryside whipping by. As a result, much of Florida has escaped the commercial development that has overtaken and changed so much of the landscape in southern Florida. Many parts of the panhandle, as well as northern and central Florida, are free from crowds and high-rises, and have retained much of the idyllic natural beauty and charm that first began drawing visitors to the state years ago. For these reasons, this guide concentrates on these less-populated and less-developed areas of Florida, though a few of the mountain bike rides described are located in the state's southern reaches.

Florida is rich with natural attractions that serve as a magnet to cyclists. There are trails and roads that skirt pristine coastal areas adorned with swaying sea oats, crystal-clear lagoons, gushing springs, and well-landscaped islands. There are trails that zip through salt marshes, flushing hundreds of screeching and squawking wading birds from their feeding grounds. There are trails that meander through old ghost towns like O'Leno and even trails that loop through grassy prairies dotted with roaming bison.

The quiescent beauty of these natural areas is undeniable. As I spent more and more time on the trails and traipsing through the back roads of Florida, the languor of the landscape reminded me of Wallace Stegner's words: "It is not hills and mountains which we should call eternal for nature abhors an elevation almost as much as it abhors a vacuum. A hill no sooner is elevated than the forces of erosion begin tearing it down." Though Stegner was referring to the vast prairies of the West, those words also ring true of the flat beauty of Florida. Gazing across dazzling beaches that stretch for miles along the Gulf, or pausing at the edge of the absolutely still waters of a haunting swamp, or looking across the green pastures of serene horse farms, you can't help but believe nature is indeed in repose in this horizontal terrain.

Apalachicola

RIDE 27 ST. VINCENT NATIONAL WILDLIFE REFUGE

Heading toward St. Vincent National Wildlife Refuge, we drove on the long bridge over the deep blue waters of the Apalachicola Bay that shimmered in the late afternoon sun. The sultry strains of Mary-Chapin Carpenter from the radio were barely audible over the growls from our empty stomachs demanding attention. Without argument from anyone in our group, all hell-bent on getting on the trail, we turned off Highway 98 (US 98) in search of a restaurant, sans dress code, that offered genuine Apalachicola oysters.

We found a small restaurant, a squatter's shack really, which precariously clung to the bank of the Apalachicola River. One good gust of wind and the place would be history. There was a weathered sign out front promising the best oysters in town, though the full parking lot at four o'clock in the afternoon was what sold us. We crunched down a path of sun-bleached oyster shells, opened a creaky screen door, and went inside to sit down. A quick look around told us that we were a little overdressed for the place, with our T-shirts actually tucked into our shorts. Country music crooned from the corner jukebox and several weather-beaten locals sat at the bar idly talking to their buddies while alternating pulls from cold beers with drags from their cigarettes.

All of the wooden tables were stocked with bottles of condiments—pickled peppers, Tabasco, etc.—for properly doctoring shellfish in true Gulf tradition. I looked through the assortment to see if there was also an antidotal bottle of Maalox tablets, but no. Even the salt blended with a few grains of moisture-absorbing white rice gave the place a characteristic coastal touch. Partially used rolls of paper towels standing on the tables and exposed ceiling lightbulbs added to the rough-hewn charm of the place. We quickly lost interest in the restaurant's trappings when our gum-snapping waitress finally slid plates of succulent oysters in front of us. Our conversation came to a grinding halt; the only sounds at our table were the spillover from the noisy bustle of the room and the locustlike whirring of our elbows as we ravenously ate.

Fat and happy as a litter of contented pups, we returned to the highway and followed the sinking sun toward the wildlife refuge. Once on our mountain bikes, our full bellies kept our pace to a slow crawl: a perfect speed for this sunset ride. As our wheels slowly spun over the glistening white sand, a variety of shore and wading birds screeched their cries of outrage as they beat their wings in an

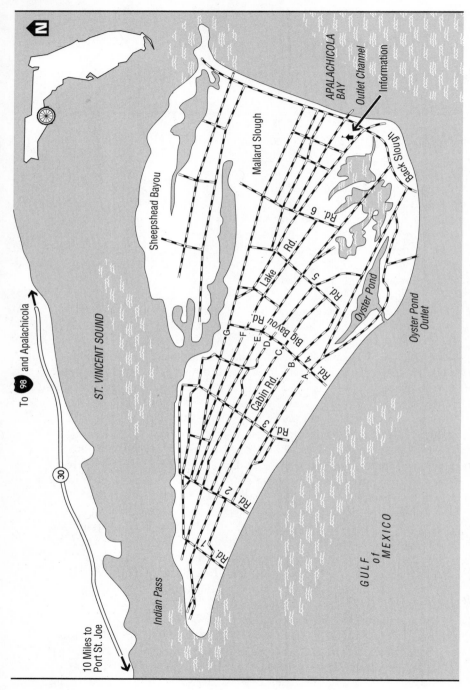

APALACHICOLA BAY

Outlet Channel

Information

Back Slough

Mallard Slough

Sheepshead Bayou

Lake Rd.

Rd. 6

Rd. 5

Rd. 4

Oyster Pond

Oyster Pond Outlet

Big Bayou Rd.

Cabin Rd.

G
F
E
D
C
B
A

Rd. 3

Rd. 2

Rd. 1

ST. VINCENT SOUND

To 98 and Apalachicola

30

10 Miles to Port St. Joe

Indian Pass

GULF of MEXICO

attempt to fly away from us. After a few miles, we got off our bikes and quietly sat to watch sandpipers delicately scamper along the water's edge. A little blue heron stood perfectly still as though posing for a painting; his slender body was silhouetted by a huge glowing orange sun slowly melting into the bay.

We were cycling along the northern shore of St. Vincent Sound, in the part of the wildlife refuge that is on the mainland. The bulk of the refuge is located on St. Vincent Island, but these few miles of cycling are perfect for a short ride if you are not interested in ferrying across the water to the island or do not have an entire day to spend exploring.

St. Vincent Island is a triangular piece of land comprised of 12,358 acres, with 14 miles of pristine beach and a labyrinth of about 80 miles of hard-packed sand roads. On the maps you will notice that the roads running from east to west are marked with letters, while the roads running north to south are numbered. Using the maps, you can custom design a ride of nearly any length less than 80 miles. Loops are easily formed using these interconnected sand roads. Most of the roads are technically unchallenging, though some sections have deep sand that will test your skills. After a storm, you may also have to make some quick moves around occasional debris littering the roads.

This island received its name in the early 1600s from Spanish Franciscan friars who were visiting Apalachee tribes. Later the island was used primarily for hunting and fishing by early white settlers and Indians until it was purchased at auction for $3,000 in 1868 by a Northerner named George Hatch. Hatch lived on the island and died here years later; his tombstone is the only one on St. Vincent Island. In the early to mid-1900s, several owners imported Old World game animals and exotic wildlife such as black bucks, zebras, Asian jungle birds, ringnecked pheasants, and others. The Nature Conservancy purchased the island in 1968; they were later reimbursed by the U.S. Fish and Wildlife Service, who now manage it.

This wildlife refuge was first established as a sanctuary for waterfowl such as brown pelicans, shore birds, and marsh and wading birds. Birders will be interested to note that ornithologists have recorded more than 180 species of birds on this island. Many of these birds begin to migrate to the island in the fall from northern climes, and by the end of December and early January reach peak population here. St. Vincent is home to several threatened or endangered species of birds such as the peregrine falcon, wood stork, and bald eagle. Certain areas of the refuge are closed during portions of each year to provide sanctuary for nesting bald eagles. The refuge's objective was later broadened to protect other endangered species, including the loggerhead sea turtle, from habitat degradation and human predation. The endangered red wolf is also bred on this island. When the pups are weaned, they are moved and reintroduced to other sites in the Southeast, such as the Great Smoky Mountains National Park.

This barrier island enclosing the Apalachicola Bay is dominated by a series of ridges and dunes and provides a unique mix of habitats—including pine palmetto flatlands, slash pine communities, magnolia and hardwood hammocks,

Late afternoon rides at the St. Vincent Wildlife Refuge offer peaceful solitude.

freshwater sloughs, and saltwater bayous—which offer good cover for wildlife and provide good opportunities for cyclists to catch glimpses of the animals. There are large concentrations of alligators, wild hogs, raccoons, and white-tailed deer. In addition, a few exotic sambar deer remain on the island. This exotic species, actually a kind of elk native to Southeastern Asia, weighs in at a whopping 500 to 600 pounds—a hefty fellow when compared to his white-tailed brother who averages 100 to 130 pounds. These two species thrive well together by occupying different areas of the island. The sambar deer prefers the wetlands while the white-tailed deer is generally found in the drier upland stretches. There are also more than 30 species of snakes, including the poisonous cottonmouth and rattlesnake.

General location: St. Vincent National Wildlife Refuge is located along the southern coast of Florida's panhandle. It is approximately 20 miles southwest of the historic town of Apalachicola. The ride along the northern shore of the St. Vincent Sound begins at the terminus of Service Road 30B. The ride on the island begins at a point decided on by you and your boat captain.
Elevation change: There is no appreciable change in elevation.

Season: Cycling during the cooler months of October through March minimizes the annoyance of biting insects. In addition, the bird population reaches its peak during December and January. Hunting is permitted three times a year; check with the refuge headquarters for the exact dates so that you can avoid cycling on the island during those times.

Services: Most services are available in the town of Apalachicola. There are several campgrounds in the area, including the Indian Pass Campground located on the St. Vincent Sound. The folks at the campground can probably assist you in finding a boat captain to ferry you across Indian Pass to the island. The staff at the Apalachicola Chamber of Commerce and the refuge headquarters should also be able to help you. The nearest bicycle shops are in Panama City (56 miles away) and Tallahassee (76 miles away).

Hazards: There are poisonous snakes and alligators on the island, though they will probably make a greater effort to avoid you than you will them. However, mosquitoes will quickly find you and dine on you if you have not anointed your skin with bug dope. Chiggers and ticks will also jump aboard and make an attempt to return with you as party favors.

Rescue index: Once on St. Vincent Island, the rescue index is poor until the boatman returns to ferry you back to the mainland. You should be certain to take plenty of food and water for the day, a well-appointed first-aid kit, maps, and insect repellant.

Land status: National wildlife refuge.

Maps: Refuge maps are available from the headquarters office. The refuge is found on two USGS 7.5 minute quadrangles, Indian Pass, Florida, and West Pass, Florida.

Finding the trail: From Apalachicola, drive 7.6 miles on US 98 West. Bear left at the fork and proceed on SR 30B for an additional 12.7 miles to the St. Vincent Wildlife Refuge and boat ramp. Park at one of the sandy pulloffs near the refuge sign.

Sources of additional information:

St. Vincent National Wildlife Refuge
P. O. Box 447
Apalachicola, FL 32320
(904) 653-8808

Apalachicola Bay Chamber of Commerce
128 Market Street
Apalachicola, FL 32320
(904) 653-9419

Apalachicola National Forest

RIDE 28 *FLORIDA TRAIL*

Looking for a ride off the beaten path? Well, look no further. This ride, well away from the crowds and bustle of the city, leads cyclists along the most remote section of the Florida National Scenic Trail. Fairly strenuous—due to its one-way length of nearly 30 miles, not to technical skill requirements—the trail traverses a west-to-east path from Camel Lake Campground to Porter Lake Campground on the Ochlockonee River. Set up a shuttle between the two campgrounds before the ride. This trail can also be enjoyed in part as an out-and-back by riding as far as you wish and then retracing your path.

Most of the ride is on narrow single-track trail, though there are several sections that follow unpaved Forest Service roads. Some sections of trail are blanketed by fallen pine needles; this thick layer of mulch muffles the sound of spinning tires and offers a silent passage through the forest. In the area near the Indian Creek Islands, the trail follows Forest Service Road 107 for several miles. There is no protective canopy of tree branches to shade cyclists from the blazing Florida sun, so during the dog days of summer this section of trail makes for a torrid, sweltering ride.

Beginning at Camel Lake Campground, the trail winds through a forest of turkey oaks, pines, and palmettos. Dense, dark titi and cypress swamps occasionally interrupt the open forest to impart an eerie flavor to this semitropical ride. Dismount your bicycles and walk across the plank bridges over low-lying wet areas.

After approximately ten miles, the trail crosses the still, black waters of the New River. The sinister-looking surroundings can cause the imagination to conjure up pictures of Lord-knows-what lurking beneath the murky surface. The ride continues past the river to the remnants of a settlement known as Vilas. During a bygone era, turpentine was harvested here from pine trees and was then shipped to market on the Apalachicola Northern Railroad, conveniently located next to the settlement. Today, all that remains are the empty shells of abandoned buildings, neglected and overgrown with weeds.

The trail then passes through stands of pine palmetto flat woods while winding toward the Ochlockonee River. This river nearly bisects the Apalachicola National Forest and serves as the natural boundary between the Apalachicola and Wakulla ranger districts. Because of the remote nature of the trail, there

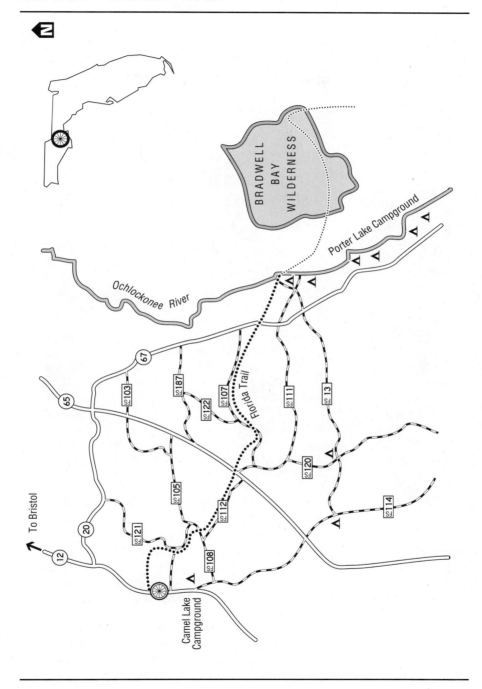

Tall pines flank many of the single-track trails in Florida.

are good opportunities for glimpsing wildlife. Keep your eyes open for gopher tortoise, fox, marsh rabbit, beaver, black bear, feral hog, river otter, bobcat, skunk, and white-tailed deer. There are also nearly 200 species of birds that have been spotted in this forest, including the endangered red-cockaded woodpecker. And, of course, there are the slithering creatures of the forest as well. Several venomous snakes inhabit this forest, including the cottonmouth, coral snake, diamondback rattlesnake, and pygmy rattlesnake. And last but not least, what would a trip to Florida be without seeing an alligator? These too are found in the Apalachicola National Forest and, because of their large numbers, will very likely be seen basking in the sun. (And to think unrestrained dogs used to be your only worry!)

General location: This trail is located west of Tallahassee in the Apalachicola District of the Apalachicola National Forest.

Elevation change: There is no appreciable change in elevation.

Season: The trail can be ridden year-round, though it is more pleasant during cooler months.

Services: All services are available in Tallahassee; some services are available in Bristol.

Hazards: A scorching summer sun will quickly fry ordinary cyclists to a crackly crunch: bring sunscreen. This same sun will also cause you to deplete your water supply quickly; be sure to bring plenty of water or some means of purifying the water taken from the creeks or rivers. Gone are the days when we could dip our water bottles into a stream for a refill—there are some bad bugs out there, one of the most noxious being Giardia. Without a doubt, you do not want this powerful protozoan parasite setting up residence in your intestines. This bad bug will keep you off the trails and close to indoor plumbing for weeks, maybe longer. Other hazards include biting insects, which can be warded off with good insect repellant. Also, poisonous snakes are in this area, so use common sense.

Rescue index: The trail is never more than 4 miles from a Forest Service road. Though these dirt roads are not well-traveled, there are two secondary highways that intersect the trail. Help could be flagged down easily from FL 65 or FL 67.

Land status: National forest.

Maps: The trail is found on the Apalachicola National Forest map. It is also found on five USGS 7.5 minute quadrangles: Estiffanulga, Woods, Wilma, Queens Bay, and Smith Creek.

Finding the trail: From Tallahassee, drive west on Interstate 10 approximately 20 miles to Exit 25, the Bristol exit. Drive south on FL 12 to the town of Bristol. From the intersection of FL 20 and FL 12 in Bristol, drive south on FL 12 for 11.3 miles. Turn left onto FS 105 and drive 2 miles to the Camel Lake Campground, which will be on the right. Park in the designated parking area on the left. The trail begins on the eastern edge of this parking area.

Sources of additional information:

Apalachicola Ranger District
P. O. Box 579
Bristol, FL 32321
(904) 643-2282

Cyclelogical Bike Rentals
P. O. Box 7412
Tallahassee, FL 32314
(904) 656-0001

Notes on the trail: There is an additional 5-mile leg of the Florida Trail that extends northwest from Camel Lake Campground. However, it is frequently wet and boggy and not recommended for mountain bikes. After heavy rains, the section from Memery Island to FL 12 may be ankle-deep in water.

RIDE 29 *CAMEL LAKE LOOP TRAIL*

This nine-mile loop of level single-track trail gives mountain bikers a good back-country pedaling experience. There are a few technical sections along this beautiful trail, but it is an easy ride for the most part. Located near the northwestern periphery, the ride begins at Camel Lake Campground, threading through stands of longleaf pine, turkey oak, water oak, post oak, sweetgum, southern cedar, trident red maple, and saw palmetto. The trail then rolls northward along the eastern edge of Johnson Juniper Swamp; this wet savannah is filled with seasonal wildflowers such as wild orchids and some carnivorous flora, including pitcher plants.

After reaching higher ground at Memery Island, the trail intersects the Florida Trail, which continues to the west. The blue-blazed Camel Lake Loop Trail continues with a right turn in a southeastern direction. Near Sheep Island and its adjacent pond, the trail crosses Big Gully Creek and actually winds up and over several buckles in the landscape that are the closest thing to hills you will find in this neck of the woods.

The trail joins the Florida Trail at an intersection near Bonnet Pond and continues with a right turn into the forest. There is another crossing of Big Gully Creek on a bridge before the trail spills into a clearing. The pathway finally winds through a stand of pines and hardwoods with thousands of palmettos nipping at their heels before reaching the end of the loop at Camel Lake Campground.

General location: This ride is located near the western edge of the Apalachicola National Forest, south of Bristol and southwest of Tallahassee.

Elevation change: There are several slight changes in elevation of about 50 feet as the trail climbs away from Big Gully Creek near Sheep Island and near the second Big Gully Creek crossing on the Florida Trail section of the loop.

Season: This loop can be ridden year-round, though summer rides are least enjoyable due to heat, humidity, and biting insects.

Services: All services are available in Tallahassee; some services are available in Bristol. There are a number of established campgrounds in this national forest, including the Camel Lake Campground.

Hazards: There are venomous snakes in the forest, such as the diamondback and pygmy rattlesnakes, eastern coral snake, copperhead (this location being the

The lush, semitropical surroundings make the trails in the Apalachicola National Forest especially inviting.

southern limit of its range), and cottonmouth. A little common sense goes a long way in avoiding these fanged reptiles, however. There are alligators in the ponds along this route; if you spot one, keep your distance and do not attempt to feed it. These are powerful, quick animals that see you, at close range, as little more than Gator Chow.

Rescue index: The trail is intersected at four points by Forest Service roads, so the rescue index is fairly good. The trail is also just a short distance from the campground, where help could probably be obtained.

Land status: National forest.

Maps: The trail can be found on the Apalachicola National Forest map. The ranger station also provides a free vicinity map on a photocopied sheet that features this loop. The trail is also found on the USGS 7.5 minute quadrangle for Woods, Florida.

Finding the trail: From Tallahassee, drive west on Interstate 10 for approximately 20 miles to Exit 25, the Bristol exit. Drive south on FL 12 to the town

RIDE 29 *CAMEL LAKE LOOP TRAIL*
RIDE 30 *CAMPGROUND LOOP TRAIL*

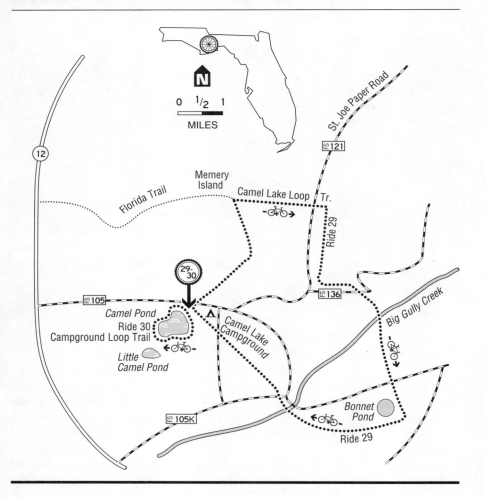

of Bristol. From the intersection of FL 20 and FL 12 in Bristol, drive south on FL 12 for 11.3 miles. Turn left on Forest Service Road 105 and continue for an additional 2 miles to the Camel Lake Campground, which will be on the right. Park in the designated parking area, which will be on your left after turning into the campground. The trail begins by crossing FS 105 and following a northerly direction.

Sources of additional information:

Apalachicola Ranger District
P. O. Box 579
Bristol, FL 32321
(904) 643-2282

Cyclelogical Bike Rentals
P. O. Box 7412
Tallahassee, FL 32314
(904) 656-0001

RIDE 30   *CAMPGROUND LOOP TRAIL*

Short and sweet, this is a good introductory mountain bike ride for young cyclists and beginners. It begins at the Camel Lake Campground on a wide single-track trail and continues for two easy miles as it loops around Camel Pond. Its proximity to the edge of the water offers good vantage points for alligator sightings during the warm months when these creatures are out sunbathing and occasionally snacking on tourists' poodles and Chihuahuas.

General location: The ride is located west of Tallahassee in the Apalachicola District of the Apalachicola National Forest.
Elevation change: There is no appreciable change in elevation.
Season: This trail can be ridden year-round.
Services: All services are available in Tallahassee; some services are available in Bristol. Camping is available at the site of the ride.
Hazards: There are alligators in the lake. The rangers of the Forest Service advise that their behavior can be erratic and unpredictable, so keep your distance. There are also some poisonous snakes in the area. The most annoying problem is biting insects during the hot summer months.
Rescue index: The rescue index is excellent because of the close proximity to the campground.
Land status: National forest.
Maps: The trail is located on the Apalachicola National Forest map. It is also found on the USGS 7.5 minute quadrangle for Woods.
Finding the trail: From Tallahassee, drive west on Interstate 10 for approximately 20 miles to Exit 25, the Bristol exit. Drive south on FL 12 to the town of Bristol. From the intersection of FL 20 and FL 12 in Bristol, drive south on FL 12 for 11.3 miles. Turn left on Forest Service Road 105 and continue for an additional 2 miles to the Camel Lake Campground, which will be on the right.

Wide, scenic dirt roads lead cyclists on a winding path through the forest.

Park in the designated parking area, which will be on your left after turning into the campground. The trail begins on the eastern edge of the campground near the established hunt camp.

Sources of additional information:

Apalachicola Ranger District
P. O. Box 579
Bristol, FL 32321
(904) 643-2282

Cyclelogical Bike Rentals
P. O. Box 7412
Tallahassee, FL 32314
(904) 656-0001

Notes on the trail: The trail can be ridden in either direction, though we rode it by beginning on the eastern leg of the loop near the hunt camp. Hikers from the campground do use this trail for exercise, so be sure to use caution and courtesy when approaching others on the trail.

RIDE 31 BRADWELL BAY LOOP

If you are not a single-track purist, you are sure to enjoy this moderately difficult loop of Forest Service roads. The 32-mile ride utilizes four different roads,
all with a nontechnical, hard-packed dirt surface. The condition of the roads
does not require much technical skill, although its length makes for a moderately strenuous day in the saddle. The scenery is beautiful as the ride skirts
the boundaries of Bradwell Bay Wilderness—a tremendous, shallow basin of
lowlands filled with mixed hardwoods, titi, saw palmetto, and blackgum. The
wilderness area is named for an early hunter named Carl Bradwell who, along
with his father, was lost for a number of days here without food or water. The
thick tangles of vegetation can quickly overcome sections of trails, but you are
not likely to become lost if you stay on the Forest Service roads.

Deep in the bay area is a virgin stand of old-growth slash pine somehow spared
by loggers in the 1800s. The wet savannah areas are host to several species of
carnivorous plants, such as bladderworts, pitcher plants, and sundews. There are
also patches of wild azaleas, orchids, lilies, and other wildflowers in season. The
dense flora provides good cover for a variety of wildlife, which draws hunters
in droves to this forest. Animals that are hunted include white-tailed deer, wild
turkey, black bear, and raccoon. There are also snakes, alligators, bald eagles,
woodpeckers, and many other birds in the wilderness area.

General location: This ride is located approximately 40 miles west of Tallahas-
see in the Apalachicola National Forest.
Elevation change: There is no appreciable change in elevation.
Season: This loop can be cycled year-round because of the mild winters in
Florida. Bugs, heat, and humidity make the ride less enjoyable in the heat of
summer.
Services: All services are available in Tallahassee. There are a number of camp-
grounds located within the national forest.
Hazards: Though there are poisonous snakes and alligators in the wilderness, it
is unlikely that you will encounter any as you cycle the Forest Service roads.
Rescue index: The rescue index is good since the ride is confined to Forest Ser-
vice roads. The city of Tallahassee is fairly close; medical care is available there
in case of a serious emergency.
Land status: National forest.
Maps: The loop is found on the Apalachicola National Forest map. It is found
in better detail on four USGS 7.5 minute quadrangles: Smith Creek, Bradwell
Bay, Sanborn, and Crawfordville West.
Finding the trail: From Tallahassee, drive west on FL 20 for approximately 35
miles to the town of Bloxham. Turn left onto FL 375 and drive south for 17.5

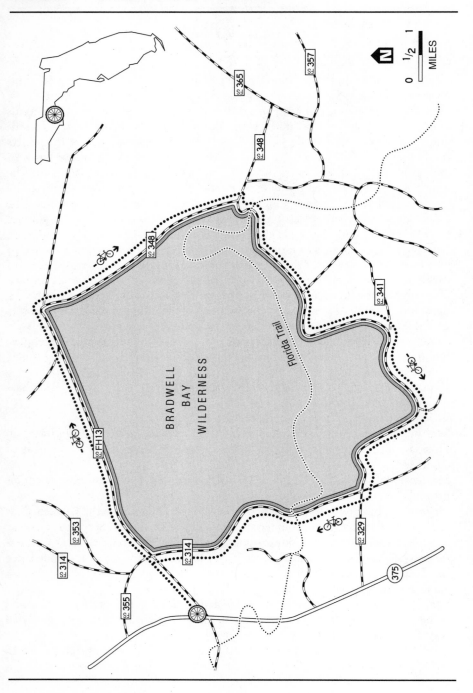

miles to the intersection with Forest Service Road FH-13. Turn left and park at any road pulloff near this intersection to begin the ride.

Sources of additional information:

Wakulla Ranger District
Route 6, Box 7860
Crawfordville, FL 32327
(904) 926-3561

Cyclelogical Bike Rentals
P. O. Box 7412
Tallahassee, FL 32314
(904) 656-0001

Notes on the trail: This loop of roads can be ridden in either direction since there are no hills to take into account. We rode it by beginning on FS FH-13 and turning right onto FS 314 to cycle along the western edge of Bradwell Bay Wilderness. After about 8 miles, a left turn onto FS 329 will lead you on a twisting, curving path along the southern edge of the wilderness. After crossing Monkey Creek, you will make another left turn, this time onto FS 348. This Forest Service road parallels the Sopchoppy River and is one of the most scenic sections of the ride. After about 2.5 miles you will turn left, back onto the well-marked FS FH-13, to return to your vehicle.

There is a 10-mile section of the Florida Trail that passes through the wilderness area but it is off-limits to mountain bikes because of its location in a designated wilderness area.

RIDE 32 *SPRING HILL RIDE*

Mountain biking by moonlight . . . the very thought conjures up words like thrilling, romantic, and maybe even spooky. The idea of pedaling along an open trail or a dirt road with only the light from a ripened moon is titillating enough to have you checking your calendar for the next full moon, regardless of where you are. Cyclists in the Tallahassee area have a first-rate location for nighttime mountain bike rides—right along the eastern edge of the Apalachicola National Forest. In fact, one of the local bicycle clubs frequently organizes full-moon rides on this moderate, 15-mile loop of dirt roads.

The ride begins near Spring Hill on glistening sand roads that seem to shine in the moonlight. Black expanses of eerie forest flank the path, while tall pine trees ominously stand guard in the half light of night farther back in the woods. The path now turns onto narrow, grassy jeep roads, which are not as well illumi-

RIDE 32 *SPRING HILL RIDE*

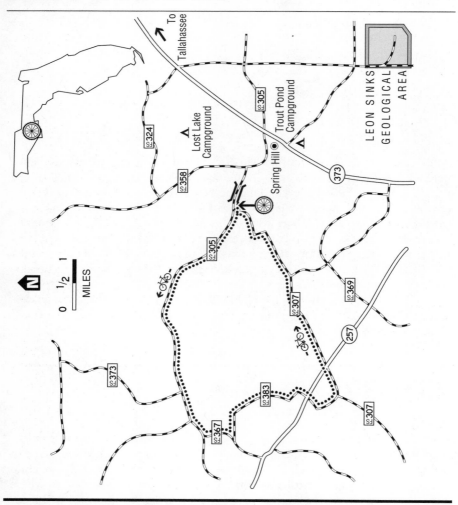

nated by the silvering moon as the sand roads. The understory of saw palmettos and other bushes is shrouded by a blanket of darkness, hiding nocturnal animals. Camouflaged by the night, these creatures slip through the forest as they forage for food. As you cycle along, you may occasionally catch the glowing eyes of an animal spying on you. It is a strange feeling to know that you are being watched—and it is especially strange in the dark of night.

Though full moons are often associated with vampires and werewolves, you probably will not spot any this far from Transylvania. On the other hand, chances

Close to Tallahassee, these dirt roads offer local cyclists a quick escape into a lush natural world.

are fairly good that you will glimpse white-tailed deer, raccoon, or opossum. Also roaming around at night are the more elusive gray fox, coyote, bear, and bobcat, though you would be extremely lucky to see one of these covert critters. You might happen upon an animal in the early morning as it prepares to bed down or in the late afternoon as it begins its nightly prowl. Your chances of wildlife glimpses are decreased if you ride during the middle of the day when the animals are less active.

General location: This loop is located in the eastern section of the Apalachicola National Forest, approximately 5 miles southwest of Tallahassee.

Elevation change: There is no appreciable change in elevation.

Season: This loop of roads can be ridden year-round. Mosquitoes and other biting insects try to crash your cycling party during the warm summer months, but a splash of bug repellant will keep them from spoiling the fun. At dusk, the bugs become especially bad.

Services: All services are available in nearby Tallahassee. There are a number of campgrounds located within the national forest, including Silver Lake Campground, which is only a few miles north of this ride. .

Hazards: Snakes are out in the forest during warmer months. Be sure to stay on the dirt roads and out of the woods at night when visibility is reduced. Sections of some of the jeep roads have a washboard surface, are rock-strewn, and are full of potholes. At night you really have to pick your line in these areas to avoid having your wheels tweaked and getting thrown from your bike. However, this element of risk only adds to the thrill of this excellent mountain bike ride.

Rescue index: The rescue index is good since you are on accessible Forest Service roads the entire time. Also, Tallahassee is quite close.

Land status: National forest.

Maps: The Apalachicola National Forest map is available from the ranger station. The ride is also found on the USGS 7.5 minute quadrangle for Hilliardville.

Finding the trail: From Tallahassee, drive south on FL 373 for approximately 4 miles to Spring Hill. Turn right onto Forest Service Road 305 and proceed for .6 mile to an intersection. Bear left to stay on FS 305, which turns into a dirt road. Drive .3 mile until you cross Fisher Creek. Park at the parking area on the right just past the creek. The ride begins by cycling FS 305 away from Fisher Creek.

Sources of additional information:

Cyclelogical Bike Rentals
P. O. Box 7412
Tallahassee, FL 32314
(904) 656-0001

Wakulla Ranger District
Route 6, Box 7860
Crawfordville, FL 32327
(904) 926-3561

Tallahassee

RIDE 33 *MUNSON HILLS TRAIL*

Another favorite of Tallahassee cyclists is this eight-mile loop of single-track trails. This is a fairly easy ride and is a popular destination for mountain bikers looking for a good ride close to the city. There are several challenging sections that require some degree of technical maneuvering and that are certain to make the ride more attractive to experienced cyclists. However, novices should not shy away from this loop because of the challenge; these technical sections of trail can be easily managed.

Located in the sandhills of the Apalachicola National Forest, the trail winds through stands of longleaf pines. The fallen needles cushion the trail floor and provide a quiet, muffled ride through the forest. On less crowded days, there is a good chance that you will glimpse some of the wildlife of the area such as gopher tortoise, wild turkey, fox, and skunk. Porcupine have even been spotted in the Munson Hills area.

The loop is reached from the northern terminus of the Tallahassee–St. Marks Historic Railroad State Trail; a 1.5-mile leg of this rail trail will bring you to the junction with the Munson Hills Trail. Adding 3 miles, round-trip, to the ride, the rail trail combined with the 8-mile Munson Hills loop creates a total ride of about 11 miles. The route can be shortened by taking Trail Pine Shortcut, which is located near the midpoint of the Munson Hills loop. By taking the shortcut, the mileage on the loop section would be decreased to 4.5 miles, resulting in a total trip distance of 7.5 miles.

General location: The trail is located in the city of Tallahassee, on the northeastern edge of the Apalachicola National Forest.
Elevation change: Though the trail's name may imply otherwise, there is no appreciable change in elevation.
Season: This trail is open year-round to cyclists. It is more enjoyable to ride in the fall and winter months because there are more temperate conditions and fewer people. During the summer, especially on weekends, the crowds tend to create a carnival atmosphere along this trail, particularly on the rail trail section.
Services: All services are available in Tallahassee. There are a number of camping areas located within the national forest, the closest being Silver Lake Campground.

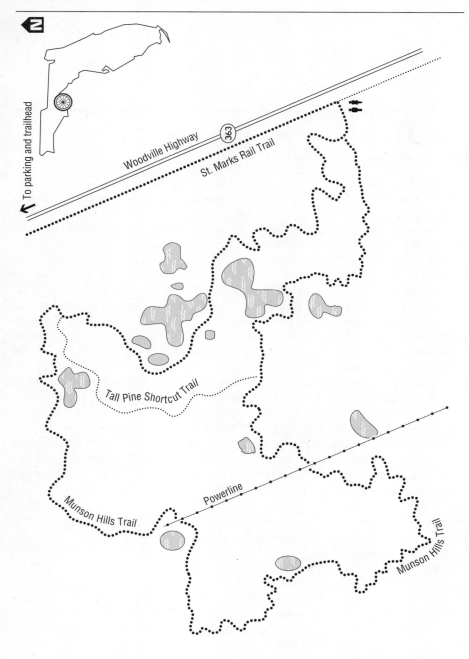

N

To parking and trailhead

Woodville Highway 363

St. Marks Rail Trail

Tall Pine Shortcut Trail

Powerline

Munson Hills Trail

Munson Hills Trail

This excellent single-track trail spins off Tallahassee's lauded rail trail.

Hazards: The only hazards on this fairly easy trail are biting insects and scorching sun during the summer months. There are some obstacles on the trail, such as exposed roots, that might throw an inexperienced rider if they are not negotiated cautiously.

Rescue index: Help is available at the bike rental shop located at the northern terminus of the Tallahassee–St. Marks railroad trail. Also, FL 363 parallels the rail trail; help could be flagged down on this highway.

Land status: The majority of the ride is on national forest land. The short portion that follows the rail trail is on state park land.

Maps: Munson Hills Trail is found on two USGS 7.5 minute quadrangles: Tallahassee and Lake Munson. It can also be found on the Apalachicola National Forest map.

Finding the trail: From the intersection of Interstate 10 and US 27 in Tallahassee, proceed south on US 27 for 3.5 miles. US 27 veers to the left; continue straight on FL 61 for an additional 2.9 miles until you reach a fork. Bear left on FL 363 toward St. Marks. Continue for approximately 2 more miles. The trail's large paved parking lot will be on the right and is well marked, as Tallahassee–St. Marks Historic Railroad State Trail.

Sources of additional information:

Florida Department of Natural Resources
Division of Recreation and Parks
3900 Commonwealth Blvd.
Tallahassee, FL 32399-3000
(904) 487-4784

Wakulla Ranger District
US 319, Route 6
P. O. Box 7860
Crawfordville, FL 32327
(904) 926-3561

Cyclelogical Bike Rentals
P. O. Box 7412
Tallahassee, FL 32314
(904) 656-0001

RIDE 34   *TALLAHASSEE–ST. MARKS HISTORIC RAILROAD STATE TRAIL*

Located right in the heart of Tallahassee is Florida's first designated state trail, a 16-mile paved pathway that provides an excellent surface for a number of different activities such as bicycling, jogging, rollerblading, and walking. Don't flip to the next chapter at the sight of the word *paved*, however, for there is an excellent single-track trail adjacent to the paved path that is ideal for mountain biking. Curving around trees and blasting through open fields, this narrow 16-mile path is thrilling to pedal. The tight turns, off-camber terrain, and natural obstacles in some sections of the trail create a fun and somewhat technical ride.

On hot summer days, this single-track offers a pleasant and shady alternative to the official state trail, which has little protective tree canopy. There are a few scenic sections of the paved path that wind beneath a gnarled live oak canopy, but most of that trail runs through open, sunny sections as it makes its way to the marshland terminus in the town of St. Marks. When you arrive, sweaty and

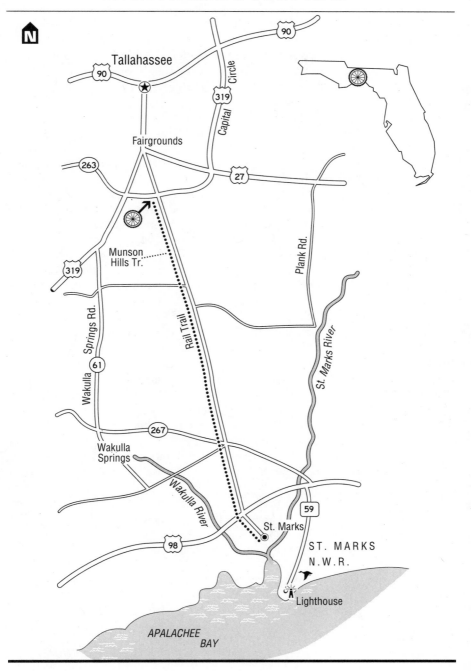

hot, at this port fishing village, you might want to take a lunch break and cool off at one of the local eateries. Smoked mullet is the locally renowned fish, but you can also get boiled Gulf shrimp or even a sandwich at any of these casual restaurants.

This is a moderate, out-and-back ride that will log 32 miles on your cyclometer if ridden in its entirety. If you have young children or out-of-shape riders in your group, you can decrease the distance and difficulty of the ride by cycling as far as you wish and then retracing your path.

Following a path along the old railway corridor of the Tallahassee–St. Marks Railroad, this rail trail is rich with historical lore. This was the first railroad to be constructed in Florida; it began operating in 1837 as a 20-mile line running on wooden rails from St. Marks Gulf port to the territorial capital of Tallahassee. The rail line was financed by wealthy cotton planters and merchants to facilitate transportation of their booming cotton crops to East Coast markets. A year after the railroad began operation, the line was extended three additional miles south to Port Leon. In 1843, just a few years later, Port Leon was destroyed by hurricane and the southern terminus was moved back to St. Marks, where it remained for 140 years.

In the early years, the rickety wooden rails were traversed by mules hauling open freight and passenger cars. One early passenger traveling on the St. Marks Railroad described it as "the worst that has yet been built in the entire world." Steel rails and locomotives replaced the wooden rails and mules in 1856. Five years later, the country was at war and the railroad was put to use in the transportation of Confederate troops from St. Marks, Camp Leon, and Camp Simkins to Tallahassee.

In the early 1980s, the Seaboard Railroad abandoned the line. Florida's Department of Transportation purchased the railway corridor to preserve the right-of-way. Private citizens organized a rails-to-trails coalition and, with assistance from the Florida Park Service, Florida's first rail trail was constructed.

The southern terminus of the trail is in the town of St. Marks, which was an important port for Tallahassee in years gone by. But its history runs deeper still. If you are interested in remnants and stories of the past, you might want to stop by Fort San Marcos de Apalache State Museum, which is located about .2 miles west of the trail's southern terminus on the St. Marks River. This fort, built by the Spanish in 1679, was used as quarters by an unlikely and diverse crew of squatters through the years. Bands of roving pirates garrisoned the fortress at times, as did British and French soldiers. Both Union and Confederate officers used the fort during the Civil War to garrison their troops (albeit at different times!). The remains of Confederate salt evaporation vats can still be found in this area today.

After returning to the northern terminus of the trail and your parked vehicle, you may wish to stop by nearby Wakulla Springs, which is located south of the intersection of FL 61 and FL 267. *Wakulla* is an Indian word that means

A father and son pedaling the paved portion of the Tallahassee–St. Marks Historic Trail.

"mysteries of strange water." It is no wonder the Indians were so mystified and intrigued with this unusual natural phenomenon, for it is considered to be one of the world's deepest springs, with underground channels of unknown proportions. The spring flows from an underground river at a rate of more than half a million gallons of gushing, tepid water each minute. Though several hundred feet deep, the water is so clear that objects can be easily seen even at the deepest point.

Birders flock to Wakulla Springs for observation of the diverse waterfowl that live and thrive here, including ibis, egrets, herons, gallinules, and widgeons. Filmmakers have also flocked to Wakulla Springs—several movies have been filmed on location here, including *Creature of the Black Lagoon*. The area has a number of recreational facilities, including picnic areas, a beach, nature trails, and a designated swimming area. A snorkler swimming in prohibited waters was killed by an alligator in the late 1980s, so use only those areas designated as safe for swimming and other recreation. Getting mauled by a Florida alligator can really put a damper on your vacation.

General location: This trail is located in the city of Tallahassee, several miles south of the downtown area.

Elevation change: There is no appreciable change in elevation.

Season: The trail is open year-round to cyclists. The trail is heavily used during summer vacation months, so expect congested, crowded conditions then.

Services: All services are available in Tallahassee. Nearby Apalachicola National Forest has a number of campgrounds from which to choose.

Hazards: The trail crosses several busy roads, so be alert when you reach the designated crossings and watch for traffic.

Rescue index: The trail parallels FL 363—a well-traveled highway—for the entire 16-mile distance, so help could easily be obtained.

Land status: State park.

Maps: Florida's park service has free maps, as does Cyclelogical Bike Rentals, located at the northern terminus of the trail. The trail is also found on four USGS 7.5 minute quadrangles: St. Marks, Florida; Woodville; Lake Munson, Florida; and Tallahassee.

Finding the trail: From the intersection of Interstate 10 and US 27 in Tallahassee, proceed south on US 27 for 3.5 miles. US 27 veers to the left; continue straight on FL 61 for an additional 2.9 miles until you reach a fork. Bear left on FL 363 toward St. Marks. Continue for approximately 2 more miles; the trail's large paved parking lot will be on the right and is well marked, as Tallahassee–St. Marks Historic Railroad State Trail.

Sources of additional information:

Florida Department of Natural Resources
Division of Recreation and Parks
3900 Commonwealth Blvd.
Tallahassee, FL 32399-3000
(904) 487-4784

Tallahassee–St. Marks Historic Railroad State Trail
1022 DeSoto Park Drive
Tallahassee, FL 32301
(904) 922-6007

Cyclelogical Bike Rentals
P. O. Box 7412
Tallahassee, FL 32314
(904) 656-0001

Notes on the trail: The St. Marks Trail Association plans a second phase of development on this trail that will extend it northward into Tallahassee via the old railway corridor along FL 363 to Gaines Street.

RIDE 35 *WAKULLA BEACH RIDE*

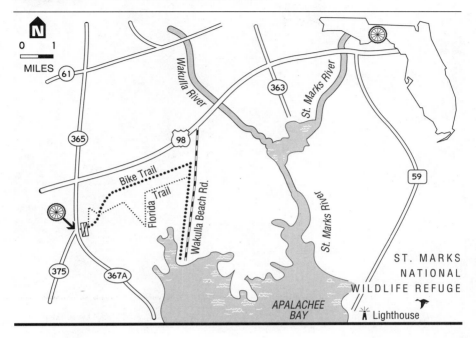

This moderately easy, out-and-back ride will take you on a tour of 15 miles (round-trip) of beautiful Florida backcountry. The surroundings vary from mixed forests of hardwoods and pines to open, grassy areas to sunny beaches. Some technical skill is needed on a few tight turns and over exposed roots and other obstacles that can make the going a little rough.

You will begin on a wide, old logging road that meanders through a mature forest of loblolly pine, longleaf pine, palmettos, and a few palm trees. This hard-packed dirt road narrows to become a single-track trail and follows an easterly course until it reaches Wakulla Beach Road. A right turn will lead you on a three-mile ride on this sandy road down to Wakulla Beach. This scenic beach is located on the northern edge of Goose Creek Bay and creates an inviting spot that may tempt you to linger for a while before retracing your path back to the starting point.

The single-track portion of this ride penetrates some thick brush in spots, which can be filled with chiggers during the summer months. These insects, also

Two female mountain bikers show the macho guys how it is done. *Photo by Owen Riley, Jr.*

known as red bugs, are among the most notorious pests of the woods. They are clandestine critters who don't even have the courtesy to notify you of their intrusion on your epidermal layers with a decent warning bite. At least mosquitoes, ants, and flies know how to fight fair and square. Their stings and bites give you a chance to respond to their attack with a defensive slap or two. But you won't even know that chiggers have waged an all-out war until you get home, start itching, and discover that the lower half of your body looks like you are reliving your childhood cases of chicken pox and red measles, both at the same time. To deter this sneaky little mite from its secret mission to make your life miserable for an itchy week or so, be sure to apply insect repellant liberally before you take off on your mountain bike.

General location: This ride is located about 15 miles south of Tallahassee.
Elevation change: There is no appreciable change in elevation.
Season: Though rideable year-round, the summer months can be unpleasant due to heat and biting bugs.

Services: All services are available in Tallahassee, including campgrounds.

Hazards: There are snakes in the woods, a few of which are poisonous. But if you keep your eyes open, and stay on the trails and out of the underbrush, you should be okay.

Rescue index: The rescue index is fairly good. The trail is close to US 98 and connecting roads.

Land status: National wildlife refuge.

Maps: The trail is found on two USGS 7.5 minute quadrangles, Crawfordville East and Spring Creek.

Finding the trail: From the intersection of FL 363 and US 98 south of Tallahassee, proceed on US 98 West. After driving 2.1 miles, you will cross the Wakulla River. Continue driving for about 5 miles to the junction with County Road 365. Turn left on this county road and proceed toward the south for 1.4 miles. Bear left on CR 367 and park at a road pulloff on the side of the county road. The trail begins at the gated logging road. Secure your vehicle and remove any valuables from plain view.

Sources of additional information:

Cyclelogical Bike Rentals
P. O. Box 7412
Tallahassee, FL 32314
(904) 656-0001

St. Marks National Wildlife Refuge
P. O. Box 68
St. Marks, FL 32355
(904) 925-6121

RIDE 36 *STONEY BAYOU TRAIL*

When I am out cycling a trail alone I sometimes pause to consider why I don't do it more often. Of course, the "parent" side of my psyche always makes arguments about safety. But on the morning that I began pedaling the Stoney Bayou Trail without a cycling companion, any arguments concerning unsafe conditions would have fallen on deaf ears. To me, this particular trail seemed ideal for a solo mountain bike ride.

The trail follows hard-packed dike roads for the entire 12.6-mile loop. It follows a flat grade and does not scream down wild descents or dangle precipitously on the edge of a steep drop-off. Nor does it blindly pick a path through tangled underbrush threatening to render a cyclist lost. It is not technical and has no downed trees or tombstone roots slyly waiting to grab front wheels, causing dramatic crash-and-burn maneuvers. It is simply a good, straightforward loop

RIDE 36 *STONEY BAYOU TRAIL*

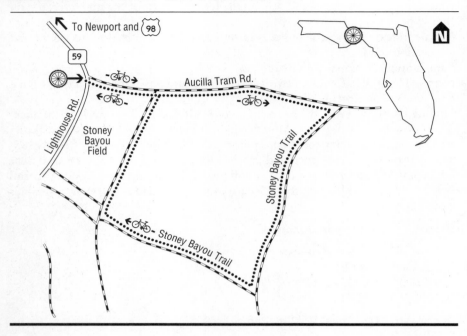

offering great mountain biking and gorgeous scenery. Whether alone or with a group, this easy trail will lead you on a good off-road ride for a few hours.

Located within the St. Marks National Wildlife Refuge, the trail traverses dike rims along grassy, wide, open routes on the edge of freshwater impoundments. More than 300 species of birds have been recorded wintering here, with more than 270 of them spotted often enough to be considered full-time residents. The birds are most active during early morning and late afternoon, so mountain bike rides during those hours will offer the best chances for sightings. Especially rewarding are rides in early morning, when the cacophony of chirps, whistles, and songs resonates throughout the refuge.

Keep your eyes peeled for the tall sandhill cranes, one of the most intriguing birds of the wetlands. When I come upon a group of different wading birds, my eyes immediately sort through the varieties in search of this five-foot-tall crane. These elegant gray birds are permanent residents, the sentinels of the swamp. When spooked, they will rise from the grass with a loud, rattling cry of warning that causes all the other birds to flee in a mad thundering of wings. In March, the sandhill cranes perform an extraordinary mating dance where they face one another, then leap into the air with extended wings and feet thrown forward.

Pines, palms, and palmettos give the typical Florida forest a tropical look.

Then they bow to each other, repeating the performance while uttering deep, croaking calls. Once they win a companion, they mate for life.

Different months offer different sightings of wildlife and waterfowl within the refuge. In January, bald eagles are nesting and waterfowl are prolific in the refuge pools; in February, great horned owls can be seen feeding their owlets, great blue herons and wood ducks begin nesting, and ospreys return to the refuge; in March, ibis and white pelicans migrate through the refuge while ducks head north; in April, ospreys and red-cockaded woodpeckers are nesting and eaglets begin to fly; in May, crabbing is at its peak; in June, turkey broods are spotted in the forest as well as white-tailed does with their fawns; in August, alligators are hatching; in September and October, swallowtail and monarch butterflies are seen in great numbers; and, by the end of the year, the waterfowl population has reached its peak due to the southern migration to the refuge.

General location: The trail is located in the St. Marks National Wildlife Refuge, approximately 20 miles southeast of Tallahassee.

Elevation change: There is no appreciable change in elevation.

Season: Wildlife activity is heightened during the fall, winter, and spring seasons. Summer's heat and humidity can make a cycling trip fairly miserable at that time of the year, particularly on this dike road path, which has no tree canopy for protection.

Services: All services are available in Tallahassee. Camping is not permitted in the refuge, but is available at Newport Recreation Area, Ochlockonee River State Park, and in nearby Apalachicola National Forest.

Hazards: Heat and the presence of biting insects can be counted on during the summer months. Though it is unlikely that you will encounter any, alligators and poisonous snakes do make an occasional appearance in the refuge, so watch out for them.

Rescue index: The trail is located within a wildlife refuge where help is readily available. Also, the trail is only about 7 miles long, so the rescue index is quite good. It is fairly well traveled by hikers and bikers who could offer or seek help if an emergency did occur.

Land status: National wildlife refuge.

Maps: The refuge Visitor Center offers free maps of the trail. For more detail, the trail is found on four USGS 7.5 minute quadrangles: St. Marks, St. Marks NE, Sprague Island, and Cobb Rocks.

Finding the trail: From the intersection of US 98 and FL 363 south of Tallahassee, drive east on US 98 for 2.4 miles to the crossing of the St. Marks River. Continue straight for .1 mile to the intersection with County Road 59; turn right. Drive for 4.7 miles (past the Visitor Center) to a gated road on the left. There is a sign marking the trails. Park at one of the road pulloffs along the edge of the road; do not block the gate.

Sources of additional information:

St. Marks National Wildlife Refuge
P. O. Box 68
St. Marks, FL 32355
(904) 925-6121

Cyclelogical Bike Rentals
P. O. Box 7412
Tallahassee, FL 32314
(904) 656-0001

Notes on the trail: Full-fledged mountain bikes are not necessary on these hard-packed dirt roads. Cruisers are perfectly adequate. This trail, due to its relatively short length and lack of technical skill requirements, is an ideal trail for beginners and families with young children. To rent bicycles, contact Cyclelogical Bike Rentals at the above address.

RIDE 37 *DEEP CREEK TRAIL*

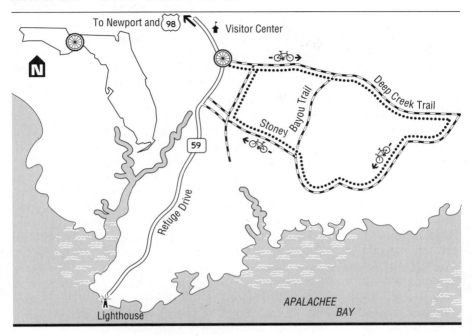

Whether you are interested in observing mammals, birds, reptiles, butterflies, and wildflowers or are simply interested in spending a few hours bicycling a good, off-road trail, the paths in the St. Marks National Wildlife Refuge offer a variety of outdoor experiences. Deep Creek Trail follows the route of the Florida Trail along hard-packed dike roads to form a 12-mile loop that is moderately difficult. This series of dikes was built to impound fresh water for the thousands of birds that winter here; more than 300 species have been recorded in St. Marks. On the afternoon I cycled this trail, I came upon two graying hikers who urged me to stop and chat when I slowed to pass them. One, a photographer, carried a camera while the other, a birder, carried binoculars. They jokingly claimed to be combining talents in order to spot and shoot some of the many varieties of birds along this trail.

The refuge extends from the Aucilla River on the east to the Ochlockonee River on the west, sprawling for about 40 miles along the Apalachee Bay. It was established in 1931 and is considered one of the oldest federal wildlife refuges.

There are about 33,000 acres of forest land; 28,000 acres of salt marshes; and 1,000 acres of natural ponds and lakes. Each of these habitats draws and supports an amazing variety of wildlife. The forest land is predominantly pine interspersed with some turkey oak, which attracts white-tailed deer, wild turkey, and other animals. The remainder of the forest is old-growth hardwood forests, live oak hammocks, magnolia groves, and hardwood swamps, which offer good cover for black bear, raccoon, otter, and a variety of waterfowl such as wood ducks. The salt marshes are filled with shrimp, fish, and shellfish that use the areas as a nursery; the protected status of the marshes makes the area ideal for this.

The wildflower aficionados in your group will be thrilled to be cycling the trails in the St. Marks National Wildlife Refuge, for the area is blessed with a diversity of habitats that support a wide selection of flora. The blooming begins early in the year with delicate blue and white violets in February. By late spring, the flowering is at its peak and the refuge is bursting with color. As you drive in toward the trailhead, look along the roadside for blue-eyed grass, Saint-John's-wort, spiderwort, wild geraniums, and blue thistle. The sunken areas and ditches near the road fill with bog buttons, hatpins, coreopsis, and the carnivorous red sundew. As you cycle the trail, you will find the canals of water dotted with floating water lily. These wet areas are also host to the carnivorous bladderwort, a unique and interesting plant whose roots freely dangle in the water while its flowers float upright. The open, grassy areas along the dike roads are blanketed with yellow jessamine and evening primrose, whose bright colors enhance this already beautiful ride.

Rich in natural history, this area abounds in human record as well. Scattered along the banks of the Aucilla River and along the coastline are old Indian mounds that date back more than 2,000 years. Remnants of Confederate salt evaporation vats can still be found in this area today. Nearby is Port Leon, a ghost town since 1843 when it was destroyed by a hurricane. This former town and deepwater port was given new life when it was chosen in 1936 as the site for the first headquarters of the newly established St. Marks National Wildlife Refuge.

General location: The trail is located in the St. Marks National Wildlife Refuge, approximately 20 miles southeast of Tallahassee.

Elevation change: There is no appreciable change in elevation.

Season: Wildlife activity is heightened during the fall, winter, and spring seasons. Summer's heat and humidity can make a cycling trip fairly miserable at that time of the year, particularly on this dike road path, which has no tree canopy for protection.

Services: All services are available in Tallahassee. Camping is not permitted in the refuge, but is available at Newport Recreation Area, Ochlockonee River State Park, and in nearby Apalachicola National Forest.

Hazards: Bugs and scorching heat are a real concern during summer months. An encounter with an alligator or poisonous snake—both of which are found in

Open refuge roads are ideal for fat-tired bicycles.

the refuge—could make for a memorable ride, but it is unlikely that you will see one.

Rescue index: Help could be obtained from the refuge headquarters.

Land status: National wildlife refuge.

Maps: The refuge Visitor Center offers free maps of the trail. For more detail, the trail is found on four USGS 7.5 minute quadrangles: St. Marks, St. Marks NE, Sprague Island, and Cobb Rocks.

Finding the trail: From the intersection of US 98 and FL 363 south of Tallahassee, drive east on US 98 for 2.4 miles to the crossing of the St. Marks River. Continue straight for .1 mile to the intersection with County Road 59; turn right. Drive for 4.7 miles (past the Visitor Center) to a gated road on the left. There is a sign marking the trails. Park at one of the road pulloffs along the edge of the road; do not block the gate.

Sources of additional information:

St. Marks National Wildlife Refuge
P. O. Box 68

St. Marks, FL 32355
(904) 925-6121

Cyclelogical Bike Rentals
P. O. Box 7412
Tallahassee, FL 32314
(904) 656-0001

Notes on the trail: Full-fledged mountain bikes are not necessary on these hard-packed dirt roads. All-terrain bikes and cruisers are perfectly adequate. To rent bicycles, contact Cyclelogical Bike Rentals at the above address.

Northern Florida

RIDE 38   *MATTAIR SPRING TRACT LOOP*

Far from civilization and far from the tourists lies the Mattair Spring Tract, a 1,189-acre piece of land located on the south bank of the Suwannee River. This eight-mile loop of single-track trails leads through thick hanging vines and past moss-draped oak trees. There is a sense of jungle that permeates the ride as you cycle along scenic trails flanked by lush tropical vegetation. It is definitely not Disney World.

The sights are certainly different from the stereotypical image of Florida—and so are the smells. There are no scents of salty sea, cocoa butter, or cotton candy; each mile of trail that flies by will bathe your nose with the earthy, fecund smell of rich soil from the moist riverbanks and the occasional, fragrant hint of blooming wildflowers. This is mountain biking Deep South–style, a great ride that will give you an entirely new perspective on what Florida has to offer.

This moderately easy loop follows the Suwannee River for nearly five miles of its entire eight-mile distance. Romantic and seductive, the winding Suwannee has captured people's hearts and attention for centuries. It was immortalized in the late 1800s by Stephen Foster's song, "Suwannee River" (or "Old Folks at Home"), which later became Florida's official state song. The river flows for more than 200 sinuous miles from Georgia's Okefenokee Swamp to the town of Suwannee at the Gulf of Mexico. Florida's "Queen of Rivers" has miles and miles of pristine natural beauty. Flanked by mature hardwood forests, swampy areas, lush moss-covered banks and limestone banks, bucolic farmlands and open fields, this river carves a curving path through a beautifully scenic section of northern Florida. Though mostly calm flatwater, there are a few sections of river that drop a substantial number of feet creating actual rapids. Whitewater in Florida, outside of Typhoon Lagoon . . . imagine that!

It is believed that the name Suwannee may have originated from the Indian word *Sawani,* meaning "echo." The Timucuan Indians, who lived in the Suwannee River area in the 1700s when the basin was first explored by Spaniards, called the river *Guasaca Esqui,* which meant "river of reeds." De Soto, in his early writings, described the Suwannee as "the river of the deer." Today, the river is still home to a healthy population of white-tailed deer, as well as fox, opossum, squirrel, raccoon, and bobcat. There are also gopher tortoises in the area and efforts are being made to improve their habitat in the Mattair Spring Tract in order to promote the species.

RIDE 38 *MATTAIR SPRING TRACT LOOP*

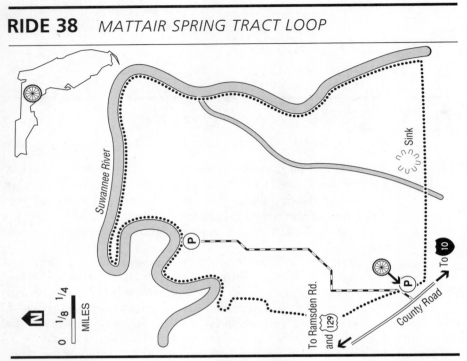

General location: This ride is located approximately 25 miles northwest of Lake City and approximately 75 miles west of Jacksonville.

Elevation change: There is only a slight change of elevation.

Season: Late fall and winter are the best seasons to cycle this trail. Spring and summer rides are plagued with swarms of relentless mosquitoes, as well as nearly unbearable heat and humidity, which make the trail fit for neither man nor beast—nor bicyclist.

Services: Most services are available in nearby Lake City, while many services are also available in the towns of Jasper and Live Oak, only a few miles away from the trailhead. Current campground information can be obtained from the Hamilton County Chamber of Commerce.

Hazards: Because of the humid conditions near the river, biting insects are a serious aggravation. There are also poisonous snakes and alligators in the area, which you should watch out for. Because the ride passes through a heavily wooded area, some sections of trail have exposed roots that can throw you from your bike if you are not expecting them.

Rescue index: The rescue index is poor. Though the trail is not terribly long, it is located in a remote, rural area that has limited rescue services. The nearest town of any size is Lake City, about 25 miles away.

Many of the rides are located in remote areas that we know as the "boonies."

Land status: State property. This tract was acquired under the Save Our Rivers Program. It is managed cooperatively by the Department of Agriculture and Consumer Services and the Division of Forestry.

Maps: Maps are available from the Suwannee River Water Management District and from Florida's Department of Natural Resources.

Finding the trail: From Interstate 10, take Exit 40 and proceed north on FL 129. After driving 1.8 miles, turn right onto County Road 136A. Continue driving an additional 1.5 miles; turn left onto Ramston Road. Proceed 1.2 miles, then turn right onto an unmarked paved road. Drive on this road for .4 miles, then bear right onto a dirt road. Drive .5 miles on this unmarked dirt road before turning left into the Mattair Spring Tract.

Sources of additional information:

Suwannee River Water Management District
Route 3, Box 64
Live Oak, FL 32060
(904) 362-1001

Department of Natural Resources
Division of Recreation and Parks
3900 Commonwealth Boulevard
Tallahassee, FL 32399
(904) 487-4784

The Bicycle Store
1871 Wells Road
Orange Park, FL 32073
(904) 278-1150

Hamilton County Chamber of Commerce
15 East Orange Street
Lake City, FL 32055-4083
(904) 752-3690

RIDE 39 *ALLEN MILL POND TRAIL*

On this ride you may spot a group of grunting wild hogs rooting for grubs or you may flush a covey of plump bobwhite quail from dense brush, but it is unlikely that you will see any two-legged beasts. Far from the neon and tinsel of Florida's tourist towns, this area is remote.

The Allen Mill Pond Trail, an easy single-track path, stretches three miles across a 461-acre tract of land located on the west bank of the Suwannee River.

RIDE 39 *ALLEN MILL POND TRAIL*

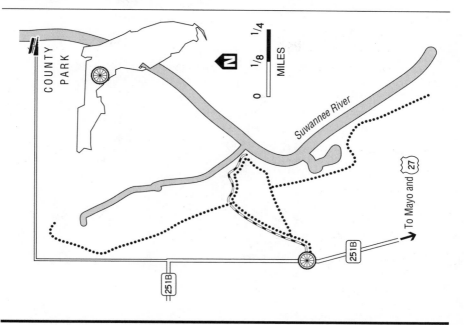

It rolls through stands of pines and through hardwood forests of black gum, sweet gum, and sweeping live oak trees. This is the only trail on the property, so it must be ridden as an out-and-back (total distance of about six miles).

The trail leads to Allen Mill Pond Spring, a second magnitude spring that produces about 45,000 gallons of water per minute. It runs for approximately half a mile before emptying into the Suwannee River. During the mid-1800s, a corn-grinding mill was built over the Allen Mill stream; some of its beams can still be seen. As secluded as this area is, some of the less law-abiding folks back in those earlier days were probably sorely tempted to put some of that corn to other uses, perhaps as the main ingredient in brewing backwoods distilled spirits.

General location: This trail is located approximately 80 miles northwest of Gainesville and about 100 miles west of Jacksonville.

Elevation change: There is no appreciable change in elevation.

Season: A cool-season ride is most enjoyable. Expect a ride during the sweltering summer season to be accompanied by heat, humidity, and ferocious bugs that will make for a miserable day in the saddle.

Services: Some services are available in the town of Lake City, located about 40 miles east of the trail. All services are available in Gainesville and Jacksonville.

Florida's easy, flat trails offer good introductory rides for children and beginners.

Hazards: Keep your eyes open for snakes and stay out of the brush to avoid any encounters with ticks.

Rescue index: The remote nature of this trail makes the rescue index poor. If you have a mechanical breakdown or medical emergency, you are pretty much on your own. Cars occasionally pass on the nearby country roads, but there is not a close town of any size that has the capability of offering much help. Bring a tool kit and well-appointed first-aid kit with you on the ride and save the kamikaze daredevil riding for a trail that has a better rescue index. (Like a trail within a stone's throw of a trauma center.)

Land status: Suwannee River Water Management District. Managed cooperatively by the Department of Agriculture and Division of Forestry.

Maps: Good maps are available from the Suwannee River Water Management District. Maps are also available from Florida's State Bicycle Program. The trail is also found on two USGS 7.5 minute quadrangles: Dowling Park and Day.

Finding the trail: From Interstate 10, take Exit 37 and proceed south on County Road 53. Drive for 17.7 miles before turning left onto CR 348A. Continue straight for 3.3 miles to the Allen Mill Pond Conservation Area, which will be on the left. Park at any road pulloff.

Sources of additional information:

> State Bicycle Program
> Department of Transportation
> 605 Suwannee Street, MS 82
> Tallahassee, FL 32399-0450
> (904) 487-1200

> Suwannee River Water Management District
> Route 3, Box 64
> Live Oak, FL 32060
> (904) 362-1001

> Bikes & More/Gator Cycle
> 2133 NW 6th Street
> Gainesville, FL 32609
> (904) 373-6574

RIDE 40 *OSCEOLA TRAIL*

This long, 23-mile stretch of trail in the Osceola National Forest offers a number of different ride possibilities. It can be ridden as a moderately strenuous one-way ride by setting up a shuttle at both ends of the trail. Or, for true hammerhead mountain bikers, it can be ridden as a god-awful, out-and-back ride of 46 (will I ever make it back?) miles. If you are not interested in such masochistic moves or are concerned that a rescue helicopter might not be able to fit between the pine trees to land and airlift you out, then you might want to consider an easier option. There is a popular, 6-mile section of trail from Olustee to Ocean Pond that can be ridden as a fairly easy out-and-back, giving you a trip total of about 12 miles.

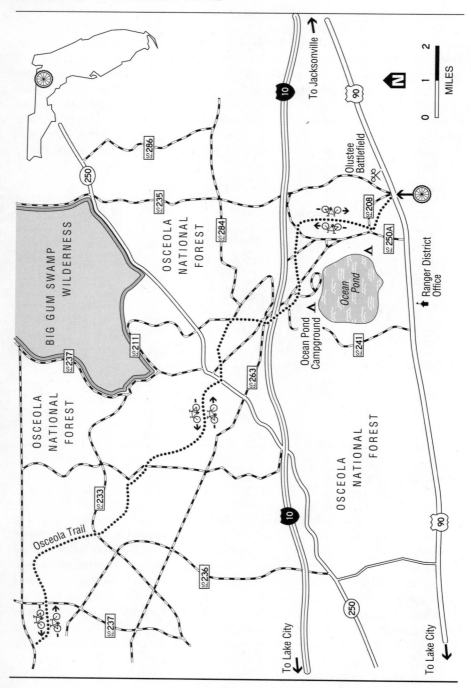

Regardless of the number of miles you decide to pedal, you will be treated to an excellent ride. The entire trail is single-track, with much of it cushioned with a thick layer of pine needles. There are more than 20 boardwalks and cat-walks located along this trail, providing bikers and hikers with dry crossings over tributary streams, swamps, and wetland areas. (These boardwalks were not designed for bike traffic, however; you must dismount and carry your bike as you walk on the catwalks and boardwalks.) Very little technical skill is required on this flat path, which gently winds through a striking forest of pines and saw palmettos.

The Osceola Trail begins at the historic site of the Olustee Battlefield, where Florida's largest Civil War battle was fought. This bloody skirmish claimed heavy losses before the Confederate troops finally turned back Union forces march-ing on Tallahassee. Brigadier General Joseph Finegan chose this site to defend Florida when the Confederate army was informed that Union troops were mov-ing west from Hilton Head, South Carolina. Finegan reasoned that Olustee was the best defensive position, with Ocean Pond on his left, a virtually impassable swamp on the right, and only a narrow passage in between. On February 20, 1864, more than 5,000 Union troops armed with 16 cannons marched into the area. They were met by a Confederate line of nearly as many men. The soldiers fought in the open forest, for neither side had constructed foxholes. The bloody battle raged into the night, with nearly 3,000 men dying before the Union troops finally began to retreat.

This state historic site includes a monument built in 1912 and dedicated in 1913, less than 50 years after the battle. There is also an interpretive center fea-turing exhibits chronicling this Confederate victory. The battle itself is reenacted each February by the people of Lake City and Columbia County. Don't be sur-prised to hear the boom of a cannon or catch a whiff of gunpowder if you cycle this trail on that day.

General location: The eastern terminus of the Osceola Trail is located about 45 miles west of Jacksonville and 15 miles east of Lake City.

Elevation change: There is no appreciable change in elevation.

Season: The trail can be ridden year-round, though the cooler months of Octo-ber through April are more pleasant. This trail tends to be rather wet; even during dry weather you will still find puddles of standing water. After periods of heavy rain, trying to mountain bike this trail becomes a joke. You may find yourself asking your buddies, "Did we come here to pedal or paddle?" When you have to wear a PFD to prevent drowning on a mountain bike ride, that is generally a good indicator that the trail is too wet to ride.

Services: Most services are available in Lake City; all services are available in Jacksonville. The Ocean Pond Campground, located within the Osceola National Forest, offers 50 campsites, drinking water, and hot showers. Primitive camping is permitted everywhere in the forest except at Olustee Beach. During big game hunting season, camping is restricted.

Trails cleave through sharp-edged saw palmettos and tall pines.

Hazards: Follow blazes to avoid getting lost on this trail. Be sure to carry a map and a compass, and know how to use them. Dehydration during the summer is a real concern on this long trail. If you are cycling the entire length of the trail, you should consider this a three- or four-water-bottle ride. There are ponds and other sources of water along the way, but you must filter or chemically treat this water before drinking. The trail is narrow and cleaves thick pockets of palmettos and other lush understory that could easily hide poisonous snakes. Stay alert for these fanged reptiles.

Rescue index: The rescue index varies from fair to poor, depending on what section of the trail you are on. Of course, the deeper into the woods you go, the farther a runner will have to travel to seek help and the farther help will have to travel to assist you. Be prepared for minor emergencies and mechanical breakdowns with a first-aid kit and a tool kit.

Land status: National forest.

Maps: Maps of the trail are available from the Forest Service. The trail is also found on three USGS 7.5 minute quadrangles: Deep Creek, Big Gum Swamp, and Olustee.

Finding the trail: From the intersection of Interstate 10 and FL 90, proceed west on FL 90 toward Lake City. Drive 5.5 miles and turn right at the Olustee Battlefield State Historic Site. Park in the parking area provided. The trail begins on the western edge of the field at a wooden fence.

Sources of additional information:

Osceola Ranger District
Highway 90 East
P. O. Box 70
Olustee, FL 32072
(904) 752-2577

The Bicycle Store
1871 Wells Road
Orange Park, FL 32073
(904) 278-1150

RIDE 41 *O'LENO STATE PARK TRAIL*

Located on the banks of the Santa Fe River is the O'Leno State Park, whose miles and miles of outstanding single-track trails beckon cyclists from all over. The park is more than 6,000 acres big, yet most of its visitors congregate around the swimming area and rarely venture outside of the first 200 acres of the park.

When you first arrive, you are likely to see chubby babies splashing in shallow water, moms pulling out potato salad and other picnic regalia, and dads singeing their eyebrows as they fire up the grills for cooking burgers. But there will be no mountain bikes this close in. It's over the river and through the woods, to the trails we go.

During the mid-1800s, a town was founded here and was named Keno, after a game of chance. Later, the name was changed to Leno. The town was located along the Santa Fe River, where a dam was built to provide power to a growing lumber mill. The town flourished and soon a livery stable, a general store, and a hotel sprung up. Leno claimed its fame, though, when the first telegraph line linking Florida to the outside world ended in this small town. In fact, the bicycle trail follows a section of the old Wire Road, along which the first telegraph line in the state was strung.

However, the boom years did not last. The supply of standing timber dwindled and then the first railroad bypassed the town. It was only a matter of time before the life and livelihood of the settlement withered. As in the manner of so many of the early Florida towns, Leno finally became a ghost town. The mill dams and Wire Road are the only remaining artifacts and evidence of this turn-of-

RIDE 41   *O'LENO STATE PARK TRAIL*

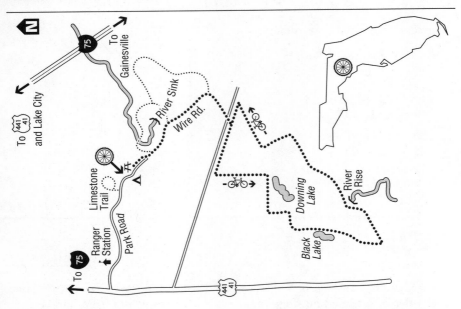

the-century lumber town. Its memory survives in the park's moniker, which is a variation on the local name for the once-thriving community, "Old Leno."

There are two loops of single-track trails that can be cycled to appreciate the variety and uniqueness of the natural areas in this park. The Limestone Trail is an easy, short, single-track trail about half a mile long. It is an ideal ride for out-of-shape cyclists, beginners, or for young children. The trail makes a curving path through a hardwood hammock, then stretches past a limestone outcropping before finishing up in a stand of pines. The second loop, about 13 miles long, offers cyclists an exceptionally beautiful ride. This moderate loop of single-track trail follows a gently rolling grade along the banks of the Santa Fe River. The river, a tributary of the Suwannee River, disappears and flows underground for more than three miles before it rises to the surface again. The trail begins at the river sink on Wire Road and follows the park fenceline past Black Lake, the river rise, and Downing Lake before returning to Wire Road.

General location: O'Leno State Park is located 6 miles north of High Springs, approximately 30 miles northwest of Gainesville and 50 miles southwest of Jacksonville.

Elevation change: There is no appreciable change in elevation.

Season: The trail can be cycled year-round. It passes through well-canopied for-

Single-track trail runs above the banks of the Santa Fe River.

est and is more pleasant to cycle during the summer than some of the trails in the area. Spring can often be a wet season, which can make mountain bike trails quite soggy. The first time I cycled this park was in early March; the river was very high and some of the trails were closed because of the heavy spring rains.

Services: All services are available in the town of High Springs. There is a campground with 64 sites in the state park. It is frequently full on summer weekends, so you might want to call ahead to make reservations. There is also primitive camping available, as well as a group camp with 18 cabins, a dining hall, and meeting building. While in the area, you may wish to picnic, swim, fish, canoe, or take a horseback ride; all activities are available in the park.

Hazards: Alligators live in this area and should be regarded as dangerous animals. They should not be approached, teased, or fed. Feeding alligators is extremely dangerous and is also a violation of state law.

Rescue index: The rescue index is excellent as the park has a ranger on duty most of the time.

Land status: State park.

Maps: Maps are available at the park's ranger station and through the Department of Natural Resources, Division of Recreation and Parks.

Finding the trail: From Interstate 75, take Exit 78 and proceed north on FL 441 for 11.5 miles. Turn right at the entrance to O'Leno State Park. There now, that was easy enough.

Sources of additional information:

O'Leno State Park Headquarters
Route 1, Box 1010
High Springs, FL 32643
(904) 454-1853

Department of Natural Resources
Division of Recreation and Parks
3900 Commonwealth Blvd.
Tallahassee, FL 32399
(904) 487-4784

Notes on the trail: Since there are no climbs to consider in planning this route, the bike trail can be ridden in either direction.

RIDE 42 *GAINESVILLE-HAWTHORNE RAIL TRAIL*

Unlike many rail trails that blaze a straight, unwavering, and unimaginative path through the countryside, the Gainesville-Hawthorne Rail Trail follows a meandering, circuitous line for much of its length. The first few miles are especially curvaceous as rail trails go, and had our group of cyclists making speculative jokes about the sobriety of the railroad worker who first blazed the path for the grading of the railway corridor. The winding nature of the path does seem to call up images of a happy-go-lucky town lush trying to walk a straight line after a little too much time bellied up to the bar.

The trail extends for 17 miles, from Boulware Springs State Park in Gainesville to Hawthorne, along a scenic railway corridor. Ridden as an out-and-back in its entirety, a total length of 34 miles can be cycled, making this a moderately strenuous mountain bike ride.

The trail follows a gently rolling grade on a surface of crushed limestone, which makes it suitable for a fat-tired bicycle, but not its thin-tired cousin. It

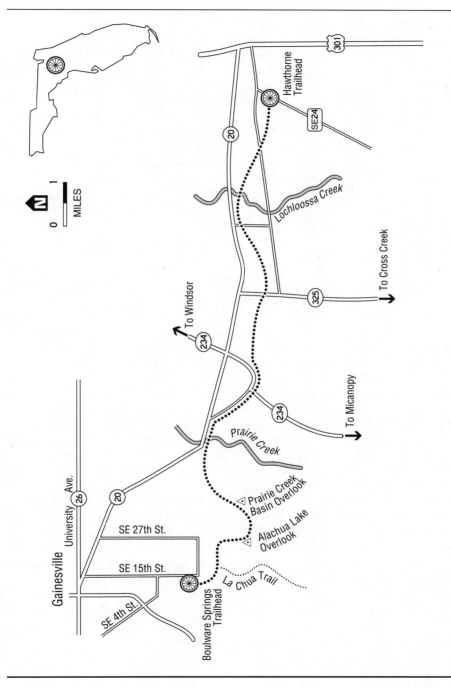

passes a number of sinkholes, which offer excellent opportunities for observing alligators, birds, and other wildlife. The sinkholes are formed when slightly acidic water dissolves limestone rock, thus forming a large depression in the earth. These depressions provide an excellent, fertile environment for extremely rare vegetation that tends to flourish in these low-lying areas. To prevent damage to these plants, you should not climb into the sinkholes. This rail trail pathway also passes a number of ponds that are home to an extensive population of waterfowl. Observant cyclists might also notice the osprey nests in some of the dead live oak trees on the south side of the corridor.

The trail passes the south border of Paynes Prairie State Preserve, a 19,000-acre state preserve of pine flatwoods, upland hammocks, and wetlands. This reserve, with its tremendous and stunning diversity of flora and fauna, is home to more than 800 species of plants and more than 350 species of animals, including bison. These large animals lumbering about the plains give the prairies a look of the Wild West, an almost surreal look. If there were also a few staged, authentically attired Indians brandishing tomahawks and loping past on horseback, you might swear you had stumbled onto the set of *Dances with Wolves*.

Historically, the Gainesville-Hawthorne railroad was first constructed in the mid-1800s as part of a plan to connect New York and New Orleans through a network of waterways and railroads. This particular stretch of railroad connected the Atlantic Ocean, at Fernandina, with the Gulf Coast, at Cedar Key. This passage proved to be less dangerous and easier than the only other passage, which was through the Florida Keys.

Alachua Sink, a large sinkhole located in the vicinity of the railroad, formed a vast lake after becoming naturally dammed around 1870. The lake was actually deep enough to accommodate steamboats that would unload goods destined for delivery by train. Cattle, produce, and other supplies were transported on the railroad, and excursion trains were used to bring people to Oliver Park, near the springs, in the late-1800s. Near the turn of the century, the natural plug that had dammed the sinkhole and caused the formation of the huge lake burst, causing the lake to drain. This left the large steamboats, once buoyant and slipping across the surface of the lake, stranded and beached like great Pacific whales.

As it turned out, the railroad was of monumental importance in the founding and early development of the city of Gainesville. In 1853, a community meeting was held at Boulware Springs (which is now the site of the beginning of the trail), where it was determined that the county seat would be moved from Newnansville to a new town on the railroad. That new town was named Gainesville. In the words of Paul Harvey, "Now you know . . . the rest of the story."

General location: This trail is located in the city of Gainesville.
Elevation change: There is no appreciable change in elevation.
Season: The trail can be ridden year-round. Cool-season rides are more enjoyable because of lower temperatures and lower humidity.

Eastern terminus of the Gainesville-Hawthorne State Trail.

Services: All services are available in the city of Gainesville. The city is home to the University of Florida, so bike shops are prolific, as they are in most college towns.

Hazards: Be extremely careful when crossing County Road 20, which carries high-speed traffic.

Rescue index: The rescue index is excellent as the trail passes well-traveled roads a number of times. In addition, the trail is in close proximity to a major city where medical help is available should an emergency situation arise.

Land status: State park property.

Maps: Good, detailed maps are available through the City of Gainesville and the Paynes Prairie State Preserve.

Finding the trail: From Interstate 75, take Exit 76 and proceed east on County Road 26, which becomes University Avenue. After driving 6.7 miles, bear right on CR 20 (Hawthorne Road) and proceed for .1 mile. Turn right onto SE 15th Street and proceed for 2 miles to Boulware Springs State Park. Turn right and park in the large parking lot for the Gainesville-Hawthorne State Trail.

Sources of additional information:

Gainesville-Hawthorne Rail Trail
c/o Paynes Prairie State Preserve
Route 2, Box 41
Micanopy, FL 32667
(904) 466-3397

City of Gainesville
Traffic Engineering Department
City Bicycle Coordinator
P. O. Box 490 - MS 28
Gainesville, FL 32602
(904) 334-2107

Bikes & More/Gator Cycle
2133 NW 6th Street
Gainesville, FL 32609
(904) 373-6574

Ocala National Forest

RIDE 43 *LAKE EATON LOOP*

This moderately easy 12-mile loop of Forest Service roads is located in the oldest national forest east of the Mississippi River—the Ocala National Forest. In addition to boasting the superlative of oldest, Ocala is also the southernmost forest in the United States. Located between the Oklawaha and Saint John rivers in central Florida, the forest contains more than 430,000 beautiful acres that sprawl eastward from the city of Ocala toward the Atlantic Ocean.

This is a land of rich, diverse topography with its natural springs, swamps, hundreds of ponds and lakes, coastal lowlands, rolling sandhills, towering palms, and subtropical palmettos. Stands of turkey scrub oak and scrubby sand pine that dominate the high ridges have caused this forest to be known as scrub country, or "Big Scrub." Its interesting features and its beauty draw so many visitors each year that it is regarded as one of the most heavily used national forests in the nation. Even filmmakers have succumbed to its lure: *The Yearling,* based on Marjorie Kinnan Rawlings' Pulitzer prize–winner, was filmed here.

This loop winds past some of these scenic areas on hard-packed Forest Service roads for the entire distance of 12 miles. It is a ride that requires very little technical skill except along occasional sandy stretches of road, which makes it an ideal ride for beginners or families. With its terminus at the Lake Eaton Sinkhole, the trail also gives cyclists an opportunity to visit this interesting natural feature after the mountain bike ride.

Lake Eaton Sinkhole is a depression measuring 80 feet deep and 450 feet in diameter at its rim. It was formed when the porous limestone beneath the earth's surface was dissolved by slightly acidic water, causing the land to collapse. This example of a dry sinkhole is unusual because most sinkholes in Florida extend below the water table, which means a lake or pond forms in their bottoms. Based on the amount of organic material deposited at the sink's base and the size of the trees, scientists believe that this sinkhole was formed less than one hundred years ago.

The sinkhole can be reached by hiking an easy interpretive trail about half a mile long. The trail meanders through an extraordinarily beautiful forest of palmetto, sand pine, and scrub oak. Songbirds serenade hikers as they stroll quietly along the trail carpeted with pine needles. The flora at the site of the sinkhole, though, is more like that of an oak hammock. Florida's state tree—the sabal

RIDE 43 *LAKE EATON LOOP*

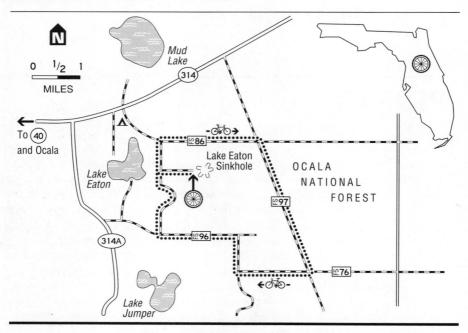

palm—is found here, along with live oak, dogwood, loblolly pine, and hickory. There are also large magnolia trees with dark green, glossy leaves and fragrant, huge white blossoms that look like doves resting on the branches. Resurrection ferns grow along the branches of some of the hardwood trees. During dry conditions, this small fern turns brown and appears to wither and die. However, after a good soaking rain it uncurls and turns green again: it "resurrects." After a few hot hours of deep summer mountain biking in Ocala, you might wish that you had the same capability.

General location: This ride is in the central section of Ocala National Forest, between the city of Ocala and the Atlantic Ocean.
Elevation change: There is no appreciable change in elevation.
Season: Late fall through early spring are the best times to cycle this loop. During the summer, expect heat and high humidity.
Services: All services are available in Ocala. The national forest is thick with campgrounds, from primitive sites to full-service facilities. Reservations can be made at some campgrounds and should be considered during the period of peak use between May and September. The ranger station can provide current information on camping. There are also a number of recreation sites that offer

Dirt roads can be technically challenging in sandy sections.

additional activities other than mountain biking, such as fishing, hiking, swimming, canoeing, water skiing, and scuba diving. Again, the ranger station can provide complete information on these areas as well.

Hazards: There is a possibility that you could meet up with a poisonous snake, though staying on the dirt roads of the loop will minimize chances. Alligators are found in certain areas of the forest, though it is unlikely that you will see one strolling down any of the Forest Service roads that comprise this loop. Your biggest threat will be mosquitoes and other biting insects; cool-season rides or insect repellant are your best defenses.

Rescue index: As you cycle, you will never be more than a few miles away from Service Road 314, from which help could be flagged down from a passing motorist.

Land status: National forest.

Maps: The loop is found on the Ocala National Forest map, available from the ranger station. It is also found on two USGS 7.5 minute quadrangles: Lake Kerr and Halfmoon Lake.

Finding the trail: From the intersection of Interstate 75 and FL 40 in Ocala, drive east on FL 40 for 13.1 miles. Turn left onto FL 314 and drive an additional 9 miles to Forest Service 86. (There will be a sign to Lake Eaton Loop and Sinkhole trails). Turn right onto FS 86 and drive 1.1 miles to FS 79. Turn right onto FS 79 and drive .3 miles to the Lake Eaton parking area, which will be on the left. Park here to begin the loop and to visit the sinkhole.

Sources of additional information:

> Lake George District Ranger
> Route 2, Box 701
> Silver Springs, FL 32688
> (904) 625-2520

> USDA Forest Service
> 40929 State Road 19
> Umatilla, FL 32784
> (904) 669-3153

> Allen's Bike Shop
> 5320 NE Jacksonville Road
> Ocala, FL 34479-1663
> (904) 622-1950

RIDE 44 *ALEXANDER SPRINGS LOOP*

This moderate mountain bike ride covers 17 miles of low-lying, swampy backcountry, offering a visual delight for cyclists. The loop, comprised of light-duty Forest Service roads, unimproved dirt roads, and a short, two-mile section of paved road, will guide you into one of the most beautifully rugged and remote sections of the Ocala National Forest. Pale sand flows beneath the wheels of mountain bikes as the roads wind past small lakes and ponds and meander through pine hammocks, hardwood, and cabbage palm.

The ride begins at Alexander Springs Recreation Area, which is located adjacent to the extraordinary Alexander Springs, the largest of the many springs in Ocala National Forest. Eighty million gallons of water surge into the springs daily, thus creating a sparkling, crystal-clear pool so lucent that you can see brightly colored fish swimming about the rocks, crevices, and swaying underwater flora. There are usually a few two-legged mammals mingling with the fish in these 72-degree waters; swimming, snorkeling, and scuba diving are permitted.

Prefer to stay dry? Hop in a canoe and paddle your way along the designated canoe run, which offers a good look at the springs and the lush surroundings of a subtropical forest. Canoes are available for rent from a concessionaire, though

RIDE 44 *ALEXANDER SPRINGS LOOP*

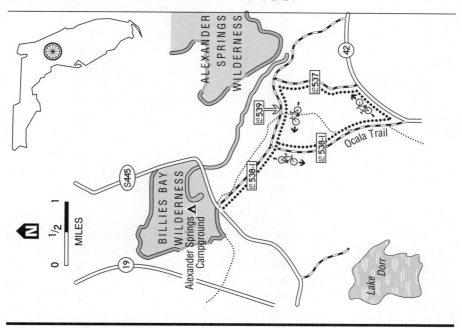

private boats can be used. Still on a dry note, you can also hike the 1.1-mile Timucuan Nature Trail. Named for the Indians that are believed to have occupied Ocala for at least 10,000 years prior to written records, the trail highlights local vegetation used by these early Indians. The trail skirts the bank of Alexander Creek and winds through a verdant, tropical forest of palm, hardwood swamp, and sand pine. If you have never visited Alexander Springs and its offerings, you might want to plan to spend a few hours cooling off and playing here after working out on this excellent mountain bike ride.

General location: This ride is in the southeastern section of Ocala National Forest, which is between the city of Ocala and the Atlantic Ocean.

Elevation change: There is no appreciable change in elevation.

Season: Late fall through early spring are the best times to cycle this loop. During the summer, expect heat and high humidity.

Services: All services are available in Ocala, and some services are available in the town of Umatilla. Camping is available in the Alexander Springs Recreation Area; sites in two of the loops can be reserved by calling 1-800-283-2267. The national forest also manages quite a few other campgrounds, from primitive sites to full-service facilities. Reservations can be made at some campgrounds and

Some of the live oak trees of the South are hundreds of years old.

should be considered during the period of peak use between May and September. The ranger station can provide current information on camping. There are also a number of recreation sites that offer additional activities such as fishing, hiking, swimming, canoeing, water skiing, and scuba diving. Again, the ranger station can provide complete information on these areas.

Hazards: You should exercise caution on the 2-mile, paved leg of this ride since it carries more automobile traffic than most mountain bikers are accustomed to. Follow the rules of the road and watch out for one another. There is a possibility that you could meet up with a poisonous snake when cycling the Forest Service roads, but chances are slim. Alligators are found in the swampy areas of this part of the forest, though it is unlikely that you will see one sauntering down any of the dirt roads that comprise this loop. Your biggest threat will be mosquitoes and other biting insects; cool-season rides or insect repellant are the best defenses.

Rescue index: The ride is sandwiched between FL 42 and County Road S445, from which help could be flagged down from a passing motorist.

Land status: National forest.

Maps: The loop is found on the Ocala National Forest map, available from the ranger station. It is also found on the USGS 7.5 minute quadrangle for Alexander Springs.

Finding the trail: From Umatilla, drive approximately 8 miles north on FL 19 to the intersection with CR S445. Turn right onto CR S445 and drive east for approximately 5 miles to Alexander Springs Recreation Area, which will be on the left. Park in this parking area. The ride begins on a dirt road, Forest Service Road 538-1, which is on the opposite side of CR S445 from the springs.

Sources of additional information:

Lake George District Ranger
Route 2, Box 701
Silver Springs, FL 32688
(904) 625-2520

USDA Forest Service
40929 State Road 19
Umatilla, FL 32784
(904) 669-3153

Allen's Bike Shop
5320 NE Jacksonville Road
Ocala, FL 34479-1663
(904) 622-1950

Central Florida

RIDE 45   *VAN FLEET STATE TRAIL*

Also known as the Green Swamp State Trail, this former railway corridor is one of Florida's most recently developed rail trails. It stretches for 29 miles from the town of Mabel to Polk City, affording cyclists with such highlights as views of Bay Lake and the black waters of the Withlacoochee River along the way. Though the grade is gentle and the hard-packed dirt surface makes fat tires sing, this ride is moderately difficult if ridden in its entirety. To make it even tougher, an out-and-back ride (for hard-core cyclists only), would bring the total distance to 58 serious miles.

When my friends and I cycled this trail, we were quite impressed with its beauty. At one point during the afternoon, I stopped to change the film in my camera and sent my buddies on ahead. Alone for a few minutes, I had an opportunity to really appreciate the solitude that the trail offered. Late afternoon sun painted the trunks of pines with warm, yellow light. A small stream gurgled contentedly somewhere off in the woods. Open fields of swaying grass wrapped around this ribbon of trail and extended for acres before dissolving into a stand of pines. A flash of wings snared my attention from the landscape and tilted my gaze toward the bird passing overhead. Then my eyes caught a glimmer of silver through the trees as my fellow mountain bikers swung around the elbow of the trail and railed noisily toward me, disrupting the tranquility.

The Van Fleet Green Swamp State Trail gives cyclists a true taste of the outdoors yet is only 35 miles away from the attractions in Orlando. Though Pluto and Goofy won't make an appearance, don't be surprised to see white-tailed deer, marsh rabbit, gray squirrel, bobcat, or any of the other animals that live in the woods that border this trail. If you are vacationing in the area, this ride would be a peaceful "recovery day" from the celluloid amusements nearby.

General location: The trail is located 35 miles west of Orlando.
Elevation change: There is no appreciable change in elevation.
Season: The best times to ride this trail are in the winter months. There is no protective canopy of tree limbs on this abandoned railroad right-of-way, so this can be a sweltering ride in summer. There are several trail shelters along the path that are good places for taking a break and getting out of the sun.
Services: Some convenience stores are available in Polk City and Clermont for

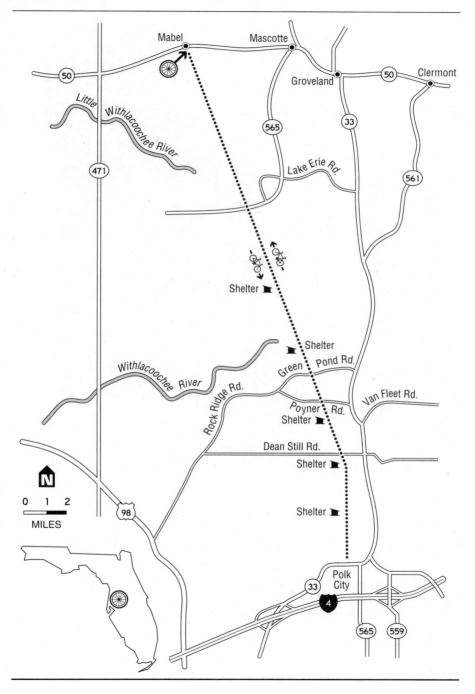

Railroad crossties once decorated Florida's popular rail trails.

juice and snacks. For bike shops, lodging, campgrounds, and restaurants, you will have to drive to the Orlando area. Lake Louisa State Park, located in the northwest corner of the Green Swamp, is close by but does not have camping facilities. It does have frontage on Lake Louisa—one of 13 lakes in the Clermont Chain of Lakes—which gives park visitors opportunities to canoe, fish, and swim.

Hazards: Watch for broken glass in some areas near road crossings. Anticipate the road crossings and be alert to traffic.

Rescue index: The trail crosses 4 roads along the way, so help could be flagged down if necessary.

Land status: State park.

Maps: Good maps are available from the Department of Natural Resources, Division of Recreation and Parks. The Seaboard Coast Line railroad is also seen on any detailed Florida road map.

Finding the trail: From Orlando, drive west on FL 50 for approximately 35 miles to the town of Mabel. Turn left at the brown sign for the Van Fleet State Trail. Continue driving for .2 miles to the well-marked northern terminus of the trail. Park here.

Sources of additional information:

> Department of Natural Resources
> Division of Recreation and Parks
> 3900 Commonwealth Boulevard
> Tallahassee, FL 32399
> (904) 487-4784
>
> Green Swamp State Trail
> c/o Lake Louisa State Park
> 12549 State Park Drive
> Clermont, FL 32711
> (904) 394-2280

Notes on the trail: To ride the entire 29 miles of this trail, you will have to ride it as an out-and-back or set up a shuttle by leaving a vehicle at Polk City to return you to a second vehicle at Mabel. There are also two other trailheads at Bay Lake and Green Pond, both of which also have designated parking areas. If you start at one of these trailheads, you can shorten the ride.

RIDE 46 *LOWER SUWANNEE NATIONAL WILDLIFE REFUGE—WEST RIVER RIDE*

This seven-mile, out-and-back mountain bike ride offers an easy morning or afternoon of cycling through the wilds of Florida's outdoors. The nontechnical ride offers the safety and comfort of cycling primary dirt refuge roads while at the same time offering a good vantage for wildlife glimpses and good views of their beautiful habitat.

The Lower Suwannee National Wildlife Refuge is one of the country's largest undeveloped river delta–estuarine systems. It is bisected by the Suwannee River, which dips and curves on its way to the Gulf of Mexico. Before reaching the Gulf, it is fattened and fed by fingers of creeks and small rivers such as Flag Creek, Shingle Creek, and Gopher River. The sinuous waters of the Suwannee and the great expanse of the Gulf have inspired many writers throughout American history to pen their thoughts, including John Muir on his 1,000-mile walk to the Gulf at the age of 29:

RIDE 46 *LOWER SUWANNEE NATIONAL WILDLIFE REFUGE WEST RIVER RIDE*

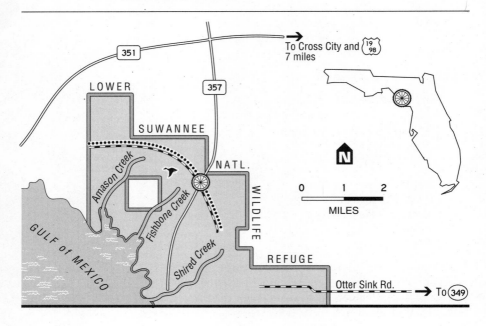

For nineteen years my vision was bounded by forests, but today, emerging from a multitude of tropical plants, I beheld the Gulf of Mexico stretching away unbounded, except by the sky. What dreams and speculative matter for thought arose as I stood on the strand, gazing out on the unburnished, treeless plain!

General location: The beginning of this ride is approximately 10 miles south of Cross City and 50 miles southwest of Gainesville.

Elevation change: There is no appreciable change in elevation.

Season: This ride can be cycled year-round, though the cooler seasons of late fall, winter, and early spring are more enjoyable.

Services: Most services are available in the town of Cross City. All services are available in the city of Gainesville. Camping is available at a county campground located off County Road 357 on Shired Island within the refuge.

Hazards: Though the ride stays on refuge roads and does not slip along over-grown single-track trails, you should still keep an eye open for poisonous snakes. Also, hunting is permitted in the wildlife refuge; wearing bright, unnatural colors is advised.

Swamps of the wildlife refuges are thick with ancient cypress trees and rounded cypress "knees" rising from the murky water.

Rescue index: Cyclists could easily be rescued on this ride since it is never far from CR 357, a paved county highway.
Land status: National wildlife refuge.
Maps: Excellent maps are available from the refuge headquarters.
Finding the trail: From Cross City, proceed west on CR 351 for 7 miles to the intersection of CR 351 and CR 357. Turn left on CR 357 and proceed south for approximately 3.5 miles to the permit/check station. Park at any road pulloff and begin cycling on the refuge road located west of CR 357, across from the permit station.

Sources of additional information:

Lower Suwannee National Wildlife Refuge
Route 1, Box 1193-C
Chiefland, FL 32626
(904) 493-0238

Bikes & More/Gator Cycle
2133 NW 6th Street
Gainesville, FL 32609
(904) 373-6574

RIDE 47 LOWER SUWANNEE NATIONAL WILDLIFE REFUGE—EAST RIVER RIDE

This 20-mile, moderately difficult loop of hard-packed primary refuge dirt roads, grassy secondary refuge roads or trails, and paved roads creates an excellent mountain bike ride through outstanding scenery. This route can also be ridden as an out-and-back ride if you wish to avoid the section of paved road. The ride carves a path through the Lower Suwannee National Wildlife Refuge, one of the newest refuges in the nation. It was established in 1977 for the purpose of protecting and managing the unique natural ecosystem along the Suwannee River.

The ride begins along a primary refuge road that is flanked by floodplain wetlands consisting of a forested area of oak, elm, ash, hickory, and other hardwoods. You will also see enormous palm trees, some 30 to 40 feet tall, standing at full attention in the forest. Majestic cypress trees canopy the brackish waters of the tributary creeks; turtles are often seen perched on logs in these creeks and basking in the filtered sunlight. These wetlands support white-tailed deer, wild turkey, black bear, otter, alligator, and even armadillo.

This area is obviously a haven for birds as the trees are decorated with a profusion of nests. Over 250 species of birds have been identified on the refuge, including swallow-tailed kite, osprey, and the endangered bald eagle. As I rounded a bend in the road on my bicycle one afternoon, I apparently surprised a trio of vultures. They, in turn, surprised me as they violently thundered away from their perch on the limb of a tree. These massive, dark birds were startling when viewed from such close quarters. I stopped to still my beating heart and watched with stark attention as these wildly ominous creatures slowly heaved their heavy bodies over the tree line with deliberate movements of their broad, leathery wings. When the evil-looking trio finally disappeared from my sight, I felt a momentary surge of relief.

The forest and wetlands also provide an ideal habitat for long-legged wading birds such as heron, egret, and ibis. Many of these birds use the area for nesting

RIDE 47 *LOWER SUWANNEE NATIONAL WILDLIFE REFUGE EAST RIVER RIDE*

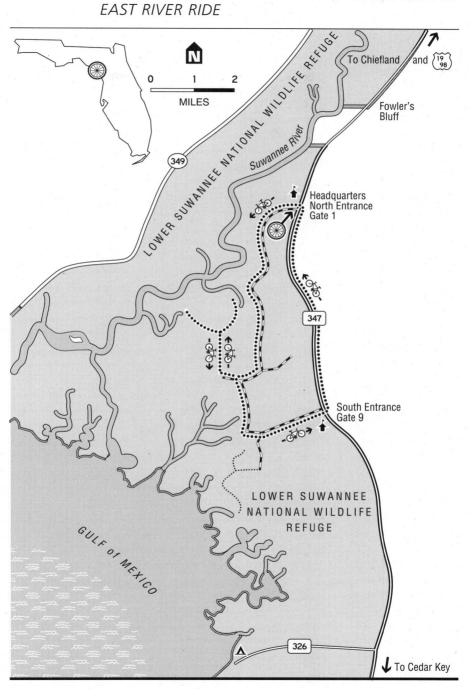

N

0   1   2
MILES

To Chiefland and (19)(98)

Fowler's Bluff

Suwannee River

LOWER SUWANNEE NATIONAL WILDLIFE REFUGE

Headquarters
North Entrance
Gate 1

347

South Entrance
Gate 9

LOWER SUWANNEE
NATIONAL WILDLIFE
REFUGE

GULF of MEXICO

349

326

To Cedar Key

during the peak period from May through July. The major nesting sites, called rookeries, are located on the nearby offshore islands of Cedar Key Refuge, which is also managed by the Lower Suwannee National Wildlife Refuge.

Radiating from the spine of the primary roads are grassy, secondary refuge roads that lead past numerous tidal creeks filled with freshwater fish, including channel catfish, bluegill, Suwannee bass, and largemouth bass. You will encounter these trails after several miles of cycling along the main dirt roads. These grass roads lead past tidal flats and natural salt marshes that attract thousands of screeching shorebirds. These waters are a valuable nursery site for populations of shellfish, shrimp, and fish. After reaching the creeks, you will then turn around and retrace your path to complete the ride.

General location: This section of the Lower Suwannee National Wildlife Refuge is located approximately 13 miles southwest of Chiefland and approximately 50 miles southwest of Gainesville.

Elevation change: There is no appreciable change in elevation.

Season: The ride can be ridden year-round, though the cooler times of the year are preferred. Because the ride sticks to refuge roads almost exclusively, this is a good ride after a period of heavy rains, when single-track trails in the area should be avoided.

Services: Many services are available in nearby Chiefland. All services are available in the town of Gainesville. Cedar Key lies a few miles south of the refuge; you might be tempted to splurge on a seafood dinner at one of the island's many casual restaurants after the ride. You will find a county campground on County Road 326 near Shell Mound, just south of the site of the ride.

Hazards: Hunting is permitted in the refuge during certain times of the year; you should check with the refuge headquarters for exact dates. If you cycle this route during hunting season, you might want to avoid the grassy secondary roads and stick to the primary refuge roads, especially during the prime hunting hours of early morning and late afternoon. These more remote areas away from the main traffic are the most likely sites for hunting. The hunters will appreciate your consideration, and you will avoid the risk of being mistaken for an odd-looking deer and returning to town strapped on the hood of a vehicle belonging to an overanxious, trigger-happy hunter. Despite the fact that many mountain bikers probably fit into the category of "wildlife," and the fact that many hunters would like to have the opportunity to bag noisy, insensitive cyclists disturbing their hunts, the U.S. Fish and Wildlife Service still does not offer hunting permits for Lycra-clad beasts. However, accidents do happen so you would be well advised to wear some bright, unnatural color to avoid being mistaken for a deer. Or, better yet, cycle elsewhere during the hunting season.

Rescue index: Since the ride follows refuge roads for most of its distance, a cyclist with a broken derailleur or a broken ankle could easily be rescued.

Land status: National wildlife refuge.

Lovely forest trails stem from the dirt refuge roads.

Maps: Good maps are available on brochures available from the refuge management office.

Finding the trail: From the intersection of US 19/98 and CR 345 in Chiefland, turn onto CR 345 and proceed south toward Cedar Key. Drive 5.5 miles and then turn right onto CR 347 to the Lower Suwannee National Wildlife Refuge. Proceed 3 miles before turning right at the North Entrance (Gate 1) of the refuge. Park at any road pulloff near the entrance.

Sources of additional information:

> Lower Suwannee National Wildlife Refuge
> Route 1, Box 1193-C
> Chiefland, FL 32626
> (904) 493-0238

> Bikes & More/Gator Cycle
> 2133 NW 6th Street
> Gainesville, FL 32609
> (904) 373-6574

RIDE 48   WHISPERING PINES PARK

This three-mile (round-trip) ride through Whispering Pines Park, a wildlife and bird sanctuary, offers an ideal ride for children, beginners, or less active cyclists. The ride stays on paved, sparsely traveled roads the entire time so riders will need no technical skill to easily negotiate this out-and-back route. Also, the roads are gently graded, giving cyclists an easy ride with no tough hills to climb.

Leading from the main parking area near the entrance to the park, the ride passes through a traffic circle and then stops at a children's playground and picnic shelter. The lack of traffic and the forested setting create a pleasant and scenic ride. The short cycling distance, excellent riding surface, and (particularly) the lure of a fun playground, are all sure to delight any children in your group.

General location: This ride is located in the Whispering Pines Park within the city of Inverness, which is approximately 30 miles southwest of Ocala and 50 miles north of Tampa.

Elevation change: There is no appreciable change in elevation.

Season: The park is open year-round.

Services: Most services are available in the town of Inverness, while all services are available in Ocala.

Hazards: Though the roads are lightly traveled, you should still exercise caution and watch for automobile traffic.

RIDE 48   *WHISPERING PINES PARK*

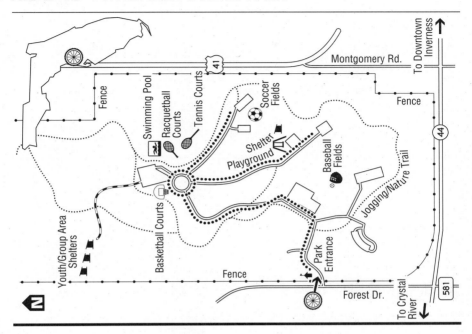

Rescue index: Since the park is located within a city and the ride stays on open roads the entire time, the rescue index is excellent.

Land status: City park.

Maps: Maps are printed in a park guide, which is available from the park's administration office and from the Inverness Chamber of Commerce.

Finding the trail: From Interstate 75, take Exit 66 onto FL 44. Drive west for 15 miles on FL 44. At the traffic light, turn right onto FL 41 and proceed north for 1.6 miles. Turn right on Forest Road and drive .2 mile to Whispering Pines Recreation Area. Park in the first parking area, which will be on the right.

Sources of additional information:

Whispering Pines Park
1700 Forest Drive
Inverness, FL 32650
(904) 726-3913

Citrus County Chamber of Commerce
208 West Main Street
Inverness, FL 32650
(904) 726-2801

Allen's Bike Shop
5320 NE Jacksonville Road
Ocala, FL 34479-1663
(904) 622-1950

Notes on the trail: There are three jogging/nature trails measuring 2.4, 3.0, and 3.2 miles each. No bicycles are permitted on these dirt trails because of heavy foot travel, especially on weekends.

The park has a number of other facilities, including 4 tennis courts, 5 racquetball courts, 1 basketball court, and 6 shuffleboard courts. There are also a swimming pool complex and youth camping area available to visitors of the park.

RIDE 49   *WITHLACOOCHEE STATE TRAIL*

The Withlacoochee River, whose Indian name means "crooked river," does indeed crookedly snake through verdant Florida country. This rail trail, a converted railroad corridor, closely parallels the river for the first 11 miles. As pleasing to the eye as it is to the quads, this gently graded, dirt and gravel trail is flanked by oak thickets, sandhill scrub, and stands of tall pines. This 11-mile section was the first segment of trail opened to mountain bikers and other recreationists after the railroad right-of-way was cleared and crossties were removed.

Currently, the trail extends from its southern terminus and trailhead near Trilby to the town of Nobleton and can be cycled as an out-and-back, resulting in a 22-mile (total), moderate ride requiring little technical skill. When completed, this rail trail pathway will extend all the way to Citrus Springs and will compete with Tampa's Pinellas Trail for the title of Florida's longest rail trail; both are projected to be 47 miles long.

As you pedal along, be sure to notice the three-sided, white concrete mileage posts located on the side of the trail. These columns were erected by the railroad company at one-mile intervals along the railway right-of-way. The numbers (825 in Trilby and 778 in Citrus Springs) represent the distance in miles to the midpoint of the James River Bridge in Richmond, Virginia, which was the site of the former headquarters of the Seaboard Railroad Company. Today, they continue to serve a useful purpose as a reference point for cyclists and other trail users. They also serve as a reminder of days gone by and preserve a small slice of America's railroad history.

General location: This rail trail is located in central Florida, approximately 45 miles west of Orlando and approximately 50 miles northeast of Tampa.
Elevation change: There is no appreciable change in elevation.
Season: The trail can be ridden year-round, though late fall through early spring

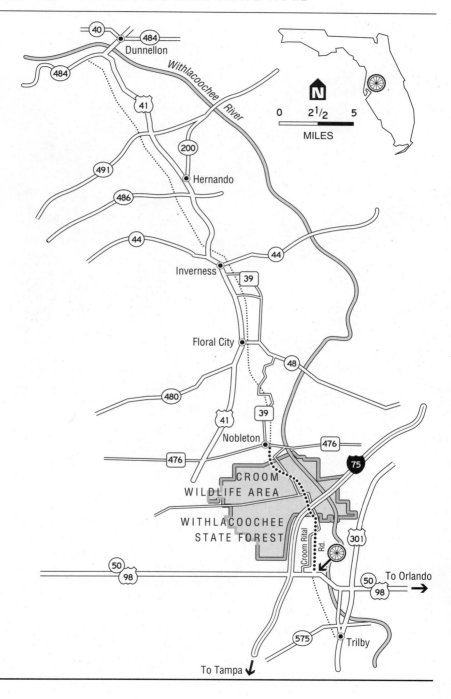

Dirt roads surrounded by the natural beauty of Florida's forests beckon mountain bikers.

are the best times. There is little or no tree canopy to offer relief from the scorching summer rays of the sun. The heat, as well as the bugs, make a summertime ride fairly miserable.

Services: Most services, including commercial camping facilities, are available in the town of Nobleton. Camping is also available in the Silver Lake Recreation Area of the Withlacoochee State Forest.

Hazards: Heat exhaustion, heat stroke, and serious sunburn are all possible on this open trail during the summer season. Liberally apply sunscreen, drink plenty of water, and try to avoid riding during the middle of the day when the sun's rays are most intense. Also, the trail crosses several busy county roads, so be sure to watch for traffic when crossing.

Rescue index: The rescue index is good as the trail passes several busy county roads, from which help could be flagged down. Several towns that could offer help are nearby.

Land status: State park.

Maps: Detailed maps are available from Florida's Division of Recreation and Parks and from Florida's State Bicycle Program.

Finding the trail: From Interstate 75, take Exit 61 and drive east on County Road 50 for one mile. Turn left and proceed north on Croom Rital Road. The parking lot for the trailhead will be on the right and is well marked.

Sources of additional information:

Withlacoochee State Trail
3100 Old Floral City Road
Inverness, FL 32650
(904) 726-0315

Department of Natural Resources
Division of Recreation and Parks
12549 State Park Drive
Clermont, FL 34711
(904) 394-2280

State Bicycle Program
Department of Transportation
605 Suwannee Street, MS 82
Tallahassee, FL 32399-0450
(904) 487-1200

Withlacoochee State Forest

RIDE 50 *HOG ISLAND RIDE*

Withlacoochee State Forest is comprised of four separate districts—Croom, Citrus, Richloam, and Jumper Creek—which form a complex of nearly 125,000 acres of land. The state forest is named for the river flowing through two of its districts; Withlacoochee meant "crooked river" to the Indians living here so many years ago. The description certainly seems befitting when one glances at a map to trace the river's 70 twisting, curving miles from the Green Swamp to its mouth south of Cedar Key at the Gulf of Mexico. It is here, within the Croom District, that the river reaches its widest expanse to form Silver Lake.

This out-and-back ride begins at the Hog Island Recreation Area and follows unimproved, dirt Forest Service roads for its entire distance. Though the road condition is good and requires little or no technical maneuvering, cycling the total out-and-back distance of 12.2 miles might prove to be fairly challenging for beginners. More experienced mountain bikers will easily cycle this path and might wish also to ride some of the other described rides in the area.

As the road rolls down toward Silver Lake, it parallels the slow-moving river and is flanked by a forest of sandhill scrub, slash pine, and longleaf pine. Growing along the edge of the river are towering live oak and cypress trees. The rounded knees of the cypress, combined with the gnarled arms of the live oaks, give this area a unique and beautiful appearance.

General location: The Withlacoochee State Forest is located in central Florida, about 40 miles north of Tampa and about 60 miles west of Orlando.

Elevation change: There is no appreciable change in elevation.

Season: This ride can be pedaled year-round. It stays on unimproved dirt roads, so it is virtually unaffected by rain (unlike single-track trails, which can become boggy and flooded after heavy rains).

Services: Most services are available in the nearby towns of Nobleton and Brooksville, while all services can be found in Tampa or Orlando. There are several full-service campgrounds managed by the Withlacoochee State Forest. Check with the Forestry Center Headquarters for a complete listing and further information.

Hazards: During the summer months, Florida's trio of heat, humidity, and biting insects can be expected. Be prepared with insect repellant, lots of water, and cool clothing.

198

RIDE 50 *HOG ISLAND RIDE*

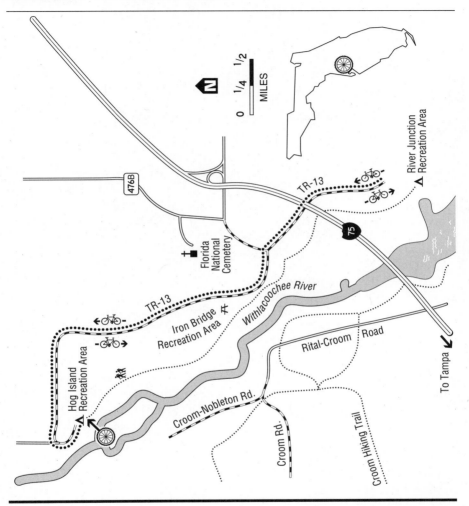

Rescue index: Help could easily be obtained or a runner could quickly find help since the ride does not extend deep into backcountry, but stays on Forest Service roads the entire distance.

Land status: State forest.

Maps: The Withlacoochee State Forest Mapguide will help you find your way, as will the individual district maps, which are also available from the Forestry Center Headquarters.

Finding the trail: From the intersection of US 41 and FL 476 at the Withla-

Saw palmettos are prolific in central Florida's Withlacoochee State Forest.

coochee Forestry Center Headquarters, drive east on FL 476 for 6.8 miles. Turn right onto FL 635 and continue driving for an additional 1.3 miles. Turn right onto Forest Service Road 13 and drive about 1 mile to the Hog Island Recreation Area. Park here.

Sources of additional information:

Withlacoochee Forestry Center Headquarters
15019 Broad Street
Brooksville, FL 34601
(904) 796-5650

Notes on the trail: From the Hog Island Recreation Area, you will reach the Iron Bridge Recreation Area after cycling about 4 miles. At the 5-mile mark, you will cross under Interstate 75. For a shorter ride, you may wish to turn around at either of these mile markers.

RIDE 51 *CROOM ROAD LOOP*

This easy loop of Forest Service roads carves a path that gives cyclists a glimpse of the majority of the Croom District of the Withlacoochee State Forest. The route rambles for about 11 miles along hard-packed dirt roads that require little or no off-road bike handling skills. This district is laced with other unimproved Forest Service roads that can be explored and cycled, thus lengthening the loop.

Mountain bikers will be treated to the scenic beauty of central Florida's sand-hill scrub, longleaf pine hills, hardwood hammocks, live oak thickets, prairies, and ravines. Occasional rolling hills spice up the typically flat terrain to give cyclists cause actually to change gears.

General location: The Withlacoochee State Forest is located in central Florida, about 40 miles north of Tampa and about 60 miles west of Orlando.

Elevation change: There is only a slight change in elevation.

Season: This loop can be ridden year-round. It is virtually unaffected by rain since it stays on unimproved dirt roads rather than trails, which can become soggy after heavy rains.

Services: Most services are available in the nearby town of Brooksville, while all services can be found in Tampa or Orlando. There are several full-service campgrounds managed by the Withlacoochee State Forest. Check with the Forestry Center Headquarters for a complete listing and further information.

Hazards: During summer months, you should come armed with heavy-duty insect repellant and a good attitude. Heat and humidity should be expected; you might wish to plan your ride during the cooler hours of early morning or late afternoon. Hunting is permitted in the forest; check with the headquarters for exact dates.

Rescue index: Help could easily and quickly be obtained since the ride follows Forest Service roads exclusively.

Land status: State forest.

Maps: The Withlacoochee State Forest Mapguide will help you find your way, as will the individual district maps that are also available from the Forestry Center Headquarters.

Finding the trail: From the intersection of US 41 and FL 476 just south of the Withlacoochee Forestry Center Headquarters, drive south on US 41 for 5.1 miles. Turn left onto Croom Road (FL 480), and drive an additional 5.3 miles to the Tucker Hill Fire Tower. Park at any of the road pulloffs in this area.

Sources of additional information:

Withlacoochee Forestry Center Headquarters
15019 Broad Street

RIDE 51 *CROOM ROAD LOOP*

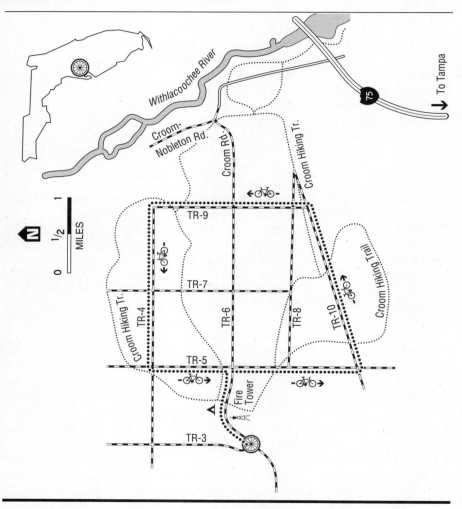

Brooksville, FL 34601
(904) 796-5650

Notes on the trail: Beginning at the fire tower, cycle east on Forest Service Road TR-6 (Croom Road) to the first intersection of dirt roads. Turn right onto FS TR-6 where the Croom Hiking Trail soon crosses. Cycle past FS TR-8 before turning left onto FS TR-10. You will cycle several miles before turning left again,

Dirt roads twist and curve through the Withlacoochee State Forest.

this time onto FS TR-9. You will cycle past Croom Road, across Croom Hiking Trail, and onto FS TR-4. A left turn onto this dirt road, and then another left turn onto FS TR-5 will loop back to FS TR-6 (Croom Road). A final right turn will take you on a short ride back to the fire tower.

RIDE 52 *TILLIS HILL LOOP*

These 15 moderately difficult miles of backcountry Forest Service roads are certain to entice mountain bikers to the Citrus Tract part of the Withlacoochee State Forest. Winding through beautiful woods and past scenic, interesting highlights, these loop roads pass through a diverse forest of longleaf pine, sand pine, thickets of oak, sandhill scrub, and hardwood hammocks. Natural features along the way—such as rock outcroppings, limestone sinkholes, swamps, and ponds—lend additional interest to the ride. Though the majority of the ride follows hard-

RIDE 52 *TILLIS HILL LOOP*

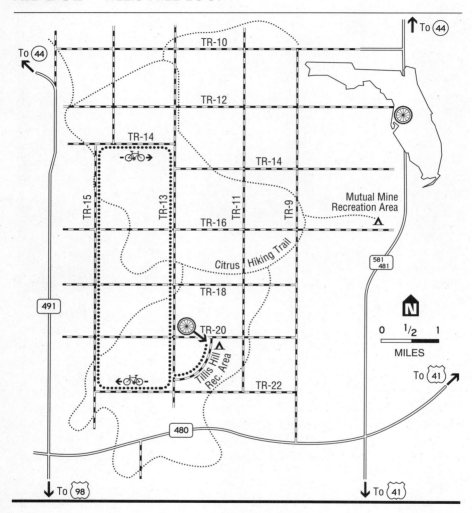

packed Forest Service roads that are in good condition, there are a few deep, sandy sections of road that require good bike handling skills and some technical know-how to negotiate them successfully.

The ride begins at Tillis Hill Recreation Area, at the forest's highest point, at 215 feet. Within the Citrus Tract are 44 miles of hiking trails and a separate network of blue-blazed equestrian trails, but these trails are prohibited to mountain bikers. As tempting as bandit riding might be, stay off these trails. After cycling a few miles, you will see the Citrus Hiking Trail on the right; here, you may wish to dismount and walk your bike for a short distance to the Lizzie Hart Sink. This sinkhole was formed when slightly acidic water dissolved the porous limestone rock, creating a large depression in the earth. This rich soil supports a host of flourishing flora and attracts a variety of herbivorous wildlife, the most notable being the white-tailed deer, who come here to feed. With more than 2,000 deer roaming this tract, it is easy to understand why this is one of Florida's most popular bow-hunting sites.

Farther along the loop, you can again dismount and walk your bike along the hiking trail to observe the raucous, chirruping profusion of birds at Mansfield Pond. In addition to the feathered friends, there are also raccoon, opossum, coyote, wild turkey, rabbit, and many other animals in the area. The Citrus Tract is one of the few places that can boast the presence of large numbers of fox squirrel. With so many of these large, colorful critters scampering about, chances are good that you will spot one as you cycle this mountain bike route.

General location: This loop is located near the city of Inverness, within the Citrus Tract of the Withlacoochee State Forest.

Elevation change: There is an elevation gain of about 200 feet at the end of the ride as you climb back up to Tillis Hill Recreation Area.

Season: This loop is a 4-season ride, though the heat and humidity of summer can make mountain biking unpleasant.

Services: Most services are available in the town of Inverness. There is safe drinking water available at Holder Mine and Mutual Mine recreation areas. You can fill your water bottles at one of these sites or bring it from home, but do not drink the water from the creeks, ponds, or streams without filtering, boiling, or otherwise treating it. There are improved camping facilities available within the Citrus Tract of the state forest at Holder Mine, Mutual Mine, and Tillis Hill recreation areas.

Hazards: Watch for potholes that riddle some sections of these Forest Service roads. Also, be aware that the air can be thick with mosquitoes and other biting bugs during the summer months, so bring along some good bug dope. When visiting the sinkhole, be on the alert for poisonous snakes slinking around the area.

Rescue index: Though the ride follows ungated Forest Service roads, vehicle traffic is extremely light. In the event of an emergency, you should be prepared to handle it yourself or send the fastest, strongest rider in your group for help.

Land status: State forest.

Maps: The Withlacoochee State Forest Mapguide is an adequate map, though some of the gated or less-used Forest Service roads are not marked on it. The forestry center offers better-detailed maps of the individual tracts.

Finding the trail: From the intersection of Service Road 44 and FL 481 near Inverness, proceed south on FL 481 for approximately 7 miles to the intersection

They just don't make grandfathers like they used to.

with FL 480. Turn right onto FL 480 and drive west for 3.5 miles to the intersection with Forest Service Road 13. Turn right onto FS 13 and drive 1.8 miles to the turnoff to Tillis Hill Recreation Area. Park here to begin.

Sources of additional information:

Withlacoochee Forestry Center Headquarters
15019 Broad Street
Brooksville, FL 34601
(904) 796-5650

Notes on the trail: Beginning at the Tillis Hill Recreation Area, cycle downhill on the dirt access road that leads to the recreation area. At the bottom of the hill, turn left onto FS TR-13, a wide dirt road that is one of the main thoroughfares through the forest. You will almost immediately turn right onto FS TR-22. After cycling about a mile, you will reach FS TR-15. (A left turn here will lead you to the Citrus Hiking Trail, which can be hiked but not biked, for a look at Lizzie Hart Sink.) Turn right onto FS TR-15 and cycle north toward Mansfield Pond.

A right turn onto FS TR-14, followed by a right turn onto FS TR-13 will return you to the access road to Tillis Hill Recreation Area.

RIDE 53   *HOLDER MINE LOOP*

Located in the northern portion of Withlacoochee State Forest's Citrus Tract lies this moderately difficult, 16.5-mile loop. Though the entire route follows hard-packed Forest Service roads, don't be fooled into thinking that your technical skills will be unchallenged on this ride. There are several loose, sandy sections of road that, if not negotiated with some degree of technical dexterity, will separate you from your trusty mountain bike and send you on an aerial tour of the forest.

The ride begins at Holder Mine Recreation Area and turns northward through a dense forest of turkey oaks. The name of the tree is derived from the delicate, splayed ends of its branches, which look like turkey feet. There are also quite a few different species of pines in this section, with some individual specimens that are more than 200 years old. The route continues on, hugging the perimeter of the northern part of the tract, and then bisects the width of the tract to return to the recreation area.

General location: This loop is located near the city of Inverness, within the Citrus Tract of the Withlacoochee State Forest.
Elevation change: There is no appreciable change in elevation.
Season: This loop is a 4-season ride, though the heat and humidity of summer can make mountain biking unpleasant.
Services: Most services are available in the town of Inverness. There are improved camping facilities available within the Citrus Tract of the state forest at Holder Mine, Mutual Mine, and Tillis Hill recreation areas. You can fill your water bottles with safe drinking water, available at the Holder Mine and Mutual Mine recreation areas.
Hazards: Watch for potholes that riddle some sections of these Forest Service roads. Also, be aware that the air can be thick with mosquitoes and other biting bugs during the summer months, so bring along some good bug dope.
Rescue index: Though the ride follows ungated Forest Service roads, vehicle traffic from which help could be flagged down is extremely light. In the event of an emergency, you should be prepared to handle it yourself or send the fastest, strongest rider in your group for help.
Land status: State forest.
Maps: The Withlacoochee State Forest Mapguide is an adequate map, though some of the gated or less-used Forest Service roads are not marked on it. The forestry center offers better-detailed maps of the individual tracts.
Finding the trail: From the intersection of Service Road 44 and FL 481 near In-

RIDE 53 *HOLDER MINE LOOP*

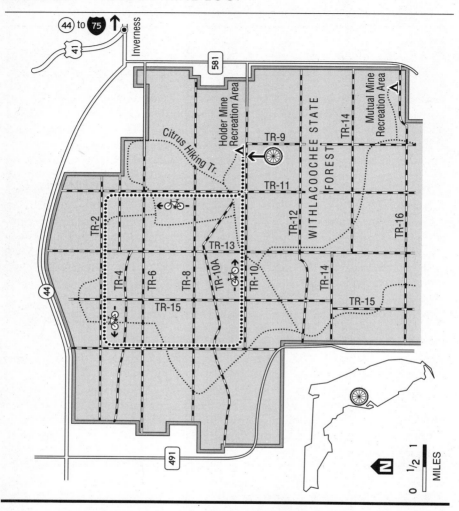

verness, proceed south on FL 481 for approximately 2.5 miles to the intersection with Forest Service Road 10. Turn right on FS 10 and drive approximately 1.5 miles to the Holder Mine Recreation Area. Park here.

Sources of additional information:

Withlacoochee Forestry Center Headquarters
15019 Broad Street

On winter days, rides on these sunny, open roads are great.

Brooksville, FL 34601
(904) 796-5650

Notes on the trail: From the Holder Mine Recreation Area, you will begin the ride by cycling west on FS TR-10. At the intersection with FS TR-11, turn right onto FS TR-11 to continue the ride. The Citrus Hiking Trail crosses the road twice before you turn left onto FS TR-2. Once on this dirt road, watch for sandy sections of road that can make for a rough-and-tumble ride. The hiking trail closely parallels this road for about 1.5 miles before it disappears into the woods, only to reappear and cross the road again. (Unfortunately, this lovely single-track trail is for foot travel only and is closed to mountain bikes. The turkeys.) You will turn left onto FS TR-17 about half a mile past the point where the hiking trail crossed FS TR-2. You will then cycle FS TR-17 past 4 dirt roads before turning left again, this time onto FS TR-10. This dirt road will then lead you back to the Holder Mine Recreation Area and your parked vehicle.

RIDE 54 *RICHLOAM TRACT LOOP*

If you are a seasoned mountain biker looking for a fairly strenuous workout through scenic surroundings, then this 32-mile loop is sure to appeal to you. Located in the Richloam Tract of the Withlacoochee State Forest, the ride passes through miles and miles of territory along unimproved Forest Service roads for the entire distance. Even though little technical skill is needed, this ride still holds great appeal to serious cyclists. The long, uninterrupted expanse of road gives mountain bikers a chance to slide the ol' chain onto the big ring and pump away at high speeds through a blur of forest. Sections of these sparsely traveled dirt roads are incorporated as legs of the Florida Trail, which makes a 31-mile loop within this tract, so you may see hikers or backpackers as you ride.

As you barrel past the pine plantations and elegant sabal palms, keep one eye open for the "Cracker" ponies that graze in this area along with the cattle that also share this land. Locals call the ponies "Crackers" for the cracking noise that the whips of Florida cowboys made years ago while they tended their herds. These ponies are the offspring of those cowboys' horses and are direct descendants of the Spanish horses first brought to Florida in the 1500s. Four mares and a stallion were donated by a horse breeder to the Florida Department of Agriculture in the mid-1980s in an effort to preserve this breed of animal.

The cattle of Richloam also lay claim to a historical Spanish background. Descendants of the Andalusian cattle brought by the Spaniards when they first arrived in Florida, they actually remind many folks of the Texas longhorns. There are more than 100 head of cattle grazing the land of Richloam, so chances are good that you will spot an animal.

I myself never spotted any of these historic animals on my rides in Richloam and might have been disappointed had I not been treated to a surprise appearance by America's national bird—the majestic bald eagle. I had stopped under the shade of the full summer foliage of a live oak tree to munch on an apple that had been tucked away in my fanny pack. After a short rest and a few sips of water, I slipped my water bottle back into its cage, tiredly mounted my titanium mountain bike and slowly rounded a bend in the road. To my delight, a large bald eagle saw or heard my approach and defensively soared from his perch in a hardwood tree. I immediately stopped and, with my bike listing against my leg, watched as thermals slowly lifted him over the treetops and out of my sight.

Aside from the bald eagle, there are also other threatened species in this forest, including the red-cockaded woodpecker and Eastern indigo snake, which are also protected by the forest management. More common inhabitants of the forest include white-tailed deer, wild turkey, feral hog, quail, skunk, bobcat, armadillo, and racoon. The woodlands of pines, oaks, palmettos, cypress, and

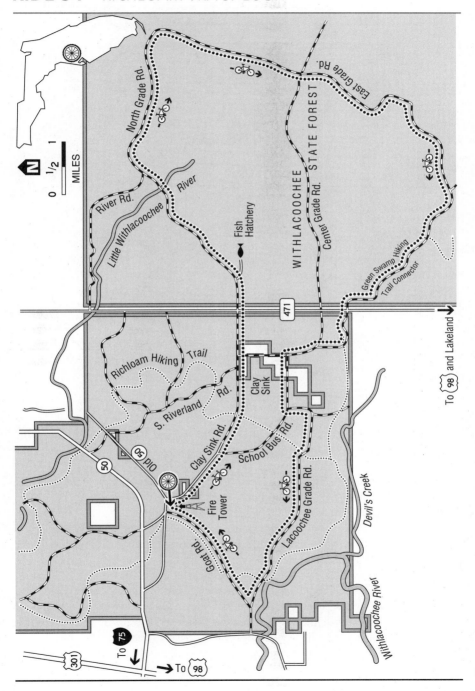

Racers use the loops of long dirt roads for training.

cabbage palms, which flourish in the rich, loamy soil (from which comes the name of this tract), are a haven for these animals.

General location: The Withlacoochee State Forest is located in central Florida, about 40 miles north of Tampa and about 60 miles west of Orlando.
Elevation change: There is no appreciable change in elevation.
Season: This loop can be ridden year-round. It is virtually unaffected by rain since it stays on dirt roads, rather than on single-track trails, which can become soggy and flooded after heavy rains.
Services: Most services are available in the nearby towns of Bushnell (19 miles to the west) and Dade City (10 miles to the south), while all services can be found in Tampa or Orlando. Potable water is available at the fire tower for filling your water bottles. Do not drink any water from the creeks, streams, or rivers without filtering, boiling, or otherwise treating it. There are several full-service campgrounds managed by the Withlacoochee State Forest. Check with the Forestry Center Headquarters for a complete listing and further information.

Hazards: During the summer months, Florida's trio of heat, humidity, and biting insects can be expected. Be prepared with insect repellant, lots of water, and cool clothing.

Rescue index: The rescue index is fair. Though cyclists will not be deep in the backcountry on single-track trails, the dirt roads see very little traffic. You should be prepared for mechanical emergencies by bringing a tool kit and spare tube, and be prepared for minor medical emergencies by bringing a first-aid kit.

Land status: State forest.

Maps: The Withlacoochee State Forest Mapguide will help you find your way, as will the individual district maps that are also available from the Forestry Center Headquarters.

Finding the trail: From Interstate 75, take Exit 61 and drive east on Service Road 50 for 7.2 miles. Turn right onto Clay Sink Road. Drive approximately half a mile to the intersection of Clay Sink Road and Goat Road; park at any of the road pulloffs near the Richloam Fire Tower.

Sources of additional information:

Withlacoochee Forestry Center Headquarters
15019 Broad Street
Brooksville, FL 34601
(904) 796-5650

Notes on the trail: From the fire tower, you will begin the ride by cycling east on Clay Sink Road, a paved road that changes to a dirt surface after about 1.5 miles. You will stay on this dirt road for quite a distance as it loops through the forest. When you see the Green Swamp Hiking Trail Connector cross the road for the second time, you will soon make a left turn onto School Bus Road, another dirt road. You won't be on this road for very long before it is time to make another left turn, this time onto an unmarked dirt road. (If you miss the turn you will see the Richloam Hiking Trail cross the road and know that you have gone too far.) After only about half a mile of cycling, turn right onto Lacoochee Grade Road. This road will bring you back to Goat Road, thus returning you to the Richloam Fire Tower and your parked vehicle.

RIDE 55 *CLAY SINK LOOP*

This ride is a much shorter version of the Richloam Tract Loop, described in the previous chapter. Its length of only 12.5 miles makes this route more appealing to cyclists looking for an easier mountain bike ride. Little or no technical skill is required to negotiate this path along unimproved Forest Service roads, which should make beginners happy. The route passes Clay Sink, a large depression

RIDE 55 *CLAY SINK LOOP*

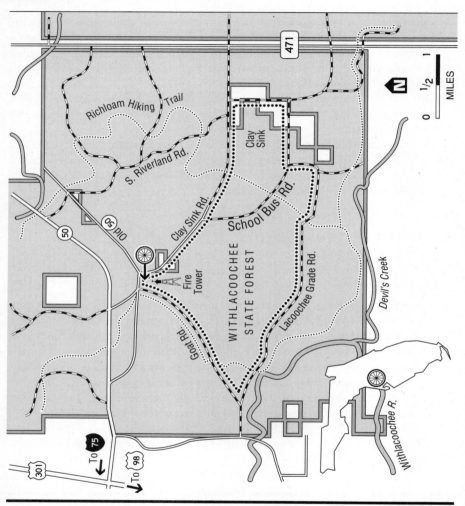

in the earth formed by acidic water dissolving underlying rock. Sinkholes are geologic features unique to Florida.

The name of this tract—Richloam—comes from the rich, fertile soil, which supports a healthy, productive forest. Timbering is of primary importance in this tract of the Withlacoochee State Forest and cyclists may catch sight of forestry activities in progress, such as tree planting and harvesting. There are a number of cypress ponds along one section of this ride; other sections of road pass pine flatwoods and hardwood hammocks. Saw palmettos carpet the forest floor and

Rides on flat dirt roads appeal to seasoned cyclists, as well as beginners.

provide good understory and good cover for many of the animals that live in this tract.

General location: The Withlacoochee State Forest is located in central Florida, about 40 miles north of Tampa and about 60 miles west of Orlando.

Elevation change: There is no appreciable change in elevation.

Season: This loop can be ridden year-round. It is virtually unaffected by rain since it stays on dirt roads, rather than on trails, which can become soggy and flooded after heavy rains.

Services: Most services are available in the nearby towns of Bushnell (19 miles to the west) and Dade City (10 miles to the south), while all services can be found in Tampa or Orlando. Potable water is available at the fire tower for filling your water bottles. Do not drink any water from the creeks, streams, or rivers without filtering, boiling, or otherwise treating it. There are several full-service campgrounds managed by the Withlacoochee State Forest. Check with the Forestry Center Headquarters for a complete listing and further information.

Hazards: During the summer months, Florida's trio of heat, humidity, and biting insects can be expected. Be prepared with insect repellant, lots of water, and cool clothing.

Rescue index: The rescue index is fair. Though cyclists will not be deep in the backcountry on single-track trails, these dirt roads see very little traffic. You should be prepared for mechanical emergencies by bringing a tool kit and spare tube, and be prepared for minor medical emergencies by bringing a first-aid kit.

Land status: State forest.

Maps: The Withlacoochee State Forest Mapguide will help you find your way, as will the individual district maps, which are also available from the Forestry Center Headquarters.

Finding the trail: From Interstate 75, take Exit 61 and drive east on Service Road 50 for 7.2 miles. Turn right onto Clay Sink Road. Drive approximately .5 miles to the intersection of Clay Sink Road and Goat Road; park at any of the road pulloffs near the Richloam Fire Tower.

Sources of additional information:

Withlacoochee Forestry Center Headquarters
15019 Broad Street
Brooksville, FL 34601
(904) 796-5650

Notes on the trail: From the fire tower, you will begin the ride by turning left and cycling onto Goat Road, a hard-packed dirt road. The Richloam Hiking Trail parallels the road on the right for several miles before crossing it. About a mile after the trail crosses Goat Road, you will make a hard left turn onto Lacoochee Grade Road. The hiking trail crosses the road twice; about 2 miles after the second crossing, Meg's Hole Road enters the Lacoochee Grade Road on the right. Continue on Lacoochee Grade Road by bearing left. You will arrive at a T-intersection, where you will need to turn right. At the next T-intersection, a left turn will lead you past the Clay Sink area. Your last turn will be a left turn onto Clay Sink Road. On this final leg of the ride the dirt surface changes to a paved surface, marking your approach to the fire tower.

Southern Florida

RIDE 56   PINELLAS TRAIL

The Pinellas Trail—an extremely popular Florida rail trail—is proposed to be 47 miles long when completed, with 36 of those miles on abandoned rail line. It will extend from St. Petersburg through the communities of Seminole, Clearwater, and Dunedin to Tarpon Springs. At the time of this writing, 22 miles had been developed for recreational use. Though the surface is asphalt and there are no tough hills to climb, the total round-trip distance of 44 miles makes this a moderately difficult bike ride. Since it is ridden as out-and-back, you can decrease the distance and the difficulty of the ride by riding as far as you wish and then turning around to retrace your path. Since it does not require a long drive into the country, the trail offers a great outlet for residents looking for a late afternoon's respite from the hassles of a hard day's work in the office.

Although the Pinellas Trail is a predominantly urban bike path, it is actually a tour of Pinellas County backyards. Some of the most popular miles lie between Taylor Park and Seminole City Park and offer peaceful residential interludes. The homes and gardens of Belleair, Largo, and Seminole line the route. Often walled for privacy, these lawns and flower beds nevertheless display a dazzling variety of showy tropical plants cultivated by the residents. Every few hundred yards, a large blossom peeks over the palings of a high fence, lending its exotic color to the lush green of the trail's margins. In fact, some portions of the route resemble an interpretive trail through a botanical garden. Though horses are not allowed on the Pinellas Trail, they can still be seen off the trail in some sections. Ponies grazing in small corrals beneath a canopy of tree limbs impart a pastoral look to these suburbs of central Florida.

The trail connects or closely approaches a number of city and county parks. At Seminole City Park, be sure to visit the aviary housing peacocks, as well as other attractions. Just off Bay Pines Boulevard is the War Veterans' County Park, which displays an impressive sundial and a battle tank, and offers an outstanding view of the waters of Boca Ciega Bay.

General location: The trail is located near Clearwater, along the Gulf coast.
Elevation change: There is no appreciable change in elevation.
Season: Because of the warm year-round weather along the Gulf coast of Florida, this is considered a 4-season trail. Summer rides can be quite hot and sticky due to heat and humidity, especially during the middle of the day.

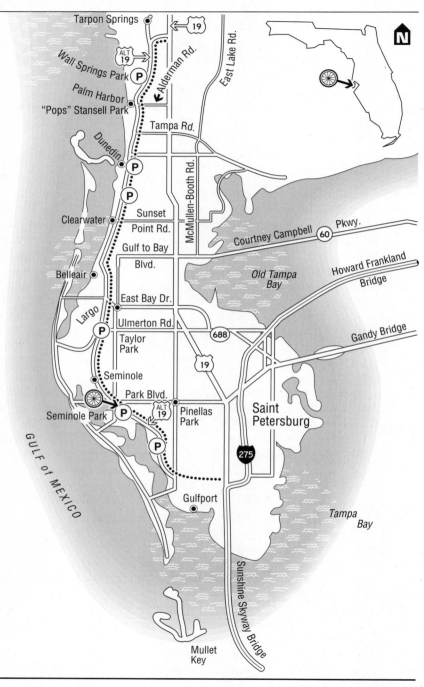

Tarpon Springs

19

ALT 19

Wall Springs Park

Alderman Rd.

East Lake Rd.

P

Palm Harbor

"Pops" Stansell Park

Tampa Rd.

Dunedin

P

P

McMullen-Booth Rd.

Courtney Campbell 60 Pkwy.

Clearwater

Sunset
Point Rd.

Gulf to Bay

Blvd.

Old Tampa
Bay

Howard Frankland
Bridge

Belleair

East Bay Dr.

Largo

P

Ulmerton Rd.

Taylor
Park

688

US 19

Gandy Bridge

Seminole

Park Blvd.

Seminole Park

P

ALT 19

Pinellas
Park

Saint
Petersburg

275

P

Gulfport

Tampa
Bay

GULF of MEXICO

Sunshine Skyway Bridge

Mullet
Key

N

Services: All services—restaurants, convenience stores, bike repair, bike rentals, gas stations, motels, campgrounds, storm shelters, hospitals, picnic tables, drinking water, and telephones—are available on the trail itself. The *Guidebook to the Pinellas Trail,* a mile-by-mile, flip-top guide, is available gratis from the Pinellas County Planning Department. The book uses icons on the map to depict the type of service available along a particular stretch of trail. This guide is an excellent reference for trail travelers. (No black-tie restaurants or snooty shops are listed. What's the use in knowing about a service if the provider is not amenable to folks showing up in Lycra, with perspiration beading on the brow?)

Hazards: Traffic is the biggest threat to cyclists along this trail. Though the pathway is well marked at intersections with busy streets, bikers are still urged to exercise extreme caution when cycling crossroads. Also, this is a multi-use trail, with pedestrians and roller blades, so watch out for them.

Rescue index: This trail is basically a metropolitan bike route where help can be readily obtained. There are station numbers posted every 500 feet along the trail; providing rescue personnel with the exact location of your group on the trail would greatly facilitate a quick rescue. In case of emergency, dial 911.

Land status: County park.

Maps: The *Guidebook to the Pinellas Trail* is available from the Pinellas County Planning Department. This is an excellent map and reference, providing cyclists with all the information needed to pedal this trail. A city map of the St. Petersburg/Clearwater area is helpful in locating the various parks providing access to the trail.

Finding the trail: From Tampa, drive on Interstate 275 across the bay and take the Park Boulevard exit. Drive east on Park Boulevard for approximately 8 miles. (You will pass the Seminole Mall.) Turn left onto Ridge Road and find the Seminole City Hall and City Park on the right. The trail runs along the east side of the complex.

Sources of additional information:

Pinellas County Planning Department
315 Court Street
Clearwater, FL 34616-9874
(813) 464-4751

Pinellas County Park Department
631 Chestnut Street
Clearwater, FL 34616
(813) 462-3347
or (813) 581-2953

Pinellas Trails, Inc.
Suite 900B
1100 Cleveland Street
Clearwater, FL 34615-4805

Notes on the trail: Since this ride is located in an urban setting, you should be aware that Florida law requires that bicyclists observe and obey all traffic controls and signals. Bicyclists must obey the posted speed limits; there is no racing permitted on the trail. Though these laws apply to all bicycling in the state, many mountain bike rides are located in remote settings devoid of traffic and speed limit signs. It is also Florida law that bicyclists cannot wear headphones while pedaling. This law is for your protection—you cannot hear warnings or the sounds of traffic when R.E.M. is blasting in your ears.

RIDE 57   *FLATWOODS AND MORRIS BRIDGE PARKS*

Great scenery and great cycling await fat-tire enthusiasts along the Gulf coast. Within a complex of county parks lies a network of roads and trails seemingly custom-made for mountain bikers. Though there are a number of ride possibilities in these parks, this chapter is devoted to the most popular route. Ten miles long, this loop ride begins along the seven-mile paved Flatwoods Park hiking/biking loop, which is an easy warm-up for the rest of the ride. Once it hits the Old Road Trail to Morris Bridge Park, however, the difficulty increases because of technical sections that must be negotiated. This dirt single-track trail has one sandy patch that demands steady handling and cadence. The creek crossings are made more challenging by intertwining roots on the approaches and exits, which are tight and abrupt. Sand, roots, and steep plunges into creek beds contribute to the technical challenge of the numerous trails in this general area.

Despite the forested areas of the ride, the most powerful impression that you may receive from this area is that of great space and uniformity of flora. Above the pines, the Florida sky streams overhead and flocks of birds fly in loose formation high above. Underfoot, the carpet of pine needles is littered with cones. The pavement occasionally crosses marshy areas and, during wet weather, water becomes a major concern in this designated flood retention area.

Old Road Trail, favored by cross-country runners and mountain bikers alike, transports cyclists quickly from the sunny pine and sabal palm forest to the deep shade of hardwoods. Live oaks, water oaks, and some hickories help create a pleasant passage into the hardwood swamp near Hillsborough River. Bald cypress trees, actually related to the sequoia, flourish near the river. Their fluted bases are bordered by distinctive "knees" where they meet the water. The Hillsborough River is particularly picturesque at Morris Bridge and Trout Creek parks at the end of this portion of the trail. Fishing docks front the river and layers of water lilies cover the dark water. Morris Bridge is a good spot to park your bikes to explore the boardwalks provided at this point on the river.

In an attempt to try to beat the heat on a late-spring ride, we reluctantly rolled out of the bed very early and were soon on the trail. The early morning ride

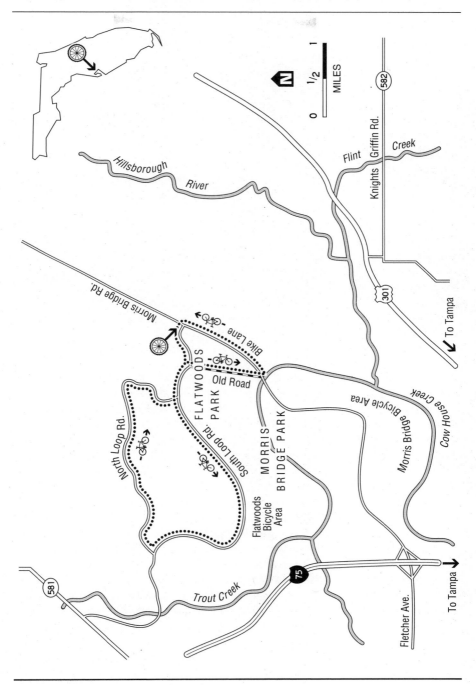

MILES

Hillsborough River

Knights
Flint
Griffin Rd.
582
Creek

301

To Tampa

Morris Bridge Rd.

Bike Lane

FLATWOODS PARK

Old Road

MORRIS BRIDGE PARK

Morris Bridge Bicycle Area

Cow House Creek

North Loop Rd.

South Loop Rd.

Flatwoods Bicycle Area

581

Trout Creek

75

Fletcher Ave.

To Tampa

Some of the wooden bridges aren't much help at creek crossings.

turned out to be well worth the dawn wake-up call for a number of reasons. The heat was not yet oppressive and the pine woods were filled with indigo shadows. Though we didn't see any, this is normally the ideal time of day to see deer browsing for a final bite of vegetation before bedding down for the day. A band of cabbage palms and scrub palms almost a mile beyond the gate became a place of mystery. Shafts of sunlight pierced the ground mist, silvering the Spanish moss hanging from a lonely oak. Beneath the palms, a veritable maze of sandy paths tempted us off the asphalt and into the woods. As the Florida air heated up, wood storks ascended from the cypress near the river and quickly became small, white-and-black specks in the cerulean sky. The wetlands provide food for other stately waders, such as great egrets and white ibis.

Off the middle of the paved loop, a fire road may bear the tracks of raccoon, bobcat, or wild turkey. Feral hogs are frequently seen rooting in the swamp areas. The Florida panther has been reported in the area, but it would be very unlikely that you would have the good fortune of actually seeing this elusive, rare cat. Armadillos are not so rare, and can frequently be seen grubbing along the shoulders of the road.

General location: The trails and roads in these two parks are located in Tampa, Florida.

Elevation change: There is no appreciable change in elevation.

Season: This trail can be ridden year-round, though deep summer temperatures and humidity are stifling. Nasty mosquitoes and other winged biting annoyances are usually associated with these types of semitropical conditions, and this area is no exception. Keep the bug dope close at hand. A late fall or winter ride is generally more pleasant due to cooler temperatures, generally in the 80s. The loop is open to automobiles Friday through Sunday. So, if you are interested in more of a back-to-nature experience (sans fumes), you might enjoy a midweek ride more.

Services: All services are available in Tampa. There is drinking water available at the Morris Bridge site.

Hazards: This is an extensive wilderness area and the possibility of first-time visitors becoming lost is real. Though the Old Road Trail parallels Morris Bridge Road and is clearly defined and heavily traveled, the widespread network of tracks and trails poses a threat of disorientation even to experienced backwoods mountain bikers. Ticks and poisonous snakes are a concern in the denser areas along the ride. Summer thunderstorms can produce severe lightning, which is a serious threat in this area. The Tampa area, along Florida's Gulf coast, sees more lightning strikes than any other area in the nation. If you are biking when a storm hits and are too far away to hightail it back to your vehicle, then take appropriate cover. Do not huddle together under the cover of a big tree unless you want to be served up at the next bike club picnic as "extra crispy." Last of all, you should exercise caution at all road crossings and when riding Morris Bridge Road.

Rescue index: Help could be obtained fairly easily and quickly along Old Road Trail, which closely parallels Morris Bridge Road. Rescue would be more difficult on the backwoods trails.

Land status: County park.

Maps: A leaflet of the area is available from the Hillsborough County parks department. There are maps on display at the park information pulloff as well. This ride is detailed on four USGS 7.5 minute quadrangles: Thonotosassa, Sulphur Springs, Wesley Chapel, and Lutz. The Southwest Association of Mountain Bike Pedalers (SWAMP) and the Water Management District are in the process of preparing maps of the trails at the time of this writing.

Finding the trail: From Interstate 75, take Exit 55 at Fletcher Avenue. Turn north (away from Tampa) on Morris Bridge Road. Drive about 5 miles (passing Morris Bridge and Trout Creek parks) to Flatwoods Park, which will be on the left. Park in the spaces provided near the gated entrance to the hiking/biking loop. The Old Road trailhead is on the left of the paved loop and is marked.

Sources of additional information:

Hillsborough County Parks and Recreation Department
1101 East River Cove Street

Tampa, FL 33604
(813) 975-2160

Wes Eubank
SWAMP
9401 Takomah Trail
Tampa, FL 33617
(813) 988-6435

Chainwheel Drive
1805 Drew Street
Clearwater, FL 34616
(813) 441-2444

Notes on the trail: At the time of this writing, the Hillsborough County Department of Parks and Recreation was reviewing the Southwest Florida Water Management District's proposal to include additional trails and dirt roads in the parks' mountain bike trail network. Prior to riding, cyclists should check with the Hillsborough County Department of Parks and Recreation for current trail information.

Much additional mileage is available on the jeep tracks, fire roads, and single-track trails extending from the paved loop at Flatwoods to a grassy levee paralleling I-75.

Much of this area is a designated flood retention area and is not rideable during periods of heavy rain due to water covering the trails. Mountain bikers are advised to avoid wet areas at all times to prevent trail deterioration and disturbance of sensitive ecosystems. During periods of limited rainfall, the trails are in excellent condition.

RIDE 58 *GRAN CANYON LOOP*

Hard-core mountain bikers, listen up. A technical, moderately strenuous eight-mile loop of single-track trails—a patch of mountain biking paradise—is waiting for you in southern Florida. If you like thrills, you will love the roller-coaster dips and screaming descents on technical, rutted portions of trail. Steep sprint climbs will have you dropping into lower gears and will have your heart rate rising.

Located in an old limestone quarry, these rolling trails are in good condition, with a hard-packed dirt and crushed limestone surface. The site advertises "No Sand," and the scarcity of the wheel-bogging stuff is welcome. Mountain bikers commonly repeat favorite loops, plunging into the "canyon" many times in the course of an afternoon, thereby increasing the total day's mileage to a respectable off-road figure. To say the least, this loop that resembles some of the true moun-

RIDE 58 *GRAN CANYON LOOP*

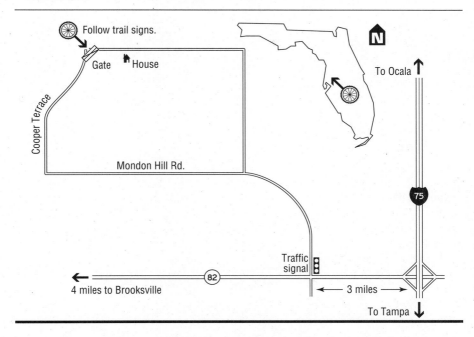

Follow trail signs.

Gate House

Cooper Terrace

Mondon Hill Rd.

To Ocala

N

75

Traffic signal

82

← 4 miles to Brooksville

← 3 miles →

To Tampa

tain rides is a welcome change from most of the rides through the flat scrubs and palmetto barrens of Florida.

Looking down from the pine woods, the first-time visitor is sometimes startled by the depth of the quarry, an impression heightened by the hilliness of this portion of Florida. Hundreds of feet below, the hardy grass is crosshatched by fine white trails of crushed limestone. Weathered outcrops of this rock spring up from the ground and remain visible along the walls of the quarry despite the vines and shrubs. At noon, the bowl of the pit is flooded with sunshine, and the cool thickets of oak waiting up and over the rim are a pleasant change of scenery.

Several notable features of the trail deserve special mention. One, a sunken, corkscrew switchback, requires a good deal of mettle to enter and as much finesse to exit right side up. Likewise, there is a dropoff within the quarry that demands nerves of steel and an indifferent attitude toward shattered collarbones and face-plants. Many of the downhills are straightforward and offer delicious speed, but riders unfamiliar with the trail should take the gullied, rock-cluttered chutes cautiously at first to familiarize themselves with the best line.

General location: This trail is located in Brooksville, Florida.
Elevation change: There is an elevation gain of approximately 500 feet. The

Gran Canyon—a resounding favorite of serious mountain bikers!

stiff climbs and exciting downhills result from a combination of fairly deep excavation and hilly countryside.

Season: The trails at Gran Canyon can be enjoyed year-round, but summers can be unpleasant, with oppresive heat and humidity.

Services: All services are available in nearby Brooksville. There is drinking water available at the trailhead.

Hazards: The technical terrain and kamikaze riders pose the most significant hazards.

Rescue index: Help is available at the residence of the property owner. Also, a portion of the Long Loop parallels Mondon Hill Road, from which help could be flagged down.

Land status: Private property. Open, with restrictions, to the public for a fee.

Maps: There are no official maps available yet for the Gran Canyon. Local bike shops can give you a good bit of information about the trails. There are directional arrows that will show you the way. These arrows change direction for different events.

Finding the trail: From Interstate 75, take Exit 61. Drive west on US 98 toward Brooksville. Drive about 4 miles to the intersection with Mondon Hill Road. Turn right onto Mondon Hill Road and drive about 3 additional miles to Cooper Terrace. Turn right. The gate to Gran Canyon is on the right and is marked with an arrow showing cyclists where to begin. Park at any nearby road pulloff.

Sources of additional information:

Chainwheel Drive
1805 Drew Street
Clearwater, FL 34616
(813) 441-2444

Azalea Bicycle Shop
7100 9th Avenue North
St. Petersburg, FL 33710
(813) 345-7584

John Benifield (property owner)
9008 Cooper Terrace
Brooksville, FL 34601
(904) 796-8955

Notes on the trail: The trail is open to the public only on weekends. You must pay a $3 admission fee and must wear a helmet. Admission during the week is by appointment only.

RIDE 59 *BOCA GRANDE BIKE PATH*

This 13-mile (total), out-and-back bike path offers an easy ride up and down Gasparilla Island. The path is the converted railway corridor of the original Seaboard Airline Railroad and passes the historic Boca Grande Railroad Depot.

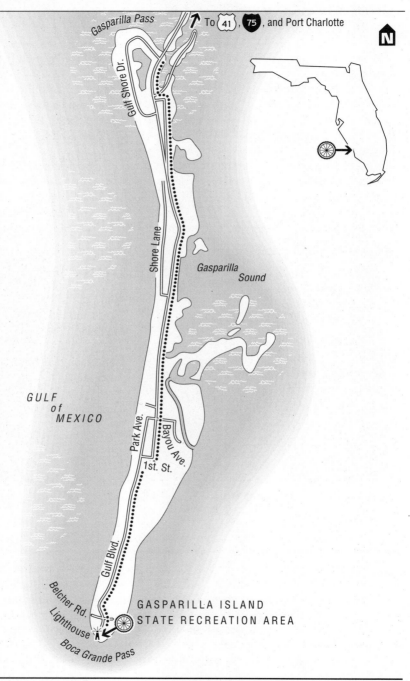

Gasparilla Pass

To (41), (75), and Port Charlotte

N

Gulf Shore Dr.

Shore Lane

Gasparilla
Sound

GULF
of
MEXICO

Park Ave.

Bayou Ave.

1st. St.

Gulf Blvd.

Belcher Rd.

Lighthouse

Boca Grande Pass

GASPARILLA ISLAND
STATE RECREATION AREA

Boca Grande's paved bike path.

Now housing a restaurant and a number of shops, this refurbished structure is a handsome reminder of the past.

This rail trail is intended for recreational use and safe, convenient travel along the length of this attractively developed barrier island. The paved surface is well maintained, though all-terrain bicycles and mountain bikes will fare better on its occasional potholes and road blemishes than a skinny-tired road bike. The terrain is flat, the surface is good, and no technical skill is required—it is a perfect ride for cyclists of diverse abilities.

From the trail, there are occasional glimpses of stunning vistas of shoreline and sparkling water. For the first few miles, you will follow a straight path through the civilized setting of a well-landscaped, seaside village. But the scenery becomes a bit wilder along the northern third of the path. Here the path is enclosed in a hearty wall of shrubbery punctuated with tall palm trees. Stiff breezes and the lapping sounds of water hitting the shore prevail, while occasional silver flashes of water between fronds and leaves grab your attention. Though the path is touted as functional, the aesthetics of this island trail are too beautiful to be ignored.

Gasparilla Island is one of the beautiful, major barrier isles making up the "Shell Coast" in southwest Florida. With thousands of islands, some large and some tiny, the Shell Coast has more islands than any other region in the state. Named for the legendary pirate José Gaspar, this island was used as a hiding place by his roving band of men in the 1700s. Later, in the early 1900s, the island's rich resources of fish and shellfish made it stand out in commercial fishing circles. It became a fishing haven for the nation's most prominent sport fishermen and played host to some of America's most affluent, infuential families. The strikingly beautiful Gasparilla Inn, circa 1910, still operates today as a hotel and as a historical testament to the boom years of tourism at the turn of the century.

The historic Boca Grande Lighthouse should be on your list to visit if you are interested in traces of the past. Placed on the National Register of Historic Places in 1980, this attraction draws droves of camera-snapping visitors each year. This wooden lighthouse was built in 1890 to guide mariners seeking the entrance to Charlotte Harbor and Port Boca Grande. It was closed in 1966 and stood vacant for a number of years. Finally, after restorative work was performed, the light was relit in 1986 and continues to blink brightly across the shimmering waters of the Gulf of Mexico.

General location: This bike path is located on Gasparilla Island, northwest of Fort Myers.

Elevation change: There is no appreciable change in elevation.

Season: Boca Grande Bike Path can be ridden year-round, though late fall through early spring are more pleasant, due to milder temperatures and lower humidity. However, migrating "snowbirds" from the north make south Florida their vacation destination for the same reason, so expect a much more congested bike path during the peak tourist season of November through April. Locals use the bike path during the summer when the tourists are gone and rely on cool, refreshing breezes from the Gulf to offset the heat of the season.

Services: Almost all services are available on this popular resort island. Additional services can be found on the mainland in Port Charlotte or in Fort Myers.

Hazards: The chief hazard is the traffic on the roads that the bike path crosses at several points. Be sure that any exuberant, charge-ahead children in your group know to stop at all road crossings.

Rescue index: This bike path sits in the midst of a busy resort community, so rescue could be effected very quickly.

Land status: County property.

Maps: Maps of the bike path are available from the Lee County Department of Transportation and from the Gasparilla Island Conservation and Improvement Association, Inc. Gasparilla Island is also detailed on two USGS 7.5 minute quadrangles: Placida and Englewood.

Finding the trail: From Interstate 75, take Exit 35 to Jacaranda Boulevard. After crossing US 41, turn left and proceed south on FL 776 toward Englewood. From FL 776, turn onto County Road 775 toward Placida. Drive about 9 miles until you see the Gasparilla Road Toll Bridge on the right. Cross the toll bridge and proceed to Gasparilla Island and downtown Boca Grande. From Park Avenue, turn right onto 1st Street and then left onto Gulf Boulevard. Park at any of the Gasparilla Island State Recreation sites along Gulf Boulevard. You will find the bike path on the opposite side of the road.

Sources of additional information:

Bicycle Planning Coordinator
Lee County Department of Transportation
P.O. Box 398
Fort Myers, FL 33902
(813) 335-2220

Gasparilla Island Conservation and Improvement Association, Inc.
P.O. Box 446
Boca Grande, FL 33921
(813) 964-2667

Gasparilla Island State Recreation Area
c/o Cayo Costa State Park
P.O. Box 1150
Boca Grande, FL 33921
(813) 964-0375

Notes on the trail: To visit the Boca Grande Lighthouse, proceed from the parking lot back into town north on the bike path, or cross Belcher Road.

Afterword

LAND-USE CONTROVERSY

A few years ago I wrote a long piece on this issue for *Sierra* magazine that entailed calling literally dozens of government land managers, game wardens, mountain bikers, and local officials to get a feeling for how riders were being welcomed on the trails. All that I've seen personally since, and heard from my authors, indicates there hasn't been much change. We're still considered the new kid on the block. We have less of a right to the trails than horses and hikers, and we're excluded from many areas, including:

a) wilderness areas
b) national parks (except on roads, and those paths specifically marked "bike path")
c) national monuments (except on roads open to the public)
d) most state parks and monuments (except on roads, and those paths specifically marked "bike path")
e) an increasing number of urban and county parks, especially in California (except on roads, and those areas specifically marked "bike path")

Frankly, I have little difficulty with these exclusions and would, in fact, restrict our presence from some trails I've ridden (one time) due to the environmental damage and chance of blind-siding the many walkers and hikers I met up with along the way. But these are my personal views. The author of this volume and mountain bikers as a group may hold different opinions.

You can do your part in keeping us from being excluded from even more trails by riding responsibly. Many local and national off-road bicycle organizations have been formed with exactly this in mind, and one of the largest—the National Off-Road Bicycle Association (NORBA)—offers the following code of behavior for mountain bikers:

1. I will yield the right of way to other non-motorized recreationists. I realize that people judge all cyclists by my actions.
2. I will slow down and use caution when approaching or overtaking another cyclist and will make my presence known well in advance.
3. I will maintain control of my speed at all times and will approach turns in anticipation of someone around the bend.
4. I will stay on designated trails to avoid trampling native vegetation

and minimize potential erosion to trails by not using muddy trails or short-cutting switchbacks.

5. I will not disturb wildlife or livestock.
6. I will not litter. I will pack out what I pack in, and pack out more than my share whenever possible.
7. I will respect public and private property, including trail use signs and no trespassing signs, and I will leave gates as I have found them.
8. I will always be self-sufficient and my destination and travel speed will

be determined by my ability, my equipment, the terrain, the present and potential weather conditions.

9. I will not travel solo when bikepacking in remote areas. I will leave word of my destination and when I plan to return.
10. I will observe the practice of minimum impact bicycling by "taking only pictures and memories and leaving only waffle prints."
11. I will always wear a helmet whenever I ride.

Now, I have a problem with some of these—number nine, for instance. The most enjoyable mountain biking I've ever done has been solo. And as for leaving word of destination and time of return, I've enjoyed living in such a way as to say, "I'm off to pedal Colorado. See you in the fall." Of course it's senseless to take needless risks, and I plan a ride and pack my gear with this in mind. But for me number nine smacks too much of the "never-out-of-touch" mentality. And getting away from civilization, deep into the wilds, is, for many people, what mountain biking's all about.

All in all, however, NORBA's is a good list, and surely we mountain bikers would be liked more, and excluded less, if we followed the suggestions. But let me offer a "code of ethics" I much prefer, one given to cyclists by Utah's Wasatch-Cache National Forest Office.

Study a Forest Map Before You Ride
Currently, bicycles are permitted on roads and developed trails within the Wasatch-Cache National Forest except in designated Wilderness. If your route crosses private land, it is your responsibility to obtain right of way permission from the landowner.

Keep Groups Small
Riding in large groups degrades the outdoor experience for others, can disturb wildlife, and usually leads to greater resource damage.

Avoid Riding on Wet Trails
Bicycle tires leave ruts in wet trails. These ruts concentrate runoff and accelerate erosion. Postponing a ride when the trails are wet will preserve the trails for future use.

Stay on Roads and Trails
Riding cross-country destroys vegetation and damages the soil.

Always Yield to Others
Trails are shared by hikers, horses, and bicycles. Move off the trail to allow horses to pass and stop to allow hikers adequate room to share the trail. Simply yelling "Bicycle!" is not acceptable.

Control Your Speed
Excessive speed endangers yourself and other forest users.

Avoid Wheel Lock-up and Spin-out
Steep terrain is especially vulnerable to trail wear. Locking brakes on steep descents or when stopping needlessly damages trails. If a slope is steep enough to require locking wheels and skidding, dismount and walk your bicycle. Likewise, if an ascent is so steep your rear wheel slips and spins, dismount and walk your bicycle.

Protect Waterbars and Switchbacks
Waterbars, the rock and log drains built to direct water off trails, protect trails from erosion. When you encounter a waterbar, ride directly over the top or dismount and walk your bicycle. Riding around the ends of water-bars destroys them and speeds erosion. Skidding around switchback cor-ners shortens trail life. Slow down for switchback corners and keep your wheels rolling.

If You Abuse It, You Lose It
Mountain bikers are relative newcomers to the forest and must prove them-selves responsible trail users. By following the guidelines above, and by participating in trail maintenance service projects, bicyclists can help avoid closures which would prevent them from using trails.

I've never seen a better trail-etiquette list for mountain bikers. So have fun. Be careful. And don't screw up things for the next rider.

Dennis Coello
Series Editor

Glossary

This short list of terms does not contain all the words used by mountain bike enthusiasts when discussing their sport. But it should serve as an introduction to the lingo you'll hear on the trails.

ATB
all-terrain bike; this, like "fat-tire bike," is another name for a mountain bike

ATV
all-terrain vehicle; this usually refers to the loud, fume-spewing three- or four-wheeled motorized vehicles you will not enjoy meeting on the trail—except, of course, if you crash and have to hitch a ride out on one

bladed
refers to a dirt road that has been smoothed out by the use of a wide blade on earth-moving equipment; "blading" gets rid of the teeth-chattering, much-cursed washboards found on so many dirt roads after heavy vehicle use

blaze
a mark on a tree made by chipping away a piece of the bark, usually done to designate a trail; such trails are sometimes described as "blazed"

BLM
Bureau of Land Management, an agency of the federal government

buffed
used to describe a very smooth trail

clean
while this may describe what you and your bike *won't* be after following many trails, the term is most often used as a verb to denote the action of pedaling a tough section of trail successfully

deadfall
a tangled mass of fallen trees or branches

diversion ditch
a usually narrow, shallow ditch dug across or around a trail; funneling the water in this manner keeps it from destroying the trail

double-track
the dual tracks made by a jeep or other vehicle, with grass or weeds or rocks between; mountain bikers can ride in either of the tracks, but you will of course find that whichever one you choose, and no matter how many times you change back and forth, the other track will appear to offer smoother travel

dugway	a steep, unpaved, switchbacked descent
feathering	using a light touch on the brake lever, hitting it lightly many times rather than very hard or locking the brake
four-wheel-drive	this refers to any vehicle with drive-wheel capability on all four wheels (a jeep, for instance, has four-wheel drive as compared with a two-wheel-drive passenger car), or to a rough road or trail that requires four-wheel-drive capability (or a *one*-wheel-drive mountain bike!) to negotiate it
game trail	the usually narrow trail made by deer, elk, or other game
gated	everyone knows what a gate is, and how many variations exist upon this theme; well, if a trail is described as "gated" it simply has a gate across it; don't forget that the rule is if you find a gate closed, close it behind you; if you find one open, leave it that way
Giardia	shorthand for *Giardia lamblia,* and known as the "backpacker's bane" until we mountain bikers expropriated it; this is a waterborne parasite that begins its life cycle when swallowed, and one to four weeks later has its host (you) bloated, vomiting, shivering with chills and living in the bathroom; the disease can be avoided by "treating" (purifying) the water you acquire along the trail (see "Hitting the Trail" in the Introduction)
gnarly	a term thankfully used less and less these days, it refers to tough trails
hammer	to ride very hard
hardpack	a trail in which the dirt surface is packed down hard; such trails make for good and fast riding, and very painful landings; bikers most often use "hard-pack" as both noun and adjective, and "hard-packed" as an adjective only (the grammar lesson will help you when diagramming sentences in camp)
jeep road, jeep trail	a rough road or trail passable only with four-wheel-drive capability (or a horse or mountain bike)
kamikaze	while this once referred primarily to those Japanese fliers who quaffed a glass of saki, then flew off as human bombs in suicide missions against U.S. naval vessels, it has more recently been applied to the idiot mountain bikers who, far less honorably, scream down hiking trails, endangering the physical and mental safety of the walking, biking,

and equestrian traffic they meet; deck guns were necessary to stop the Japanese kamikaze pilots, but a bike pump or walking staff in the spokes is sufficient for the current-day kamikazes who threaten to get us all kicked off the trails

multi-purpose   a BLM designation of land which is open to many uses; mountain biking is allowed

out-and-back   a ride where you will return on the same trail on which you pedaled out; while this might sound far more boring than a loop route, many trails look very different when pedaled in the opposite direction

portage   to carry your bike on your person

quads   bikers use this term to refer both to the extensor muscle in the front of the thigh (which is separated into four parts) and to USGS maps; the expression "Nice quads!" refers always to the former, however, except in those instances when the speaker is an engineer

runoff   rainwater or snowmelt

signed   a "signed" trail has signs in place of blazes

single-track   a single, narrow path through grass or brush or over rocky terrain, often created by deer, elk, or backpackers; single-track riding is some of the best fun around

slickrock   the rock-hard, compacted sandstone that is *great* to ride and even prettier to look at; you'll appreciate it even more if you think of it as a petrified sand dune or seabed, and if the rider before you hasn't left tire marks (from unnecessary skidding) or granola bar wrappers behind

snowmelt   runoff produced by the melting of snow

snowpack   unmelted snow accumulated over weeks or months of winter—or over years in high-mountain terrain

spur   a road or trail that intersects the main trail you're following

technical   terrain that is difficult to ride due not to its grade (steepness) but to its obstacles—rocks, logs, ledges, loose soil . . .

topo   short for topographical map, the kind that shows both linear distance *and* elevation gain and loss; "topo" is pronounced with both vowels long

trashed   a trail that has been destroyed (same term used no matter what has destroyed it . . . cattle, horses, or even mountain bikers riding when the ground was too wet)

two-wheel-drive   this refers to any vehicle with drive-wheel capability on only two wheels (a passenger car, for instance, has two-wheel-drive); a two-wheel-drive road is a road or trail easily traveled by an ordinary car

water bar   an earth, rock, or wooden structure that funnels water off trails to reduce erosion

washboarded   a road that is surfaced with many ridges spaced closely together, like the ripples on a washboard; these make for very rough riding, and even worse driving in a car or jeep

wilderness area   land that is officially set aside by the federal government to remain *natural*—pure, pristine, and untrammeled by any vehicle, including mountain bikes; though mountain bikes had not been born in 1964 (when the United States Congress passed the Wilderness Act, establishing the National Wilderness Preservation system), they are considered a "form of mechanical transport" and are thereby excluded; in short, stay out

wind chill   a reference to the wind's cooling effect upon exposed flesh; for example, if the temperature is 10 degrees Fahrenheit and the wind is blowing at 20 miles per hour, the wind-chill (that is, the actual temperature to which your skin reacts) is *minus 32 degrees*; if you are riding in wet conditions things are even worse, for the wind-chill would then be *minus 74 degrees!*

windfall   anything (trees, limbs, brush, or fellow bikers) blown down by the wind